AF446259

213

213

BOB BARTON

2022 Illuminator Publications Paperback Large Print Edition

Copyright © 2022 By Robert Barton

Photos copyright © 2022 by Robert Barton

All rights reserved

Published in the United States by Illuminator Publications

ILLUMINATOR PUBLICATIONS is a registered Trademark of
Illuminator Subversives

LIBRARY OF CONGRESS CATALOGING-IN-PUBLICATION DATA
Barton, R. G. (Robert G.)
213 / Robert Barton
ISBN:979-8-8860-959-6

1123.5813.2134.5589.144

Printed in the United States of America on Acid Free Paper

Illuminatorpublications.com

369

BOOK DESIGNED BY R.C. & D.V. BARTON

DEDICATION

I would like to dedicate this book to Clairemae Barton, a wonderful wife, mother, friend, artist, and partner; as well as a pillar of support throughout the journey of our lives together. This book would not exist without your inspiration during all of the experiences that are cataloged here as well as your encouragement to actually write them down for posterity. You are the love of my life and have made it all worthwhile.

Thank you

FOREWARD

"I want you to know that in the conversations that I have had with retired deputies from the 70's, your name is always mentioned with due respect. In fact, when we had the oldies (late 60's and early 70's) luncheons with Col. MG, your name was always mentioned when it came to respected leaders at PBSO."

-P.W.

PREFACE

These are a series of stories, some short and some long, of some of the varied calls I responded to while working as a deputy sheriff for Palm Beach County, Florida, and two police departments, Rivera Beach and Palm Beach Gardens. These are by no means all the calls I answered in my career, they only represent a small portion of them. I wrote these stories years ago while they were still fresh in my memory, but as most people, I procrastinated and they have sat idle for years, moved numerous times and stored. My wife and Kids have for the longest time asked me to write them in book-style or at least put them on a computer. So, as I record them, some are funny, and some might bring a tear to the reader. They are in no order of occurrence and are written at random, but all are true. I thank my family for never giving up that one day I would eventually write these stories. I hope as a reader, you will enjoy them, and realize just what police officers and deputy sheriffs go through daily and appreciate them and what they do. All statutes or laws are what was in effect in the state of Florida at this time (1967 through 1977), and as you read these, I'm sure that some have been rescinded or changed.

ACKNOWLEDGEMENTS

Where do I even begin, Chris, my son, the bright and shining star of my life. You carry the torch of my legacy; I am so proud of you. Knowing that you would be born someday gave me the strength to face all of the danger with confidence. I am forever grateful to have been given the gift of being your father.

P.S. I better mention your sisters too, Heidi and Wendy.*

*Disclaimer – The Acknowledgments and Dedication were written by me, his son Chris, as this book is a gift to my father, I could not have kept it a secret if I asked him to write the acknowledgments; of course it was written in jest.

INTRODUCTION

These are stories captured from my life as a Police Officer and Sergeant in the Sheriff's Department on Road Patrol. They are all true and range from *"Motorcycle Gangs"* to *"Green Bean Fights."* A telling book about the times that I lived in while I was in law-enforcement. The years ranging from 1964 - 1978.

My law enforcement career began in Riviera Beach Florida & then Palm Beach Gardens Police Department for a brief tour. I then spent most of the time on the Sheriff's Department of Palm Beach County, in Florida. Later leaving the Sheriff's Department to go to the state of Alaska where I joined the U.S. Marshals service in Anchorage as a contract court security officer, where I spent the next 21 and a half years before retiring with my wife Claire, of almost 50 years, also my three children, Heidi, Wendy and Chris. I also have 9 grandchildren and 5 great-grandchildren.

Table of Contents

45th STREET

I lived in a housing development known as Gramarcy Park. It was located west of Haverhill Road and just east of the Florida turnpike and was a large development full of modest and mid-income families just like mine, and like most Florida communities it had lots of canals close by, most were clear and about 8 to 10 or so feet deep.

Lots of people fish in them for bass, brim, and other pan size fish. Most of these canals, if not all, were made by a drag line. Now I never fished in them, but I did use them to clean the fish I got while diving in the ocean, such as grouper, snapper, jewfish etc. It was a lot easier to filet them in the water because of all the mosquitoes and flies. They didn't bother me so much, and I could keep the meat clean as I would just throw it in a plastic cooler, besides it was close to home.

Filleting a big fish took time and being out in the hot sun when I was done, I'd just swim the carcass out to the middle of the canal, puncture its swim bladder and sink it for fish food for all the fishes. I didn't have to worry about burying the carcass. Once when I was filleting a 400-pound Atlantic goliath grouper also known as a jewfish, I heard an alligator grunting from across the canal so he must have smelled the meat, but I never did see him, and I kept a close eye out.

I was on my day off from the 4-12 PM shift and we were just through eating supper. It was about 6:30 PM, the sun was still up, and it was a typical nice Florida evening. The phone rang and it was our complaint desk wanting to know if could go and check a canal for a possible signal 26, drowning victim. The canal they wanted me to check was right by the turnpike and close to my house. I told them sure, it would only take 5 minutes to get there. The complaint desk sergeant thanked me and told me that a uniform car, zone 1, was standing by along with a detective. I hung up and told my wife, loaded up my 1963 Ford hippie van with all my diving gear and took off for the canal. I already had my cutoffs on. My wife always complained about my cut off's because I wore them diving and at home all the time and the salt water from the ocean would make them stiff so that when I took them off, they stood by themselves, and they smelled like fish.

I came over the turnpike overpass and saw the patrol car off by the canal along with a detective's car and a green pickup truck. When I pulled up, I saw the detective was one who had been assigned the case in fact used to be my road sergeant when I first came on the department. He told me he had run a 10-28, a license & registration check. It came back to a black male from Riviera Beach, the cross index of that address showed no phone listed, so he had the dispatcher call Riviera Police Department to have one of their cars go by that address to see if they knew where the owner was.

When I pulled up, the detective was still waiting for a reply from the dispatcher and any word from Riviera Beach. We stood around for about 5 or so minutes when the dispatcher called the detective back and advised that Riviera PD said it was a good address and that the owner of the truck was fishing west of the turnpike.

The detective acknowledged her and hung up the radio. Well, so far it checked out and it looked like we had a drowning. I had been beside him and told him I'd go in the canal for a look. I put my knife on my leg, put my scuba tank and weight belt on and my rubber boots. My mask was the last piece of equipment, I had spit in it and rubbed it and rinsed it so it wouldn't fog up. The water was fairly clear with 5 to 8-foot visibility. I turned on the air, checked the mouthpiece and under I went.

I swam straight down following the slope of the bank. I got down around 10 to 12 feet and it was still pretty clear even in the fading light. On the bottom I stopped to adjust my weight belt and when I looked straight ahead, I saw the bottoms of two feet, heels up. He was lying on his stomach on the bottom. The soles of his feet were a lighter color than the rest of his skin. I figured the poor guy was just standing in the water, enjoying his fishing and took one to many steps out into the canal, lost his footing and that was that. He probably panicked and just drown. I could never understand why people want to live in Florida where there's so much water and they didn't learn to swim.

I grabbed him by his belt and started up the slope I had just come down. There was no weight to the body as it had a neutral buoyancy. I guessed the guy to be about 175 pounds. I broke the surface right in front of the detective and the zone deputy and just lay the body on the canal bank at their feet. The detective was glad I found the guy and said, *"Shit Bob, it didn't take but about 9 seconds from the time you went down till you came back up."* I wasn't about to stick around as this was my day off, so I told him, *"Adios".* He had to take care of towing the truck, then he had to wait for an ambulance to respond to take the body to St. Mary's Hospital to be formally pronounced dead by a doctor. Then it would be released to a funeral director.

I went home and told my wife, *"Yea, I found the guy,"* she never liked me to go into detail about body recoveries or anything involving death or violence.

The next day at road patrol the captain knew that I had made a body recovery, but he never bothered to mention it when he saw me. He must have figured it went with the job.

****

This is one of the reasons I taught my kids to swim right away.

Besides, who needs an ATTA BOY.

ALLIGATOR STORIES

The time was in the 70's, and it was the night shift, 11 to 7 AM. I was the sergeant and shift supervisor as we had no lieutenant's (Lt.), well at least none to work on the night shift. On our department back then a Lt. were a scarce commodity. Now we had one to work the day and evening shift but none for the night shift. On the night shift it was deemed that a sergeant could be entrusted with the safety of the county, and he was capable on leading 7 to 10 troops, cause that's all we had, and they were zones 1 through 7 and possibly a cover car.

This night proved to be exceptionally quiet and nice and warm. I made my rounds with the troops just shooting the breeze, hearing complaints, getting comp days, also earned days off. It seemed that a one on one made them loosen up, more relaxed and comfortable and I'd possibly give out a subpoena or return a report to be redone or changed. Or something to that effect.

Well along about 3 AM I hear the dispatcher call zone 6 and advising him to check Congress Avenue in front of John F. Kennedy Hospital for an alligator about 15 feet long. Zone 6 acknowledges her and advises he's enroute. Hell, I figured I want to see this, so I don't say anything to the dispatcher or zone 6 and I start that way.

I don't have to say anything, they all knew that 213, my ID would be 10-51, enroute. I had a kind of surname of Mother Hen given to me by one of my troops because I was always there with a troop in a serious, or potentially serious, call. Now I never heard anyone bitch about it though.

Gators are an accepted fact of life in Florida, just like sharks are a fact of life in the ocean. All this time alligators were still on the endangered list of whoever keeps the list of endangered or about to be extinct species, it's the federal government. Now the gator at JFK Hospital had been reported several other times before. He had a habit of coming out of the water in Lake Osborne and the swampy area near by which was directly east of the hospital. He would shuffle across 2 lanes of Congress Avenue, shuffle across the median strip and then across 2 more lanes on Congress Avenue, then would saunter up to the hospital entrance and go behind to the incinerator and eat things like dressings and things to burn. There was an endless supply of food for him, and when he was done eating, he would just amble back the way he came, and he never met with any resistance. It seemed to always be a case of DGI, 'don't get involved', just call the sheriff's department while he made his way back to John Prince Park, the swampy area, and back into Lake Osborne.

It just so happened that about 2 weeks prior a 13-year-old boy had been attacked by what was described as a 13-foot alligator while he was swimming in a pond not far from this location, could have even been the same gator. The alligator had grabbed his arm and broke it, and chewed it up, but for some unknown reason had let him go. The boy was extremely lucky to be alive, so bad feelings about alligators in Palm Beach County were extremely high.

Now gators don't have real sharp teeth and what they do is just chomp down on their prey and start spinning in the water. This tends to drown the prey or to tear away an arm, leg, or something. Anyway, the gator then takes its prey to its nest or lair through an underwater opening and lets it putrefy or soften up so it can eat it. Now something like a dog or duck or turtle it just swallows whole, anyway the boy, (lucky boy) and his family most likely realize just how lucky he was to be let go. One thing you can imagine was the pure fright and terror the boy must have felt during while the attack.

I got down by J.F.K. Hospital just in time to see this big gator. He's around 15 feet long, and he's east bound just off the Avenue. I see him make it to the water, so he's gone. Now I don't know the feeding habits or sex life of the American alligator, or much care, or if he's going back for seconds or what, but a 15 feet long alligator has got to weigh over 1,000 pounds and I don't want any of my troops screwing around with one that big. I can just see animal control sending some little ole person out to capture a gator, anyway animal control only deals with domestic animals like dogs and cats etc. Now Florida fish and game are recognized experts on gators and have a sergeant whose job it is to go around and trap alligators from populated areas and transplant them to isolated areas of the state, so I tell the dispatcher to contact Fish and Game and tell them about the gator. Besides, they enforce Florida statutes concerning deer, wild hogs, and gators.

Now while I'm waiting for her to call Fish and Game and get an answer, I shoot the breeze with zone 6 about gators and the lucky little boy who was attacked and the big article in the paper about it. Now in about 15 minutes the dispatcher comes back with, *"Palm Beach to 213,"* I acknowledge, and she continues, *"a captain, pissed off, advises that complaints are handled 8 AM through 5 PM, Monday through Friday at the Military Trail office."* Now I thank her and think, that SOB, he don't like to get woke up and just likes his administrative job on Mondays through Fridays and his banker hours. Hell, captains are all alike. I then came back on the air with, *"213 to all zones, if*

you encounter any alligators on the road shoot 'em, as a hazard."
Now I was hoping that Fish and Game monitored our radio channel. All 9 zones acknowledged my order by chicks on their radios and some even added additional mic clicks.

****

Now needless to say, gator calls at the hospital for some reason had stopped and the department had no more calls of an alligator at the incinerator. I never heard from Fish and Game or from captain, don't bother me.

So, in this case a 125-grain jacketed hollow point would have been well worth the 1,000 pound plus cause.

****

I worked another alligator case in John Prince Park. The time again was in the 70's, and I was on the day shift, one of the few times I got on day shift as I think they tried to play down having a Polish sergeant on the sheriff's department. Anyway, I used to go and hide when it was not busy. So, I'd go to John Prince Park to get away from people and definitely from Road Patrol, it was out of sight, out of mind concept, anyway I'd drive into the park and down by the Lake Osborne close to the camping area. Now people used to, and still do, swim in the lake at the camping area. Lake Osborne had lots of water ski schools and you could always watch novice and expert water skiers.

I was parked in the shade, engine running and the air conditioner going full blast looking out over the lake with my binoculars when I see this head that looked close to 30 inches long, and it's a gator, a big gator and he's not 50 feet offshore only about 300 feet from the camping area. Hell, I couldn't believe it. Well, I had the dispatcher call it into Fish and Game and had her make sure that she advised them that it was a big gator, and he was right in the vicinity of the camping area, and he posed a real danger to any unsuspecting folks, especially swimmers.

Well, I kept watching the gator and the dispatcher comes back with a 10-39, message delivered. Well, I took off, got with zone 6, and advised him about the gator, where it hung out, and the possible danger to campers, and swimmers.

Now about a week later, my shift had changed from day shift, 7 AM to 3 PM to the afternoon shift 3 PM to 11 PM. Now zone 6 was a different deputy and didn't have the information on the J. P. Park gator.

I hear the dispatcher call zone 6 and tell him to, 10-17, a possible signal 33 at J. P. Park involving a dog, investigate a possible shooting. Now it sounds like someone had shot a dog. Zone 6 acknowledges and advises he's 10-51, enroute. As the sergeant, I advise that I also respond. Well, me and zone 6 arrive at J. P. Park about the same time and pull up to the lake on the narrow causeway that goes to the camping area. Now all we could find was this white male who was just standing there, when he saw us, he called us over and tells us he had called the department from the camping area office. Then went on to explain that he was fishing right there when this young white male, driving a pickup truck with a dog in its bed. The guy, who reported went on stating that when the pickup stopped the dog jumped out and ran into the water and started to swim out away from shore, meanwhile the owner got out of his truck and was watching his dog swim when all of a sudden, he spied the gator just as it grabbed his dog. In a split second he grabbed a rifle hanging in the back window of the truck, and the guy reporting said that the rifle had a lever. When the dog owner jacked a round into the chamber and aimed at the gator, with the now dead dog in its jaws, and fired. The gator with the dog in its jaws went under water and was seen no more. The guy with the riffle hurriedly jacked the empty round out of the chamber, jumped into his truck and took off.

The guy who reported, gives us the tag, make, and color of the pickup. A 10-28 registration check gave us the owner, his address, make, and model of the truck. It corresponded with the information that the guy who reported, gave us. He showed us the exact spot were the guy parked his truck and fired from, and searching we found an empty shell casing from a 30-30 caliber rifle. Zone 6 made a preliminary report and I also had him advise Fish and Game about the incident, and with that we left the scene.

Now gators that are shot sink right away and the only way to recover one is to dive for it. As far as I'm concerned, it's like playing Russian roulette with 6 rounds in the cylinder. The only other way is to let mother nature take her course, which in the semi-tropics, what south Florida is considered, is that a dead body will rise to the surface 3 days after being submerged in water due to the expansion of gases within the body and have a positive buoyancy, it floats. So true to nature, after 3 days the complaint desk got a call about a dead gator floating in Lake Osborne. Needless to say, the gator was over 10 feet long and was all bloated and looked huge. The head had a big gaping wound in it.

Well, this was for sure the gator that was shot by the guy that lost his dog 3 days ago. Now it wasn't positive that he had hit the gator when he shot at it, but now we were sure that we had a crime scene and so I called for a detective and a Dan Hicks was the one who responded. I told him the whole story and gave him the suspects name, address, and tag number of his truck. The projectile (bullet) was removed from the carcass, and it was weighed at well over 600 pounds. A search warrant was obtained by Hicks based on all the information that he gave, and the rifle was taken from the residence as evidence. The guy was arrested. Our crime lab matched the casing with the rifle.

****

The guy coped a plea to shooting the alligator because he was mad about the gator getting his dog like that, deputy or not I'd have done the same thing.

AMARYLLIS ANCHORS

This story is an addition to another story about the Amaryllis, but it's about the anchors and chain that it had. I won't go into detail about the Amaryllis and its trip to the beach in our city as I had related that in the next story.

It was a dark and stormy night, sounds like the start of a horror story, hurricane Betsy was in progress when the Amaryllis must have been north bound in the straits of Florida and caught in a very rough ocean. Now I don't know if the ship lost power or what, but I do know that it was unable to stop its westward journey toward land, and land was only 3 miles away from the gulf stream.

I never did see the ocean as I was busy giving out warnings, I'm sure it was angry, and the waves had to be big as a storm was in full progress and pounding the whole coast of Florida. Anyway, the Amaryllis in its fatal westward journey, unknown to me if it had power or not, couldn't stop. And In desperation dropped both its anchors, which I'm sure weighed a lot.

A word about anchors, all ships have two. They are located on the bow, (front) and they have one on the port side, (left), and the other on the starboard side, (right). All anchors are connected by chain. I don't know how many feet there are on each anchor, but you can be sure it's plenty. When not in use, the chain is stored in what's called a chain locker, to be out of the way and available for instant use. Just to give the reader some idea of the great weight it has to have, the links, that's just one link of many, can weigh as much as 100 pounds apiece. The anchor to which they are attached, can weigh several tons.

Most big ship anchors are what is called Danforth

anchors, to understand just what a Danforth anchor is, just picture a big 'T', that when they are dropped and hit bottom, the bottom end of the anchor, being moveable, drops down and the two ends, (flukes) being somewhat pointed, dig in and grasp whatever, bottom, rocks or whatever can stop the ship from its forward movement. Well, the Amaryllis was in such a fix as it was steadily closing into shore during the storm. They dropped both anchors in a desperate attempt to stop or at least slow down, the anchors and all the chain played out and just snapped at the end and the ship never slowed down but continued on its shore bound journey. Well, the Amaryllis finally did stop, but it was now on shore, stuck in the sand.

I guess the insurance company that covered the Amaryllis stood to lose or at least pay out a lot of money once all the claims were settled, insurance coverage was a mandatory must. Now the insurance company must have figured that it could recoup some of the money that they surely would have to pay out by the cutting up and scrapping some of the Amaryllis, recovering both anchors and chain that was lost somewhere in the ocean. So, they did I guess what most business would do in their predicament, they advertised in the local newspaper that, all you had to do was, locate the anchors and chain and just mark the location. To be eligible for a $5,000 reward you didn't even have to raise them. Now there's not too many people in this world that would consider a $5,000 dollar reward paltry, just for finding and marking something. As for me I certainly didn't think it was paltry. To me, $5,000 was the world. I could just see my bills paid off, and maybe I could even save a few bucks, unfortunately I didn't have access to a boat and to find the anchors you definitely needed a boat because they were out there in the ocean somewhere just waiting to be found. All I had was the general path the Amaryllis took on its last journey, and I liked to dive, and all my diving was done in the ocean.

I wanted to find those anchors or a chain link as the anchors still had to be attached. Well Florida has its share of divers and I'm positive that a $5,000 dollar reward just for finding them was a heck of an enticement. Anyway, someone from the police department saw the ad in the paper and he too had visions of a nice reward, but he also didn't have a boat, nor did he dive. Now he knew that I dove and would be willing to dive to locate the anchors and the chains. Well, he asked me, and I said YES. We both could make a nice piece of change, and so he rented a 25-foot boat and a sea sled.

The boat was big as far as I was concerned, it had a cabin and a head, (toilet) a stove and refrigerator and it was way more than I expected. I don't remember the horsepower, but it was big enough to push the boat with ease and was an inboard motor. The sea sled I had never used before but anyway it was made to dive for whatever you were looking for, or to travel over a large distance or just sightseeing the wonders of the ocean.

A word about sea sleds, the one that he had rented was made from aluminum and steel pipe and it was shaped like a cross. The diver's feet, with his fins on rested on a pipe on the lower end. On the upper end where the arms reached out was a plate/plane maybe 8 or 10 inches by 6 or 7 inches with a handle on the inside and this plate/plane was moveable so that a diver when he points the plane down on both sides, the sled dives, and when he points the planes up, he surfaces for air as he's just using a snorkel. The planes are just like those of a submarine. And as the diver controls the sled, he can dive as deep as he wants, and he's only limited by how much rope was played out from the boat that he's attached to. Any sled is designed to be towed through the water, so no SCUBA gear is used. Just a mask, fins and a weight belt. Myself, I used 7 pounds of lead when I free dove. A weight belt made it easier to dive down so you didn't have to fight to go down, this burns up air in your lungs and you can't go as deep or stay as long.

Diving on a sled was easy, all you had to do is stay on and go down when you want, the boat did all the work for you. Well, the ocean was calm and settled and the water was cleared up from all the turbulence of the storm. A shade of green meant the water was still shallow, but as the ocean got deeper it changed colors from a green to a blue and blue meant deeper water.

Well back to the anchors and an easy 5 grand. I loaded up my SCUBA tank and regulator in the boat and only planned on using it once I had found the chain or an anchor, all I had to do was to drop off the sled and signal the boat driver I found something and he would stop, turn around and come back for me. I could then get back into the boat and put my SCUBA gear on after pulling in the sled. All I would have to do is take an empty Clorox bottle with some line on it, tie it on the chain or anchor and surface. We could report it to the insurance company and be the proud owners of a 5 grand reward. Sounds easy to do, but first all I had to do was find the anchors and chain.

Well, we had the sled and the SCUBA gear loaded so off we go out Palm Beach inlet, not even a1/4 of a mile away. The tides coming in, the waters clear, and the ocean is calm and it's a good day to get five thousand dollars richer.

Once we got out the inlet we turn north and now we're in the ocean. On our left right away is Palm Beach Shores and right away is Riviera Beach. This is where I'm a cop, and you can see what's left of the Amaryllis up on the shore. You can't miss it as it's so big, and anyway you don't often see a ship on shore stuck in the sand.

I figured we can start looking 3 or 4 hundred feet directly east of the wreck. Now all I had to do was get into the open ocean, put the sled in and the boat could start traversing back and forth north past the ship. Turn around and tow me south past the wreck. With each pass slowly go eastward into deeper water. We had let out about 50 feet of rope on the sled

All I had on was my mask, fins, knife and weight belt and all I had to do was aim the planes of the sled down, go down about 25 feet and turn the planes up, come up and get a breath of air and then go back down again and just look. Depth was no problem as I could see all the way to the bottom, and it was all sandy.

We had made about 4 passes and had covered a lot of water and sandy bottom, now maybe the water was close to 80 feet deep. I had just surfaced when out of the corner of my eye about 20 or so feet down, I see this Remora, it's also known as a shark sucker, remora swim with or, attach themselves to big fish like sharks, rays etc. They have an oval section on their head that they can stick to a large slow-moving fish so they get a free ride, or they can swim along with it, and when it eats, they can also have leftovers. Now I see this Remora, so I know that something big is coming my way and here I am, 50 feet from the boat, in deep water where there's no place to hide or take cover because I'm in the open ocean.

I can't turn my head to see what's coming as I was being towed and the force of the water would have pulled my mask off as it's only held on by a rubber strap. I did know that whatever it was coming was big because I saw the Remora and they only swim with something big.

Now being towed I felt like bait and here comes a big beastie. I had spent all this time on a sled looking for the anchors and chain, didn't see anything and now here comes whatever and I can't get away from it. It's going east and I'm going north and were going to meet in 1 minute and I still can't see what it is.

I figured at least I could get off the sled if I had time and try and stick it in the mouth of whatever as it comes at me. The guy driving the boat would know that something was wrong and hurry and turn around and come back and try to pick me up, but by that time, whatever was going to happen would have happened.

Well, I was on the surface and about to meet whatever was coming when I see several more Remora, then this big head comes into view, what a relief, it's a big sea turtle and it's in the 400-pound range. it's down about 25 feet and just swimming low and it didn't even bother to look up at me and it just continued east ward along with its Remora.

Well, I got to tell you, it's definitely time to get out of the water, so I signaled the boat driver to pick me up, besides I never did see any signs of the anchor or chain.

****

Well, I never did find any trace of the anchors or the chains, and I don't remember anyone else finding them either. I figure that the anchors fell right down when released and the chains also fell down when they ripped out of the chain lockers just like dominoes falling, and they were covered up with sand from ole Betsy.

The guy who rented the boat and sled had to eat the costs, pay for them himself. Me, I was just glad that the ole beastie was just a turtle and not a shark.

AMARYLLIS CARGO SHIP

This is a story about a ship, the *"Amaryllis,"* to be exact, and its encounter with police work. The time was in the mid 60's, and I was a police officer in the city of Riviera Beach Florida. Now everyone has heard of the Gulfstream. it's one of the worldwide known currents and is used by shipping companies as a fuel saver so interest and use are taken by companies that do business in the United States, especially when their ships do business on the eastern seaboard.

The Gulf stream starts its north ward journey somewhere off the Florida Keys and continues all the way north to Newfoundland, and basically hugs the U.S. coastline all the way north, so you can see that it's invaluable to those that might use it.

What most people don't know is that its true name is called the Straits of Florida, until it reaches around Jacksonville Florida and then its proper name is the Gulf stream. Palm Beach County has the distinction of having it come within 3 miles off its shore, the closest it comes to the U.S. shore on its northern journey.

Not only is it used by worldwide shipping companies, but even old Adolf of World War II fame, or infamy, used it to get his submarines close and undetected to the U.S. shore, and some of his sub crews were even reported to pull liberty, or shore leave, at the time.

Everyone knows that Florida experiences hurricanes at a certain period during any given year, and it just so happened that this was that time of year when a hurricane was predicted to hit south Florida, and so people took precautions in preparing for the coming storm.

At the time I happened to be working the 3-11 PM shift and our Chief was a man named Lennie Cotrell. Chief Cotrell had a responsibility to the people of Riviera Beach to advise them and take whatever steps he deemed necessary for their safety. As a patrolman for this great city, I wasn't consulted nor was I privy to just what those steps might be. As a slick sleeve patrolman my job was to do as told, so I did.

One thing I did know was that Chief Cotrell was to ask all his Lt. and sergeants to ask all their people if anyone cared to work over and warn people to evacuate the coastal area of his city for the coming storm. As a young patrolman and a new daddy I put my hand up when my sergeant, Jeff Waites, asked who wanted to volunteer, to let him know that I would gladly volunteer for the detail knowing that my wife and new baby would be safe, as at the time I lived several miles inland away from the coast and I wasn't worried about any flooding, besides I could use the extra cash as I had a hard time paying attention.

Now on my shift was a man named Gene Armstrong, no it wasn't Jack the all-American boy, at least so I thought. Gene was my mentor, sometime employer, and most of all, my friend at the time. He also volunteered to stay and warn the people. So Chief Cotrell had 2 patrolmen stay over and warn the coastal community residences. He, as chief, decided that 2 people staying over was enough, so we were advised just what was required of us.

First off, we had a patrol car, and our only job was to drive slowly and use the loudspeaker, or bull horn to announce that the hurricane was approaching and to evacuate the area for higher ground, or at least go inland, as Florida was in short supply of any high ground. Riviera Beach sits right on U.S. #1 and is a very busy town as most towns on the gold coast are. It sits partially inland, so water and its woes didn't seem to be of great concern. However, crossing U.S. #1 within the city is a road known as Blue Herron Blvd., it is a busy 4 lane road that runs east and west. Of concern was where, on its an east end, it crossed the inter coastal waterway which is where it turns into 2 lanes from 4. Besides all this, the bridge raised up to allow boat traffic to pass. On the east end of the bridge is what is known as, the Causeway. On one side was a beach that was used by tourists, swimmers, and residents. It was always full of beach lovers etc. On the other side of this causeway, to the north side, was what was called Phil Foster Park, a busy boat ramp, parking lot and picnic area, so it was a busy place. All this was less than 1/4 mile from the open ocean. The eastern end of this busy causeway was another bridge, but it was low and not made for boat traffic, just for cars, pedestrians and fisherman. I believe that it was built just several feet over the high tide line. Now Palm Beach Inlet is just a short distance away, so the tidal pull is strong as it goes up the inter coastal waterway returning approximately 6 hours later running back to the ocean. When the tide is running in, the water under the bridge is crystal clear so you can see bottom about 20 or 25 feet down.

Anyway, at the east end of this bridge are businesses and residences. About 2 1/2 blocks from this bridge, Blue Herron Blvd. turns north, and it becomes A1A, or the Coast Highway and the Atlantic Ocean is only about 200 to 250 feet away and is only 2 lanes wide. Now on the east side, or ocean side area, there is a line of motels and an occasional empty lot, but on the west side are numerous houses, luxury houses, and they all had a canal for a back yard that led into the inter coastal waterway. Now all these houses had boats, big boats, expensive boats, so they all had to be warned continuously of the coming storm to secure their boats and then evacuate the area, this was known as, *"Palm Beach Isles".*

Now just on the south side of Blue Herron. Blvd., just before it turned north to become A1A was the town of Palm Beach Shores. P.B.S. was just a small town maybe several blocks square, but it also was a tourist town, and its southern border was Palm Beach Inlet, and its western border was the inter coastal waterway, the eastern border was the Atlantic Ocean. So, within this town, no bigger than several blocks square, were house after house after house, and if there wasn't a house, it had a hotel or a motel or maybe a bar, but no empty lots. On the southeast corner of this town was what was known as the Colonnades, a 3-story hotel, bar and snack bar restaurant that was owned by billionaire John D, McArthur. Well, enough layout on the city and the detail. The coming hurricane was named Betsy. By now the winds came along with some heavy rain and the ocean got worse and worse. Armstrong and I were in our patrol car with the federal system on to the bull horn mode, we used the microphone to advise all that a storm was coming and the need to evacuate. We traversed all the streets on the causeway and advised all to please leave as it wasn't mandatory. Now that I think about it, I never did see a single soul as if they had waited, they might not be able to get out. There only way off was up in North Palm Beach and U.S. #1, a good 7 or 8 miles north on A1A. It might have been that the road was impassable, as A1A paralleled an angry ocean all the way north and it was getting worse. Armstrong and I hadn't seen a soul in several hours, but we still gave warnings out over the federal system for people to evacuate. Now signs, billboards and streetlights swayed hard, and some blew down, and there was lots of rain. After not seeing anyone for so long, at least 3 1/2 to 4 hours, we started to shoot at streetlights as there was no one around, just to stay awake and for something to do. It seemed that all living souls had long since left the causeway, Palm Beach Shores and its hotels and motels were all dark and deserted. I remember Armstrong was driving, I was in the passenger seat, and we were north bound on A1A at a real slow speed because you couldn't go fast anyway in all the rain and wind. I think it was about 4 AM and we were both sleepy when I happened to look east toward the ocean. I knew it had some big waves; we just passed an empty lot when as sleepy eyed as I was, I did a double take to be sure I saw what I saw. It was a ship, yeah, a big ocean liner or freighter, it's up on the beach in the empty lot and it's only about 250 feet away, its stern was still in the water. Now this ship is a good 5 to 6 hundred feet long. Needless to say, I'm not sleepy anymore and I tell Armstrong who had all he could do just keeping his eyes on the road while driving. He stops the car right away and I run over to the ship, and I see several males up on the bow, I tried to see first if any one was injured and might need help. Now the bow is a good 30 to 35 feet up over my head and the guys that I could see were waving and shouting something at me and I'm not understanding the words they were shouting down at me. This might sound corny, but what they were shouting down at me sounded like Greek, I found out later that they were Greek. All of them as far as I knew spoke no English. Now as a new rookie patrolman and never having any experience with big ships or Greeks, come to think of it, I don't know anyone who did, I got on the radio and called my sergeant and advised him what just happened. The males up on the bow, even though they were on dry land, shot a line gun from the ship to us standing on the sandy beach. I don't know why they fired the gun, but it was a good 3 or 4 hundred feet of waxed 1/4-inch line and it was orangish in color.

A short word about a line gun for landlubbers to understand what it is. A line gun is a gun that shoots a light line from one ship to another while they are at sea for whatever reason. What the ships do is to travel close to each other when the gun is fired, and a progressively heavier line is attached until a heavy enough line connects the ships so that whatever needs to be passed can safely pass over the water between them. Be it cargo, personal etc. Well by now my sergeant, Jeff Waites, came on the scene, and like all good sergeants, took charge of the ship and its crew and then let me pick up and keep the line that the crew had shot. The crew men were kept on board the ship as they weren't U S citizens. They were released later by custom officials.

****

The Amaryllis was repeatedly pulled by tugs to try and get it back into deep water, but it was never meant to be. The repairs that were attempted to patch the holes in it failed. After numerous attempts it was finally cut up, dragged off the beach, and its parts were sunk in deep water to become an artificial reef. The crew had long since departed the ship and returned to their homeland, Greece, where else!

The hooks and anchors, well that's another story.

ATLANTIS COUNTRY CLUB

Now this story occurred when I was just a new deputy sheriff. The time was in the very late evening and the shift was the 3-11 PM. I was working zone 6. Now this zone goes from 10th Avenue on the north side, to Lantana Road on the south, so it's a big zone and encompasses a large area. Now within zone 6 is a very exclusive country club and it's known as Atlantis Country Club and is located on the west side of Congress Avenue, on the south side of J.F.K, Hospital, John Fitzgerald Kennedy. Now Atlantis sits just off the avenue and has a well-manicured lawn and driveway leading up to the club house, and like all golf courses, is well maintained and groomed as Florida is known to have a few golf courses.

The club house at Atlantis was quite large and had a bar, restaurant, etc., now I can only attest to this as I was never a member

or asked to be one, and never had the occasion to go inside. So, I really didn't know the layout.

Anyway, the dispatcher came on the air with, *"Palm Beach to zone 6, a signal 27, (prowler) at the Atlantis country club and the accountant is terrified."* With that she gave me a case number and time dispatched. I acknowledged her and drove over the speed limit and in no time went 10-97, arrived, I killed my lights and drove slowly as I pulled into the club house area.

It's now late evening and dark and all seemed to be closed down. The only light came from what was the office and it had an octagon shaped window that was about face high, and this window was behind some trees and bushes, off to the side of the club house. As I pull up slowly, I see a white male trying to get in this window and you just knew was scaring the lone female inside. Now it just so happened that the prowler, or whatever he had in mind, saw me pull up so he started to run away.

I still had to stop, park my car, get out, all this time giving the male a head start. Well, I started to run after him as he ran first behind the club house and over an open space. Now off to the left was what I guess was a driving range as there were squares set up and as I ran past that's what they looked like to me. Behind that was a long two

story building set up like a motel, I don't know where the golf course is, and I don't much care.

Now this guy I'm chasing runs up a flight of stairs to the second floor and runs down the hallway about midway into a room. At the other end of this group of doors is another set of stairs. I wouldn't guess how many doors or rooms there were, just say lots as I didn't take the time to count them, I'll just say lots. This guy was just going into a room when I made it up to the second floor. So, I took my gun out, not aiming at the guy, and fired a round off over the driving area just to scare him into stopping but what it did was to make him run all the faster, doing a sharp left turn into a door which he slammed shut.

By now I'm on the second floor and I see just were the guy ran into a door and slam it shut. Now I made it down the hallway but I'm all sweaty and out of breath and I kick the door he just went in and it fly's open and all the lights are on. There in the middle of the room is a cot or rollaway bed and there's this guy in bed with his eyes closed, covers pulled up to his nose and sweating like mad. So, I walked up to the bed and said, *"you SOB,"* and I grabbed the bed and flipped it over, guy and all, and guess what, he had all his clothes and shoes on, so I grabbed him and yanked him to his feet. I cuffed him with his hands in back and started walking him back to the club house. When I got there, I was met by Detective Lt. Val Jean Haley, and he advised me that he would handle the case, so not to question him I took off my cuffs, got into my car and went 10-8, back in service.

I advised the dispatcher that the case was TOT, turned over to Lt. Haley.

****

I never did see or talk to the account secretary who had made the complaint, but I know she was relieved. I don't know what Haley did with the prowler, but I bet my life he won't do that again. Best of all, I didn't have to do any paperwork.

BOBBY LEVINE - LATHI

Everybody knows Clint Eastwood of Dirty Harry fame, or at least cops do. That's where he played Inspector Calahan, an aggressive purveyor of truth and justice for the SFPD, San Francisco Police Department) and an avowed advocate for constitutional and civil rights for all citizens, especially criminals, well at least, I think.

Well, he also played a purveyor of criminal interests in a flick, called, Thunderbolt and Lightfoot, which also stared Bo Bridges. Now I don't recall the year it came out, but it involved the use of a 20-millimeter Lathi cannon, it's an anti-tank aircraft weapon.

This story also involves a 20-millimeter Lathi cannon, but it happened before *"Thunderbolt and Lightfoot,"*.

The time was in the 70's. I was a road patrol sergeant and always busy with uniform troops and calls that required uniform personal, so I didn't concern myself to much with detectives or vice cops because they weren't my responsibility. I know everyone in both divisions, and we were all friends, and most had worked for me at some time before they were promoted and still in uniform. I didn't get involved with either division unless they asked for assistance.

It just so happened that one of the vice agents developed a stinger, a snitch or informant, on a guy by the name of Bobby Levine and that Bobby was the proud possessor of a 20-millimeter Lathi cannon, also that Bobby had some larceny in mind with its use. Now Bobby had the cannon mounted in the back end of a pickup truck that also had a camper shell to hid it in. Being mobile like that, Bobby possibly had in mind an armored car or something similar. I never did find out for sure cause poor Bobby got busted, arrested, before he got a chance to use it.

Now it's illegal to possess military ordinance and explosives or silencers unless you have a federal stamp(s) and are a class 3 dealer from ATF, Alcohol, Tobacco and Firearms, and you can also be charged under state statute. Unfortunately for Bobby, he had neither, so he was charged under state statute for possession of an illegal firearm. Sorry to say I wasn't in on the original bus, but it went down with no problems. Now Bobby didn't pass go but went directly to jail.

I just happened to be on day shift and was the road sergeant when they brought the cannon out to road patrol to be stored in our armory along with all the accessories. All I did was to help take it off the truck as it had been dismantled and was in several crates.

Our Sheriff, William Heidtman, known as the Silver Fox, had only recently been appointed Sheriff, as the one in office, Martin Kellenburger, had suffered a stroke and was unable to continue his duties of Sheriff. Now William R. Heidtman had been an insurance executive and he was a personal friend of Governor Claude Kirk who definitely had the authority to appoint Heidtman as sheriff.

It would almost make one think that politics and law enforcement go hand in hand. Now Heidtman didn't know fecal matter about law enforcement, but he was a good administrator and surrounded himself with good people who would coach him in legal ways, and besides he was fascinated by the workings of the department, and he even managed to get national recognition for clearing up Palm Beach County from motorcycle gangs, and fortunately he was good to us troops. Well, the curiosity got the best of him, and he came out to road patrol as the gun was being unloaded and said, *"Henry"*, that's Captain Sanchez, *"I'm going to take the cannon out to our pistol range as it really needs fired."*, of course, it REALLY needed fired. Anyway, he had a new shotgun that he wanted to fire it. I believe it was a model 10, I don't remember the brand name. It was one of those new 12-gauge shotguns that's made short and made to be fired with only one hand. (a people gun) It had a short U-shaped attachment that fit in the crook of the arm, and it also was designed to hold a flashlight to be mounted SOS that you hit whatever you aimed the light at. It was made strictly for law enforcement personnel. Now me and Lt. Bendick are assigned to load it up and go with the Sheriff to the range and assist him. We loaded up the long crate, the barrel, and the small ones with the clips and ammo, and now we're off to see the wizard.

Well, our range is out in the boondocks, out in the country, and when we get there, we set the gun up and load the clip. The gun is about 200 yards from a large hill that's used for a backstop for our firearms. Now I'm not an ordinance expert but the Lathi is a clip fed, top loading weapon and holds 5 rounds in the clip. I think it's an anti-aircraft weapon and it has a large spider sight. When you push the clip in and down it locks into place. Well, the Sheriff walks up and now he's looking a little skeptical on firing such a big gun. He tells Bendick to go ahead and fire it. So Bendick gets into the metal harness that's on the gun, that's 2 metal stirrups that you put your shoulders up against real snug so that you don't break them on the recoil when the weapons fired. Well, Bendick fires and there's a loud boom and the hill explodes about halfway up, when the smoke clears there's a noticeable hole where the round hit. He gets up and tells the sheriff, *"Go ahead and fire it sheriff, it's fun to shoot,"* Well the Sheriff looks like he wants to but instead he tells me to go ahead and try it. Well, I never fired anything that big, caliber wise, and it looked like it would tear your arms off, but hell, I'd never say anything. I got into the harness and made dam sure I was in tight, looked through the spider sight, closed my eyes, and pulled the trigger. WHAM! It definitely caught my attention, but it wasn't too bad. The Sheriff never did fire the weapon stating, *"We'd save the rest of the ammo and besides it fired okay."* We fired the sheriff's new shotgun. On a bare arm it gave you what looked like a hickey or a sucker bite in the crook of your arm where the U-shaped attachment was. This was supposed to be the stock, but the recessed screw on the U-shaped screw left its imprint on you when it was fired.

Well, we took the Lathi 20 mil, back to road patrol and put it in the armory and told Wagner, he was the armorer, that it needed to be cleaned first. I didn't think any more about it cause frankly we don't have much call for a cannon in our line of work. It was just several days later while I'm at road patrol, it's still day shift, and I'm waiting for my troops to come in off the road so I can check all their paperwork done that day when I hear this voice call over the PA system, public address, *"Barton, in my office."* He hated to mince words and sounded like he just gargled with battery acid, I wonder, *"shit, what did I do now or what didn't I do when I should have or what did one on my troops do that I should have known about."* Captain Sanchez was the type of man that could make a priest pray. He was the kind of CO, commanding officer, that you automatically thought, what did I do now. Well, I go into his office, and he says, commo just called, communications, and there's an attempted jail break. Take your troops down to the jail and hurry and no radio transmission. What a relief, *"yes sir I'm 10-51,"* enroute. No radio transmission as anyone monitoring our radios, if things were bad at the jail the inmates wouldn't know we were coming. Hell, that wasn't bad, I'd rather have a jail break than have the captain on my ass.

Well, the troops were all in and waiting for me to do their paperwork, so I tell them, *"Throw your paperwork in the basket and I'll check it tomorrow, were going to the jail cause there's an attempted break. No radio transmission and no guns in the jail, just night sticks, let's go."*

Now the Palm Beach County jail is in the city of West Palm Beach, and we were coming from the north side of Palm Beach International Airport, a distance of 3 or 4 miles. All nine of us go screaming code 3, that's blue lights and siren, and get to the jail in no time. The dispatcher already knew we were enroute by a landline, you can image that a lot of people ran over a curb, or onto the median strip in a hurry to get out of the way of 9 sheriff's department patrol cars driving like crazy with blue lights and sirens going.

We had arrived at the jail; the dispatcher knew it and so we went on 10-33 traffic, emergency traffic only. The city of West Palm Beach's police department had the jail ringed as the jail is in their city. We go into the first floor of the jail after everyone secured his weapon in the trunk of their car and all we had were night sticks. Well at the booking desk there stands Captain Jack, OIC, Officer in Charge, he's waiting for us and tells us that the break is on the 3rd floor and that the rest of the jail is locked down and secure.

Now there are several detectives waiting to go upstairs with me and my troops and at this time the detective bureau was in the same building as the jail just on a different floor, in fact every division of the sheriff's department was in this building except for the Uniform Division which was at the airport. Kind of makes you think they kept the uniform troops low-key and kind of out of sight.

The jail always has about 400 plus inmates, give or take a few, the 3rd floor supposedly housed the badass.

Well, me and the troops crowd into the elevator and we go up with nights sticks, no one has a gun. The elevator door opens and out we pour onto the 3rd floor. The cells are all large and they have about 6 cells within. As you enter from the elevator you first enter a lounge type area where they have a table or two and then behind this are the small individual cells. Each one is a 2-man cell with a commode, and these are open through the day as the inmates have access from cell to cell and the lounge area. Well, we went around and started checking the cell blocks systematically. By this time Lt. Humphrey, the 3 to 11 PM detective Lt, and or OD, officer of the day, and several more detectives came up, now it's really strange cause there's no noise, no cat calls from the inmates, no nothing.

Well one of my troops spots it first, it's a heavy mesh screen covering one of the air conditionings ducts up high, and it was bent and just hanging, it was right in the main hallway in front of cell number 308 and 309, but anyway none had made it up through the duct yet. This duct is up about 10 feet off the floor and all the main cell doors were locked when we first came up and they still were, someone had gotten out of a main cell and had worked on the screen and screws on the duct, and you could see that it took more than one inmate to do this.

Now bars in a jail are vertical, up & down, and are about 1 inch in diameter and about 5 or 6 inches apart, about every 15 to 18 inches there is a flat bar, horizontal, that the vertical bars pass through, I guess they reinforce the other bars, now all these go from floor to the celling. We took night sticks and ran them along these bars, just like a kid running a stick along a picket fence. Well, don't you know that we got 3 bars to fall out. They had been sawed out and put back in place and were held by soap chips and cigarette ash mixed. All jail bars are painted a battleship gray, so the soap and cigarette ash blended right in with the paint. Well, I had the troops check every bar on the 3rd floor, and no more saw throughs were found, just the first three.

Well, we had a jailer with us, and he opened a cell and that's where I met Bobby Lavine for the first time and only cause the jailer called him by his first name. We, my troops and I went into the cell and did a complete shake down starting with Bobby's cell block. We found a hack saw blade and a shank, homemade knife, the shank was made from a toothbrush. Then we lined up the 15 prisoners we had in the lounge and cell block, had them strip down and grab their ankles as we were looking for any additional contraband, which is illegal to possess.

Well, I got to tell you I called a lot of people asshole but that's the first time I had so many look at me. We checked every cell and inmate on the 3rd floor. What was nice is that the detectives did all the paperwork. Well, it was all over so myself and my troops went back toroad patrol normally, and not code 3.

****

Bobby Lavine was charged additionally with jail break. Now I didn't follow his career, but he was a con, convict. When he finally got out of prison he went to court and had his name changed and the last I heard was that he opened a jewelry store and was dealing especially in gold as it had just been declared legal to possess by Richard Milhouse Nixon. I don't know Bobby's new name or the name of his business, but the Lathi is still in the armory as far as I know.

BOBBY SPAIN

It's the 3 to 1 PM shift, and I was working my zone, that's zone 2. It was around 6:00 PM and I already had 2 arrests booked into jail, hell I was already tired and sweaty and wanted to go eat and take it easy, so I ask the sergeant, over the radio, if I could go 10-40, eat, as back at this time we had to ask the sergeant if we could go eat and not the dispatcher. Now the sergeant, George Steidley, was just a relief sergeant and was not the regular one. He told me that as zone 3 was already 10-40, my adjacent zone and I couldn't go so that killed that idea for now.

Well, I headed west on Westgate Avenue figuring I'd go and sit in the shade at Golf View Elementary School and do my paperwork on the 2 arrests I had made. That way I'd be caught up so far and maybe I wouldn't have to stay at road patrol after shift ended. Back at this time you couldn't leave road patrol until all your paperwork was completed and turned in. That's accidents, citations, reports, your trip sheet and even evidence, like guns, knives, etc. had to be turned in to the property room as it had to be tagged and a property receipt filled out.

I kind of averaged 3 or 4 hours over each night working in zone 2 as zone 2 was a busy zone and sometimes I just went from call to call, and no time to do a report.

Anyway, I'm still west bound on Westgate Avenue and I'm almost to the school when I see this car up ahead. it's east bound, coming slowly, and weaving from one lane and then back. Oh hell, it's a DWI and he's coming straight at me, so I just pull off the road and into a yard as it passes me by.

I advise the dispatcher of just what happened and tell her that I'd be on Westgate Avenue with a DWI and to put me 10-50, traffic stop. She acknowledged and tells me that the complaint desk already had phone calls on the car, and she even had the tag and description. I put on my blue lights and put the federal system on, siren, turned it to manual so I can work it off the horn and take off after the DWI. The car is still east bound and still weaving like crazy when I see it pull into the Lil General store parking lot and just stop right in the middle of it. I pull up just then and see the driver is Bobby Spain.

Now Bobby Spain lives in Westgate along with his kin folk and he represents the typical Florida red neck, always dirty, stinks and needs a bath and has an IQ in the high 20's or low 30's, and today ole Bobby is no different except he's drunk out of his head. Now Bobby stands right at 6 feet tall, and his DL, driver's license, puts him at 318 pounds. I found all this out from his DL on another arrest I made on him several months prior to this stop.

As I pulled into the parking lot Bobby was just getting out of his car and staggering toward the store. He sees me pull-up, get out and walk toward him and he recognizes me and keeps walking but continues waving and says, *"what you want Sheriff?"*

Now when I got out of my car, I took my gas billies with me. I never carried a night stick as we were issued gas billies.

A gas billie is a metal club about 10 inches long, have a hole in one end and it shoots a tear gas shell that was about the size of a 410-shotgun shell. It unscrewed in the middle to put the shell in, then you screwed it back together. Then on the other end it had a spring once it was pulled the billie was armed. The trigger was on the side, and it was just like the switch on a flashlight, all you did was push it forward to fire it expelling the gas. In addition to this it was attached to a leather thong about 15 inches long so that if it was swung at someone it generated a lot of power. We had been taught that if you had to gas someone to aim it at the chest area as the wadding from the shell was also expelled and it would also burn the individual who was gassed, of course anyone who ever got gassed got it all in the face. This incapacitated an individual immediately if not sooner and beside a deputy that had to gas someone had already gone a few rounds, so it was time for the fun and games to cease.

Anyway, Bobby sees the billie in my hand and I said, *"Bobby you're drunk, and you're under arrest, so get in the car."* I say all this slow so he can understand, and I don't make any aggressive moves towards him, nor do I point the gas billie at him. Now Bobby is too big to try and be aggressive with. I stayed away from him about 10 or so feet. Now Bobby is big, fat, and slow, but at 318 pounds he's got to have some strength and so I wanted to keep a safe distance. He says, *"I don't want to go,"* also in his slow and slurry voice, not in a mad tone. He just didn't want to go to jail but into the store, probably to buy some more beer. Well at this time I jumped right up to him and stuck the gas billie in his face and shouted, *"get in the goddamn car"*, now Bobby is slow and dumb but he's not stupid as he knows what a billie can do and so he just about jumped in the back seat of my patrol car. Boy I was sure glad that was over.

I unscrewed the gas billie, removed the cartridge and fired an empty billie. I then replaced the cartridge as it was safe to carry as long as it wasn't cocked. Bobby was safe now behind the mesh screen and he was just fumbling around and not cuffed.

I picked up the mike and advised the dispatcher that I had a 10- 15, (prisoner for DWI) and to send a rotation wrecker for Bobby's car and have the jail warm up the breathalyzer unit. The dispatcher acknowledged and told me to stand by as the sergeant wanted to see me. I gave a 10-4 and stared to make out the vehicle storage report while I was waiting, did the inventory of the car. Now while I'm doing this Sergeant Steidley pulls up. Now Steidley is pretty sharp. He's retired out of the Navy, and he made sergeant on our department in just a few years.

Well, I just stand with him by the sergeant's car, and he just wanted to make sure I didn't have any trouble with my arrest. When he saw that my prisoner was Bobby Spain, he said I should have gassed him anyway, but they would be glad to get Bobby at the jail as he was a good cook and a kitchen helper. I gave Steidley the tow slip for the car as he had offered to standby and wait for the wrecker so I could get Bobby to the jail.

Well, I walked toward my patrol car, and I see Bobby with his arm hanging out and resting on the door, the widow was completely down. Now police cars have their window and door handles removed, at least in the back seat, and inside they have a mesh screen that divides the front and rear seats and so it's actually a mobile cage. I got to my patrol car and ask Bobby, *"how in the hell did you get the window down,"* he showed me his thumb and right forefinger and said, *"I just rolled it down."*

Now I didn't want to make a big deal out of it, so I told Bobby to just get his arm inside and move to the other side of the car. Well, I got the window crank out of the glove compartment and put the window back up. As I was driving to the jail, I was thinking how much strength it must have taken to put just 2 fingers on the knob and roll the window down. I could just see my bod if ole Bobby had got his hands on me, blessed gas billies!

At the jail Bobby read .2 on the breathalyzer and he got 90 days in the slammer, besides now the jail had a good cook.

****

I arrested Bobby again for the same offense 3 1/2 years

later. If you ever take a window crank off your car for any reason, try with 2 fingers to put it down or up if you can. ALSO PLEASE Don't DRINK AND DRIVE IN MY ZONE. I'm OLDER NOW AND THEY Don't ALLOW GAS BILLIES!

BODY RECOVERY

By now I had been a road sergeant for several years and my diving for the department hadn't been as active as when I had first started as far as accident victims, drowning, evidence recovery etc. Oh, I still dove 3 or 4 times a week or more if the weather permitted, but it was for sport, spear fishing, because that's what I really enjoyed. Well, the sheriff's department had grown so much since I first started and done so many recoveries, that now the department had several certified divers along with boats, airplanes and even a helicopter and they were now called "special services". The divers were called, what else," *the harbor patrol"*. It was just past noon, and the weather was so hot and sunny, and I noticed the trees were not moving, that meant no wind blowing, meaning the ocean would be clear. So, I grabbed my diving gear and gun, spear gun, that is, threw them in my hippie van and was just about to leave the house when the phone rings. It was the complaint desk from the department, and it was the complaint desk supervisor. She wanted to know if I could go and see just what I could do at a pond in Mangonia Park, it was about two miles east of my home.

She, the supervisor, tells me that a black male juvenile had possibly drown and hadn't been seen or recovered yet and that a road unit was standing by securing the scene and that the harbor patrol units had been contacted but wouldn't be on the scene for at least 45 minutes. My name was still listed as an active diver, and it was close to my home. Well, she tells me the directions to the pond, and I recalled years ago a little black girl also drown in that same pond. I tell her that I know the pond and that I'm enroute. I hear her relay to the dispatcher to advise the road unit that '213', my ID number, was 10-51, enroute. I jumped into my hippie van dressed in my badly faded jeans and my flip flops, shoes, sort of, these were my standard clothes for diving in the ocean. Well, it only took me 8 to 10 minutes until I was 10-97, arrive. The pond was behind a business that made computer parts, I think. The pond was actually a small lake and it had been used by blacks mostly as it was close to several low-income housing projects in the Mangonia Park, Riviera Beach area. By now there's got to be 70 to 100 kids all standing quietly, scared, around the water's edge. No joking or laughing and no one in the water. I see the deputy's car and who is standing by and drive over/ around the lake to where he is, and it's Greg Vincent. He gives me a *"hi Sarge,"* and fills me in about a B/M juvenile, 9 or 10 years of age that was swimming and all of a sudden, he wasn't seen any more. Vincent points to the general area where he was last seen and then he points to a young black female standing off in the distance saying that *"it's the missing boy's mother"*. The pond/lake covers maybe two acres so it's pretty big area to search and so it would take some time to swim around and search, and it all depended on visibility, if there was any. The water didn't look bad at all, not like most canals that as you go deeper, they just got blacker and so all I could do was dive to the bottom, make an ark with one hand.

So as not to get caught under a tree or any obstruction and pull myself along with the other, and if you're lucky, you find what you're looking for. Well, I tell Vincent that I don't have any scuba gear with me, tank, and regulator, but that the water didn't look to bad, so I'll look around anyway. We got to do something positive in front of all these people until the harbor patrol arrives for a possible recovery.

Well, I put my knife on my leg, my booties and my mask and fins, and in the water, I go, with Vincent on the bank. Right away I see that the visibility is really good, 25 or 30 feet, so that's good. The lake bottom drops right away from shore and the deepest point looks to be about 18 to 20 feet. Looking down from the surface I can see a haze like cloud, that's what they call a thermocline, a layer of colder water. I can see beyond the layer all the way to the bottom of the pond. I take a deep breath and dive down to the haze/thermocline and it's like going into a cooler. The water was definitely colder but still clear and it catches your attention, the water is a good 12 to 15 degrees cooler than surface water or on top of the haze. While diving down I noticed a lot of trees, tires, and branches sticking out of the sides, plus lots on the bottom, also while swimming down I swam out from the bank/shore, and I was closer to the middle. Well, I had to go up for a breath, as I was only free diving. So up on the surface I waited a couple of minutes, rested, and hyperventilated, breathing hard, and dove back down a second time and LO, there he was, a poor little black boy, about 10 or 12 feet down, right at the thermocline with his foot jammed into the crook of a tree branch much like a wish bone but this was a deadly wish bone. What probably happened is that he dove down and not wearing a mask, hit the thermocline, colder water, and the sudden shock of the colder water made him scared and he hurriedly tried to get back to the surface, and when he did, he just jammed his foot all the harder. He still had his arms outstretched toward the surface, so close, but yet so far. Poor kid. Looking at him for a second, I could see the seven-year-old boy that I had recovered long ago in North Palm Beach, on the inter-coastal water way. He was in the very same position when I found him reaching up to the surface, arms outstretched to the surface. Well, I pulled his limp little body down just a bit to release him from the branch and held the body with one arm around him and saw I was only about 20 or so feet from the shore. I took the snorkel out of my mouth and told Vincent on the bank that I had the kid and to get a disposable blanket from his trunk, and to also advise the dispatcher that we had made a recovery, and to 10-22, disregard, the harbor patrol units responding. I pulled up to the bank and gently laid the kid down and Vincent covered him over with the yellow disposable blanket. You could hear a lot of sighs and hushed comments from all the scared kids standing around. The boy's mother came over to me, crying in her grief. and said words to me I'll never forget, *"Thank you Mr. Policeman for my boy"*. I got into my van with some wet eyes and drove home.

CAR IN CANAL OFF B LINE HIGHWAY

The time was in the mid 70's and by now the sheriff's department had grown in size right along with the population of the county. They now had three substations on the east coast, in addition to Belle Glade Sub. I was the senior road sergeant and so I got first choice where I wanted to work, and Captain Sanchez was going to be the CO, commanding officer, of the north substation. I also chose that one. Well in comparison to the central or south substations it was considered a country club and for good reason.

I was working the day shift and Lt. Fritz was the administrative Lt. He had been a team leader for one of the TAC squads, also known as SWAT teams, and I was the leader of the second team. Fritz worked three days a week with his team, and I worked the other three days, we all worked on Sundays, at least on paper. The time was around 9:30 to 10:00 AM and nothing great had happened so far, it hardly ever did on day shift except for B & Es which were mostly residential and had happened on the night shift anyway. Well, I was just coming from home in Gramarcy Park after stopping to see my wife and kids. I had just left the house when the dispatcher calls Able 4, substations were ID'd as Able, the northern most, Baker or the central region and Charlie as the southernmost. Able 4 acknowledged and the dispatcher advised him to 10-65 10-17, copy and investigation, and to check out a car in a canal on the Beeline Highway, State Road 710, just east of the intersection of Haverhill Road. She advised that it was reported by the engineer of the FEC (Florida East Coast) railroad that they were east bound.

Now the Beeline Highway has nothing on it except swamp, sand and a canal that runs parallel to the highway, so it's generally just boondocks, 15 miles west is Pratt & Whitney Experimental Plant.

The tracks are on the south side of the highway and are a good 75 to 100 feet from the roadway. Well, I happened to be close, so I told Able 4 to 10-22, disregard, that I would check it out. Now just about any place you can drive in Florida on a road has a canal, and people are forever dumping trash, cars etc. into them in addition to driving into them as the result of accidents. When you get a call like that it can be anything, so you never know, but you still have to check it out. I got to the intersection of Haverhill and ask the dispatcher for a better 10-20, location, and she advises me that it's about 1/4 mile east.

Well by now we had convertacoms, that radios that were portable and they charged up while in the cars, when you left the car, you pushed a button that released the radio, and it was portable and fully charged. I started walking toward the tracks, and then just started walking east bound on the tracks because I could see the canal. Well, I went about 150 feet and sure enough there was the roof of a car in the canal, it looked about 3 feet under the surface. From the looks of the brush and the tracks it appeared that it had been in the water for some time. Well, I tell the dispatcher that I found the car and to send a 10-70 (wrecker) from the rotation list and she comes back in 2 minutes that Karl's wrecker is 10-51, enroute, so I tell her to tell the driver that I will meet him at my car on the Beeline Highway, and she acknowledges me. Now in about 20 minutes Karl's wrecker pulls up and the drive looks like he slept with the wrecker. When he finds out that there's a car in the canal and it's way off the road and that he's going to have to stretch the cable across the railroad tracks and then that he's going to have to dive down to the car to hook it up he says, *"man, I ain't going in no canal."* Now at first, I thought he was just screwed but then I realized he wasn't and so I told him to get the hell out of here. I told the dispatcher I was taking Karl's off the rotation list as the driver refused to dive for the car. Now all this was done on the air so all who monitored our calls heard of Karl refusal. I ask her to send me the next 10-70 on the rotation list. Well, it was Leo's wrecker, and the driver was named Dick. He was the son of the owner. It's a family-owned business. A service station, wrecker service, and car body work. Both Dick and his dad are good people and I try to steer as much wrecker business as I can their way. I then had the complaint desk call FEC dispatch and advise them that we will be pulling a car of the canal and that their engineer reported to be aware that we would have a cable stretched across the tracks so to let us know well in advance when their next train was due. Well Dick took his hook along with a chain attached, dove down and hooked on to the car and I held the end while he hooked it to the cable. Then he cranks it tight, took up the slack, and starts a steady pull and up comes a 4-door compact car. Then he let it drain on the canal bank. I looked at the front seat and it was empty. Then I looked at the back seat and saw a skeleton and right away I figured a signal 5, murder, I tell Dick to just leave the car on the bank and to disconnect the cable because we'd be a while. Then I tell the dispatcher to call the north substation and tell the Lt. that I'd need a detective and a crime scene unit, she acknowledges me. I never said anything else over the air as far as a skeleton, but only that I needed both units. Well, the first thing I know, is Channel 5 has a reporter on the scene. They monitored all the sheriff's department channels, we used to have scramblers but some judicial body in all its wisdom said that was illegal and that everyone has a right to hear. Boy our detectives and crime scene should respond so quickly! The next thing I know the reporter is walking across the sand and coming up on the tracks just about to get to the car on the canal bank and he's got a camera with him, so I head him off and tell him it's a crime scene and if he crosses the track, I'm going to arrest him for it, and he backs off. Now this particular reporter I have known for a long time, and I didn't particularly like him because of the way he would come on the scene of an accident or a crime scene and try an intimidate a deputy with his right to know crap. He later lost his job over some strange circumstances involving little girl. Anyway he backs off from my possible crime scene. I give the dispatcher the tag number of the vehicle for a 10-28, registration check, and advises her to just hold the information and not put it on the air.

Lt. Fritz shows up along with a detective, he tells me that the car and its contents would be towed to, and processed, at the central substation and not to disturb anything. I found out later that the victim was a signal 8, missing person, a white female, and her case had been worked 6 months prior, also that she had lived in the same development as I did.

Now we had to build a ramp up and over the railroad tracks to get the car over easy so not to disturb the skeleton and clothes in the back seat. Well, I got the car and its contents to central substation with no problem and TOT, turned over to, the detective who had originally worked the case so he could close it out. Now I was really pissed at Karl's wrecker driver and so back at the north substation I told Lt. Fritz about it, and Captain Sanchez told me, *"I'll take care of it,"* well I wanted Karl's off the wrecker rotation list.

A couple of days later the captain tells me that Karl's had fired the wrecker driver, but that Karl's managed to stay on the list. Now I'm just sure that somebody wasn't in someone's pocket, heaven forbid!

An autopsy showed that the woman died of drowning and no foul play. The back floor of the car was loaded with empty beer cans, so it was figured that she was drunk and drove into the canal and her death was listed as accidental.

****

I'm sure there was no road there, but she drove through soft sand and scrub and just jumped the railroad tracks. Hell, she committed suicide but there's no way to prove it.

COCKFIGHTS

This is a story about birds, specifically the kind that fight and not in the barnyard or on the farmland kind. this is strictly about fighting cocks, that's in an arena. These are the kind of birds that put steel spurs on their feet, and when the price is right, and all bets have been placed. and believe me, a lot of money is bet. won, and lost over the outcome.

Now cock fighting is illegal and so it's a state law in Florida, as in most if not all states of the union. But millions of dollars are bet on cock fights, and the owners of such birds take great pride and care of their birds as they are a valuable commodity, and can have the potential of making them a lot of money, even though it is a crime,

Now as it is a crime in the state, so deputies enforce state law and anyone found fighting birds was jailed, moneys and birds confiscated etc. The crime of cock fighting, and of fighting dogs, although it was against the laws of the state, they were not crimes or

calls that a regular road deputy would normally answer as he responded to domestics, accidents and just about anything you can think of, but sorry to say, rooster and dog fighting wasn't big on his agenda.

Now these types of crimes were investigated by vice or detective units of the department, in addition to following dope deals, illegal gun deals etc. They also followed up on cock fights etc. when they had the time. Cock and dog fighting were big sports among migrants, and it was usually conducted out in the woods or farmland, always far away from civilization.

Now it just so happened that one of the vice agents developed a stinger, CI, confidential informant, who had advised that a large group of fighting cocks, and migrants were to gather at a compound that run just east of state road #7, state road #7, was also known as the Range-line. Now the area where the fighting was supposed to take place was in a very rural area, and it was all encompassed with trees and bushes etc. A big turnout would be there to watch and bet.

I was a uniform deputy at the time and the informant used must've been used in the past, so his information was reliable. The head of the vice squad, Lt. Val Gene Haley, came to the road patrol headquarters and ask if he could use some uniform deputies from the road and those that were off work who might want to go on the cock fight raid that he had planned.

The time was a Saturday afternoon and I just so happened to be off work at the time, he wanted maybe 10 or 12 uniform deputies, so it was to be a pretty big raid. He also had several vice agents going along so a lot of personal from the department would be in use. All the uniform deputies were also off work at the time so it wouldn't affect the road units any. A raid like this wouldn't affect the day shift work of the uniform patrol, and so the raid was planned.

Now all the uniform personal, of which there were more than 10, plus the vice agents also going, were to meet at road patrol headquarters. So, a sizable force was assembled to go. Now it was explained by the vice agent in charge of the raid, just what was going to take place. Arrests were to be made, and evidence was to be taken for court at a later date. The evidence was fighting cocks, spurs and money.

All the vice agents had their own cars, and all were different in color, style etc. so they blended right in with everyday traffic and would cause no alarm to anyone who saw them. But with the uniform personal, they just couldn't take that many patrol cars, as once a uniform car was spotted, everyone there would try and run into the woods and hide and there would be a lot less arrests made, and a large majority would get away. It was decided by the agent in charge, that all the uniformed personnel could hide in a, King Car/Truck Van. It was a big cube shaped 1-ton van with the King Car/Truck logo on the sides and would be plenty big enough to hide all the uniformed deputies inside and would cause no alarm when seen. After all, rental trucks and vans were a common sight on the roads, Kings Car/Truck rentals just happened to be PINK in color. Beside the cube van was so big, that anyone arrested, and they anticipated a lot of arrests would be made, could be locked up in the back end and could be taken to jail, besides a rental van didn't have any windows in it, so no one could see the uniform personal, and by then it would be too late to run and try hiding in the woods.

There would surely be a lot of money on the ground, bets etc., all the money found would be turned over to the agent in charge, a crime scene deputy would be called and take pictures of all the birds, money and migrants caught in the raid, and the department would take charge of the birds and all the evidence.

With all the preliminaries out of the way, and all explained about the raid and just what we were to do, we all went out and loaded up into the PINK van and the overhead back door was closed with all uniforms inside. I believe that most deputies also carried a shotgun in addition to their regular side arm, and we all had a supply of plastic handcuffs for arrests made.

Back at this time a deputy could carry whatever firearm he had qualified with at the gun range, so an array of wheel guns, revolvers ranging from a 38 caliber, all the way up to a 44 magnum, if he carried a shotgun as well, he could as long as he had also qualified with it. Some had single barrel pump action, and some carried double barrel shotguns, one thing they all were was 12-gauge.

Well, the van ride in the dark with all the deputies standing up as there was no place to sit down, but thankfully it was only about 20 minutes where we pulled off the Range-line. I'm sure the caravan was led by the vice agent in charge, anyway you could feel crossing a wooden bridge over a canal that ran parallel to the road. We were there and now, and the van stopped. One of the vice agents involved in the raid was our driver, he hurriedly opened the door and outran all the uniform deputies.

What we saw as we poured out of the van were several rows of cages and each cage had a fighting cock inside. The birds had to be separated as they would automatically fight another bird if they could get to him. They didn't need any steel spurs as they were for the two who would be in the ring at the time, and they tried to get to them before they killed the other bird. There were lots of Mexicans and Puerto Ricans running about, especially when they saw the deputies from the sheriff's d epartment. When the van pulled up, they must have thought it was just someone with a load of fighting cocks, when it stopped and all the deputies ran out, well SURPRISE, guess what's about to take place. Needless to say, a lot of arrests were made and every one of the fighting cocks was taken into evidence. A lot of money was taken also. The best thing about the raid was that the vice squad handled all the paperwork, the arrest forms, booking slips etc., Us in uniform didn't have to do anything. All it cost us was our time and that was well spent. And best of all, no one got shot.

The sheriff's department confiscated all the birds and moved them to another location. They had to be watered and fed and cared for. The care they received was on a daily basis and it was quite some time as the department couldn't just dispose of them as they were live roosters, and they were also evidence in the case. There had to be more than 40 birds.

Well, the department tried to pass on the expense of keeping the birds, both the watering and feeding and even the services of a veterinarian onto the owners. But lo, a suit was filed in Palm Beach County court. It was declared by the court that the sheriff's department had the birds in custody, held as evidence and so they were responsible for the care and feeding and any other expense incurred. Well, I got to tell you that the local newspaper made a big deal of it in one of their articles and the sheriff's department ended up paying for the upkeep and I got to tell you, it was more than chicken feed for 40 plus birds.

CONTINUATION OF OUTLAWS

I wrote extensively about the Outlaw M/C gang and my involvement with them. Now what follows also happened, but I was not personally involved. The story continues....

Christine Deese was a young girl, only 18 years old at the time and she was a motorcycle freak, so she got involved with the Outlaws somehow. She became somebody's old lady and to make money for the gang she prostituted herself and would give the money to her old man. Well, she was found to have withheld $10 of her hard-earned money and when the Outlaws found out about it, they decided to teach her a lesson. So, they nailed her to a tree by her hands. Well, she was treated at St. Mary's Hospital emergency room and that's how the sheriff's department became involved.

Now her father was named Tom Deese, a very big man, about 6'5" or 6" and well over 200 pounds. He worked for FPL, (Florida Power & Light.) Tom was also an auxiliary deputy sheriff, meaning he had to ride with a regular deputy sheriff so many hours a month. Tom liked to ride in the southern zones as he liked to work in the labor camps which the county had many of. He would ride with a deputy Grady Brannam, and he once threw a Puerto Rican male through a wall, so you can see he had a temper.

The sheriff figured that once Tom found out what happened to his daughter that he would go bananas and a violent crime was sure to happen. Sheriff Heidtman called someone big at FPL and had Tom transferred immediately to north Florida.

Now Tom had a brother George who was just a wee bit smaller than Tom and was the Chief of Police in the city of

Green Acres. It sat somewhat in the center of Palm Beach County. However, I don't think that he ever got involved in the case, this is only my assumption.

The case with Christine Deese got national press coverage and sometime later, Sheriff Heidtman and Lt. Haley went to the city of Detroit Michigan, and   with the help of DPD (Detroit Police Department) raided the Outlaws club house and arrests were made. Three of the Outlaws were extradited to Palm Beach County where they were tried and convicted of nailing Christine to the tree.

CORVAIR SIGNAL 7'S

This sad event occurred in 1967, I had only been on the sheriff's department about 1 or 2 months, and I was considered a rookie. The shift was the day shift, 7 AM to 3 PM. and I had been put in zone6.

Day shift on the department, as on most departments consistedof taking reports on crimes that were mostly committed on the night shift such as B&Es, breaking and entering, but weren't reported until later when people went to work. The department also had a school crossing program, all the guards were women that I can remember, but it was run by a guy named DeFazzio, also on the day shift, there was also a lot of traffic to contend with.

Day shift, especially in the morning, consisted of a lot of PR, public relations, and errands for deputies, especially unfortunateto be assigned close to road patrol headquarters, like zones 3/4, such as picking up friends of someone in high places, or picking up laundry, uniforms at some dry cleaners etc. On this day I happened to be away from all this as I was in zone 6, an area that ran from 10th Ave as its north boundary, all the way to Lantana Road, its southern border. It was definitely a large area to cover. This single event that was about to occur changed my entire career, life and what society would have thought of me. Now the southwestern part of zone 6 is mostly farmland and rural country, but it still has several labor camps within its boundary, and that means migrants as it was that time of year when the vegetables and other crops were ripening. Now it was getting into the later part of the shift and so far, there were no outstanding calls that I can remember.

Well, the dispatcher came on the air with, Palm Beach

zone 6, signal 4, accident, Lantana and Jog roads, vehicle on fire and unknown injuries. Well, I acknowledged her by advising 10-4, 10-51, code 3, that's I got her message and I was enroute with my blue lights and siren. Well, it didn't take no time at all running so fast with lights and siren on.

When I got there, I found a single car involved and it was on fire, inside were 2 women screaming and clawing on the glass, trying desperately to get out. the heat and the flames were so hot that I couldn't even get close. the car was just burning up with its two occupants. The doors of the car must have jammed when it had hit the fence. The car was a Chevy Corvair. Now I'm sure that the fire department had been called and that they were responding posthaste, but I was there in rural Palm Beach County with a car burning up and two women screaming and clawing to get out but couldn't, so not thinking that I would be tried for murder, took my gun out and was about to shoot them through the glass window, knowing there was no saving them and I wasn't about to let them die that way regardless.

Just at that very moment a car drove up and it was a vice agent named Grady Lisk, who had heard my call on his radio, and he was in the area stopped to see if he could assist me. when he saw me with my gun in hand and the burning car with its occupants, screaming and clawing on the glass, he turned white when he realized what I was about to do and he said, *"Bob, you can't do that,"* he had me put the gun back in the hoister after calming me down. By now the two occupants were dead and the car was burnt up, what a hell of a way to die.

Years later, when I made sergeant, a friend of mine fixed up and gave me a car that I used mostly for fishing as at the time I did a lot of spear fishing and I'd just tie the fish on the car's hood as I didn't want a fishy smell in the car, it looked like a hood ornament when I traveled. The car was a Corvair, when I first got it, it reminded meof the two women who had died a horrible death in one. I found out later that they were a mother and daughter just returning from Belle Glade and who lived in a coastal town. Grady Lisk, the vice agent, finally retired and was rehired to our department motor pool. Thats were detective and patrol cars are serviced.

****

Oh, by the way, a guy named Ralph Nader wrote a book about Corsairs and named it, "UNSAFE AT ANY SPEED."

DEATH & DOGS MANS BEST FRIEND

Saturday morning and its day shift. Not much is happening on Saturday mornings especially day shift except that the zones get busy with Fridays B&Es, breaking and entering, as businesses are opening and finding any vandalism's they may have had. Well, I walk into the lineup room and there sits a good-looking blond female deputy sheriff just sitting there. I recognize her as being from the airport detail. Back then the sheriff's department didn't have any females in uniform on the road. Anyway, she's really good looking, is divorced, and has two small children. I don't know her to talk to other than to say hello once or twice when I happened to be at the airport. I ask her what I can do for her, and she tells me that she has orders from her captain to get some road exposure as to the types of calls handled and to see if she could ride with a zone car. I could see no problem being that she was a deputy sheriff and that it would be fine with me thinking to myself, *"welcome to the world of crime and corruption you fox"*. Besides I didn't want her telling her captain that Sergeant Barton wouldn't let her ride.

I was never wild about airport deputies as they got almost the same money as the grunts on the road, but they didn't have any hassle at the airport, oh a drunk or a fight once in a while but most people at the airport are more concerned about flying somewhere or else picking someone up and aren't interested in causing any trouble.

It seems that airport deputies have a multitude of war stories to tell at choir practices or at department functions, such as the sheriff's annual birthday surprise when the fire water flows, and the cake is long gone. Now I don't remember this particular female deputy telling any war stories at this point in time. I was finding it hard to accept females as grunts on the road, and I'm sure I was not alone in this feeling. Now back when females first started in law enforcement, at least in our department, I had in the back of my mind where I could just hear the radio someday when one of our female deputies takes a disturbance calls at one of our red neck bars, gets into trouble and before a cover car can get to her, one of the customers gets on her patrol car radio and advises for all to hear that, *"the deputy is bar hopping in her maiden form bra"*, or something to that effect. Oh well I could go on and on about the merits of female deputies on the road, but back to the lineup.

I had nothing spectacular to pass on to the troops, just zone assignments and telling zone 3 and 4 that he would have a 10-12 passenger, and I introduced him to the airport deputy that's to ride with him. The zone man already knew her, I figured I'd put her in zone 3 and 4 as it's a central zone where myself, or someone, would always be close by in case of any trouble. Well, lineups not quiet over when in runs one of the troops from the night shift and tells me to call the dispatcher right away. Well, I call, and she tells me that Universal Ambulance had responded to Royal Palm Beach on a call, and they were requesting the sheriff's department to respond as it looked suspicious.

Royal Palm Beach is a nice growing residential community that is a town within the county, and it has its own police department, one man per shift at the time. It handled all misdemeanor calls, and felonies were handled by the sheriff's department. This came from the County Solicitors office which later became known as the States Attorney's Office. These types of situations are embarrassing to officers of small departments; all of who take pride in their city and police departments, but they can only investigate minor crimes as dictated by the Solicitors Office, and who knew the capabilities and equipment of the little department. Being that the Solicitors Office is the prosecuting agency for all crimes committed in Palm Beach County, they have the jurisdiction and the authority to designate which department must turn over to the sheriff's department, even if the crime was committed within their city. Now Palm Beach County has about 33 police departments or law enforcement agencies of which the sheriff's department is the largest. WPBPD (West Palm Beach Police Department) does handle their own felonies now.

Being that RPB (Royal Palm Beach) is in zone 3 and 4 area, I told him to break from line up, get his 10-12 and head toward RPB, and I basically filled him in on the call and to call me if any assistance was needed. It took zone 3 and 4 about 15 minutes to get his gear from his personal car, load it into his patrol car, and head toward RPB. He had about 10 miles to go to get to that city. Now I don't imagine he was on the scene but a minute when he gave me a call at road patrol where I was still doing reports from the night shift as I had just gotten the troops on the road and just called in the line up to the communication desk, name and zone assignments. Now the reports from the night shift had to be checked for errors and classified according to NCIC (National Crime Information Center) this is compiled by the FBI (Federal Bureau of Investigation) and is a directory of crime(s) and is reported by every police agency in the United States, and this is how the FBI comes out with criminal statistics for the country.

Well zone 3 and 4 informed the dispatcher that he's got a dead white male in bed, his penis is gone and no weapon to be found and yet blood is all over the kitchen and hallway and into the bedroom where the victim was found. Now first appearances look like a brutal homicide had occurred. He told me that the only ones there where the ambulance driver who originally called the department and his assistant, the RPB officer and the victim. Now the victim lived alone at this residence, and he had two poodles. I told him to just secure the scene and that I would contact the dispatcher and also get a crime scene unit and I would also contact the detective on duty and too just keep any witnesses present for the responding detective, and that while he's waiting to start a supplemental report as to his involvement in the case, that the detective would do the face sheet. I was in a hurry to get the wheels in motion and so I asked him briefly, *"how's your 10-12 like crime in the real world?"* He responded with, *"I think she's sick."* I called the dispatcher with orders to call the crime scene unit and the duty detective and also the upper echelon who would need to know, such as the detective Lt. at his home, also the detective captain at his home, the chief deputy and the sheriff himself. Well, it was Saturday, and no detective was working, and even though all detectives were titled detective sergeant they had no authority for that matter over other detectives, consequently the detective Lt. was called at his home, advised of the case and what I had done so far and who would he advise to respond to it? Now the Lt. couldn't think of any additional thing for me to do or people to contact, so he just thanked me and ask for the address. Well it appeared to be a decent homicide and I wanted to be there to make sure the crime scene was secure and to assist zone 3 and 4 with the multitude of things that need to be done at the scene of a homicide, or the scene of any major crime, but I didn't even have my gun belt on, or my shotgun, and my personal gear bag was in the sergeant's car, so I called the dispatcher and told her to send the junior sergeant to the scene.

Our department had grown from having a uniform Lt. on the day shift, Monday through Friday, to having a uniform Lt. and two uniform sergeants on all three shifts. The sergeants split the county in two with Southern Blvd. being the dividing line. Now one sergeant supervised the north end on the county and the other the south end. They basically had the same number of zones to supervise, so it was equally shared responsibility. I usually took the south end as I liked to work in the labor camps, also I was the senior sergeant, and I got my choice. Well as the forces of justice prevail, RHIP (Rank Has Its Privileges) and it just so happened that there was no uniform Lt. on duty, compensation day, and so I was the acting Lt., big deal, as it was, I ended up busy spreading happy dust, fingerprint powder, for several of the zones who had B&Es or vandalisms in their area during the night. I also assisted in a felony capias, warrant, arrest, so I didn't get a chance to personally go and assist zone 3/4 at his crime scene. Now the junior sergeant was a good supervisor, a black guy who had just recently made sergeant being promoted and transferred out of the vice squad. I was sure that he would check on the crime scene and keep all in order until the crime scene unit and detective arrived and took charge. Well time passed quickly, and I was busy and at the end of the shift had to go back to road patrol, gas the sergeant's car for the oncoming sergeant, take out my personal gear and have the car ready for the next sergeant, and also fill him in on the day's events, especially the homicide. Now this is one of the biggest bitches the troops had about incidents that happen in their zones, and they never get the word on it, or what happened that they should know about. In their zones, like domestics or B&Es or any anticipated trouble etc. Well, I filled the sergeant in on all of it and lo and behold, a live Lt. shows up to work on the 4 to 12 shift and I have to do it all over again for the Lts. benefit. About this time in comes zone 3/4 with his haggard looking 10-12, airport deputy. She didn't look so fresh and vigorous, and she did in the AM, she was just tired and glad for the end of shift. I took zone 3/4 and his 10-12 aside to check and see if they had all their paperwork in order, and make sure they had all the assistance they needed. He, zone 3/4, fills me in that the crime scene unit, along with a detective Lt., plus several detectives showed up and that the whole scene was covered. He also tells me that the other shift sergeant arrived and when he saw the crime scene unit and the detectives that he just looked in the door stating that he didn't want to taint the crime scene, but zone 3/4 thought it was because there was blood everywhere and he didn't want to get sick. He told me that a brutal homicide had occurred and that person(s) unknown at this time had entered the residence of the victim who lived alone with his two poodles, and it was determined at the time that robbery was the motive but whoever had taken a knife or a sharp instrument and had cut the victims penis off. Now this had happened in the kitchen and somehow the victim had managed to crawl from the kitchen, through the hallway and into the bedroom and got into bed and died, it was also determined that he, the victim, had called the ambulance before he expired. Now the crime scene was easy to reconstruct because of the trail of blood starting in the kitchen and ending in the bedroom. I asked zone 3 /4's 10-12 how she enjoyed riding and assisting the zone man with everyday calls and crimes that a road deputy responds to. She gave me a sheepish grin and said, *"oh Sergeant Barton, I can't wait to get back to the airport and tell my captain that I don't ever want to go on the road, and that I'm perfectly happy at the airport."* Well now, this really confirmed my feelings about females on the road and I kind of related it to having mammary glands on a boar hog.

Well, lo & behold after three days of intensive investigation and the result of an autopsy it was revealed that the victim had died of a heart attack, and he was not the victim of a homicide. The autopsy also revealed that his penis was just tore off and not cut off as originally appeared, under a microscope it showed that the area around the penis to be jagged and uneven and not having been done with a knife or a sharp object but with something dull, like maybe teeth.

Well more than probable cause existed, and a court order was obtained, and the dogs put to sleep. A necropsy was performed on both dogs, and it was revealed that parts of the victim's penis were among the contents found in the stomach. Final analysis showed that the victim had been having sexual relations with the two dogs in the kitchen, bestiality, and that at a crucial moment he had a heart attack and while he was laying there incapacitated and unable to defend himself and with both dogs in an excited state, they just chewed his penis off. The case was ruled as an accidental death and not a homicide.

****

Approximately 8 years later after this happened, I left the department for a 3-year period in Alaska. When I returned, the sheriff's department welcomed me back. I did have to start all over again as a slick sleeve deputy and not as the senior sergeant, I was now 45 years old. Even though the department gladly took me back I had to start at the airport, just like all new hires. Though I was only there for a period of two weeks the same female deputy of so long ago was still there but now made sergeant while I was still there. The deputy she had ridden with on that day is now a road sergeant. The rookie road sergeant was appointed the first black Lt. on the department. The detective in charge on that investigation is now an inspector and is the number three man on the department.

****

A word about female deputies or female cops in general. They have proven themselves time and time again to be most capable in all situations and are as good or better than their male counterparts.

DIVE SCHOOL

This story is about a dive school I attended while still an active member of the Riviera Beach Police Department, but it was conducted by the sheriff's department of the county.

My first experience with the sheriff's department came while I was still on the Riviera Beach Police Department. I had been on that department about a year and a half already and I had just come in for the 3 to 11 PM shift and my sergeant, Sergeant Jeff Waites met me at my locker in the squad room and said, *"Hey Barton, the Chief wants to see you in his office right away."* Well right away I thought shit. what the hell did I do now, as I walked down the hall to his office, as I walked, I kept trying to think of any incidents that might have happened in the last two days that might be cause of a complaint against me. Hell, these civilians, you give them a ticket, or say an unkind word, and the first thing they do is call the department and register a complaint against you.

By now I'm at the office door so I knock." *Come in,"* and I enter, the chief is seated, all neat and professional. He looks up and tells me to sit down. Now in 1 1/2 years I've been on the department I've been to the Chief's office twice and both times ended with me being suspended. The first time I got suspended for 3 days and the second time I got suspended for 5 days, and so with a command like, *"sit down Bob,"* I figured, here we go again. Well to my surprise he says, *"Bob, I know you spend a lot of time diving so I wondered if you would like to attend a diving school that is being sponsored by the sheriff's Department, it's for any county police departments that are interested in having their own recovery unit. The instructors will be the Coast Guard Diving*

Unit out of Miami and will be assisted by Sergeants Bishop and Haley from the sheriff's office, also Bo Wells from our department will attend." Bo Wells was our crime scene man. Well, my sphincter muscle released its grip on the seat, and I replied, *"I'll go,"* knowing that I wasn't on the carpet, and now to be offered the opportunity to attend a diving course. Hell, that's my sport anyway, and as far as I was concerned it would be a piece of cake.

Now I was really into SCUBA diving and at this time I was using several tanks a week, besides doing that I also free dove, just mask & fins.

At this time all my diving had been done in the ocean and it was sport diving like for coral, seashells and spear fishing. So far, I had never been in any canals, lakes or in any fresh water, just the Atlantic Ocean.

The Chief was quick to point out the purpose was that any water related incidents that required the services of a diver, be it day or night, on or off duty, that our response, me and Bo, was to expedite getting a diver to the scene of a water related accident, drowning or evidence recovery within the city limits. Now the police departments in Palm Beach County, of which there are over 30 at this time, had to call the sheriff's department for assistance in requesting a diver for any type of water recovery, and hell, it might take up to 6 or 7 hours for them to respond and it was a real embarrassment to be in uniform at the scene of a drowning, with all the people standing around and sometime even family members of the victim questioning, "hey officer, when are you going to look for the fellow or kid," or whatever the object of concern was.

The sheriff's department had two divers, Sergeant Bishop

which ran the Harbor Patrol was the only full-time deputy who's duties consisted entirely of water related accidents and enforcement within the county, and they also had Sergeant Haley, a detective, who assisted Bishop on drowning calls.

Now Palm Beach County is approximately 2500 square miles and with all its shoreline and waterways added in makes it one of the largest counties east of the Mississippi River. So, when an incident occurred that a diver was needed, the police department needing the diver would contact the sheriff's office for Bishop or Haley. Now if Bishop is out on the water, he first has to get to a dock, call, then get his car and gear, pick up Haley and then they would respond. Like I said, it could take 5 or more hours to go 10-97, or arrive at the scene, from the first time they were notified. You can see what a great benefit it would be for all police agencies to participate in the course and have their own divers.

The city of Riviera Beach is located on U.S.#1, highway, and has within its jurisdiction the Port of Palm Beach, a large and busy portion on the U.S. Inter coastal waterway, a causeway with a beach, known as Phil Foster Park and it's always loaded with tourists and native Floridians. In addition, it has a good 5 or 6 miles of beaches on the Atlantic Ocean side, it also has an island out of the Port of Palm Beach known as Peanut Island. Now Peanut Island has a Coast Guard station and detachment, it also has in addition, a deep vault bomb shelter way below the water level and I think it was built for president JF Kennedy and his family should an emergency arise.

The city of Riviera Beach has no harbor patrol or boats of its own, however, if the need ever arose that one was needed, it would present no problem as there are at least 12 boat storage yards with docks that would only be too happy to assist the police department.......

That would also be another delay in their response.

Now on Riviera PD we changed shifts every 28 days, and this diving course was due to last 2 weeks. That's Monday through Friday of each week, so being already on the 3 to 11 PM shift the course would be no problem. I'd just dive all morning until about 1 PM, leave early, go home, and get ready for work. It would make for a long day but back in 1965, police officers didn't think much about paid overtime, just figuring it went with the job. I had been looking at the course as sport diving and not as a working dive, big difference. I was soon to find out how wrong I was. I figured I was a good diver both SCUBA and free, knew theory pretty well and was not in too shabby of shape due to my almost daily diving.

Well, Chief Cotrell wished me good luck and told me to go to the Knights of Columbus swimming pool at 9 AM on Monday morning. Well, it's Monday morning, 8:30AM, and I'm waiting at the pool, dressed in cutoffs and caring my mask and fins. I had long ago given up buying nice swim trunks as the constant use in saltwater just wore them out or rotted them. So, I just cut the legs off a pair of old Levi's. My wife was mad cause I'd come home from diving, go in the back yard and hose my scuba gear and spear gun and often I'd just stick the hose down the crotch and wash my cutoffs and then when I had taken them off, I'd just stand them up to dry. They were so old and salty they would stand by themselves. I wouldn't let her wash them as they looked salty and had character. Then Bo Wells, the other police officer from Riviera Beach showed up. Bo was a good diver and was with me when I got my first jewfish, it weighed 207 pounds and he was a big help. It was about 8:45 AM so we went to the pool area, an Olympic size pool, with bleachers around it, and it's all fenced in. There were a few guys there already. Haley and Bishop from the sheriff's department, our instructors I knew, plus 4 other guys. So that meant there was only 6 students' total. Sergeant Bishop introduced me to Tom Murray and Dave Chasteen from the sheriff's department, Bob Baker from Lake Worth Police Department and Tom Rivenbark, he was a civilian who was taking the course and a good friend of Sergeant Bishop. He was going to assist with the gear and equipment and just tag along. Now Bishop took charge and seemed kind of glad the class was small. He started off by telling us that he, Haley and a Bob Cowart from the Coast Guard diving unit would conduct the course. He broke down the schedule stating that the first 2 hours would be devoted to calisthenics that started with a 2-mile run and followed by no less than 25 pushups, 50 sit-ups and 50 jumping jacks and lots of squats. All being increased daily by increments of 5. This would be followed by 3 hours of pool work that involved ditch and recovery of equipment, diving gear, underwater laps, and while we had the use of a clear water pool, we would go over various search patterns so that when we got into black water, we knew what we were doing. The last hour of the day would be devoted to the theory and physics on diving and of gases, and we would be having tests. He told us that the last week of the course we would report to the Coast Guard dock at the Port of Palm Beach where we would be using scuba gear and Descio gear, shallow water diving masks with surface supplied air. We were required to make 3 nighttime swims, one of those dives was a scuba dive with only a compass and that all 5 of us divers would be tied on a line together. This compass dive would be from the Coast Guard dock at the Port of Palm Beach, all the way to the Coast Guard Station on Peanut Island, a distance of about 1/8th to 1/4 mile. Now this dive also covered a portion of the inter coastal waterway and being it was night and in the port area it might, and normally is, a heavily traveled route, but not to worry as we were diving at night and boat traffic should be light. Besides we would be on the bottom. The other 2 dives would be with masks and fins only and would be around 2000 yards each. They would take us out in the ocean in the harbor patrol boat and drop us off in teams of 2, then we had to swim west to the town of Palm Beach. Now Bishop went on to say that we would be working divers and not weekend warriors like the vast majority of divers in Florida Well that seemed to be all the instructions he would give us so he gave us a course from the pool that 2 miles later would bring us right back, and with that he told us to hit the bricks, start running. Well, we all started running and kept a good pace for about a mile and then I started to get a pain in my side, so I slowed down, I wasn't the only one to slow down so I didn't feel too bad. Well somehow, I managed the 2 miles when I got to the pool, they were all waiting. Now running was never one of my strong traits. I thought I would get a short break, but Bishop shouted out for 25 pushups, fortunately I was able to do them, same as the squats and the sit-ups. After good hour of this it was hit the pool and believe me it was good to get in the water. Now right away it was off to the deep end, 9 feet, we put on our fins, and then shoulders to the pool wall with Bishop hollering, *"I want to see the dam wall move from all the force you generate kicking."* Now 5 minutes of this and I know you can sweat in the water. We had to do this for 10 minutes. Hell, I was thinking I don't see a dam thing wrong with sport divers or weekend warriors and this is just the first day of 2 weeks of 'fun filled' diving.

What the hell did I volunteer for, no wonder Chief Cotrell was nice to me. Well, I'm here so I might as well make the best of it and besides ole Lennie, Chief Cotrell, would probably can me or at least make my life miserable if I quit.

Now you got to remember that all these exercises were one after the other and no rest periods were given. Rest periods, it was explained, would come later during the theory hour, anyway after 10 or 15 minutes of pushing the swimming pool wall away from the pool, he made us get out and take off our fins and jump right back in the water from the wall at the deep end, made us submerge, kickoff and swim the length of the pool underwater,100 feet. Now 100 feet underwater is a long way to swim without fins, hell it's a long way with fins, but I had done a lot of free diving, so I hyperventilated, submerged, and pushed off, and I made it. Bo Wells was the only other one that made it, we continued this exercise for four more laps of the pool, and I was able to complete 2 of them all the way. I didn't feel bad cause no one else made it at all, not even Bo my department buddy. Swimming and water sports are nothing but endurance, and I think that what Bishop was testing us for.

Now we went to a game called, *"find the quarter."* This is where Bishop would line us up at the pools edge with our backs to the pool, then he would throw a quarter somewhere in the pool and hollered," *Go,"* and 6 guys scrambled around a 50 by 100-foot pool like maniacs looking for the quarter he threw in. This last exercise lasted for about 30 minutes, and I even managed to find the quarter a couple of times. By now I was so dam tired I couldn't believe I still had to go to work yet today. Finally, Bishop ended the exercise and had us sit in the bleachers while he went into the theory of diving, different ailments common to divers, and emergency treatment. Also, the use of repetitive dive tables and showing how they are used. Now these are what is known as paper dives cause you have to figure out how long and at what depth you were at, if you planned on going down a second or third time under water, if you do, you must consult the tables and they put you in a category that allows you to go to a depth for so long and then tells you how long you got to decompress and at what depth. An example is, say, 10 minutes at 40 feet, and then say 7 minutes at 30 feet, and then 5 minutes at 5 feet, all this is just hypothetical. The reason for all this is to purge and nitrogen out of the blood stream. Nitrogen or bends always forms in the body joints, elbows, knees etc. It's a little more complicated this, but it gives you a general idea of just what a paper dive is and how you use the tables. One thing it should do is show that a sport diver or any diver can get bent or get the bends real easy if the tables are read or used wrong and you need a recompression chamber immediately if not sooner. So, you can see its best to leave paper dives alone and just enjoy sport diving

Well, what seemed to be only 10 minutes Bishop says it's 1PM and see you all tomorrow. Hell, sitting in the warm sun discussing dive theory I was wishing we had only 1 hour of PTs, physical training and the rest of the time used for theory, I was so tired and sore that I didn't think I'd make it to work, fortunately the 3 to 11 shift was just routine. Sergeant Waites put me in zone 1 and all I had were a few traffic stops and several citizen complaints and that was it.

The next day's course was a repeat of the previous day and I hurt bad. When we got to the swimming pool work Bishop added an exercise, he called us out of the pool and gathered us at the 9-foot depth sign, this was right at the deepest portion where the drains are.

Now the drains ran from side to side, and they covered a 50-foot width. Bishop had one of the students jump in and with no swim aids, that's no mask or fins, handed him a weight belt with about 25 pounds of lead on it and told him to swim to the other side. Now needless to say there's not a man, or even a few beasts that could do it, at least not without fins on. Anyway, the diver pushes off the wall holding the 25-pound weight belt and starting for the other side. Well, he got about 5 feet from the wall and the belt started to take him down underwater, he couldn't stay up, so he dropped the belt to the bottom, 9 feet deep. Well, he rested, took a breath, jack knifed down, then pushed up and toward the opposite side. Well, he finally made it to the wall after about 6 dives and lunges. I know that he drank more water than he wanted too doing it. Now Bishop didn't tell him he did good, bad or indifferent, he just hollered for the next troop to hit the water and said I'll see you on the other side. Seeing what a hard time the first troop had, the second one figured he'd do it a little differently and swim the weight belt over to the other side. So, with one hand on the wall, he laid back in the water and laid the belt over his chest, lungs, and gives a big push off the wall, he did get about 5 to 7 feet out and then the weight belt just sank him, so he let it fall to the bottom, well from there he finished just like the first troop. Bishop then called for me, so I jumped in the water and held onto the wall while he walked back from the far side. Now as he was walking back, I was thinking, *"hell no one can swim with that kind of weight on the surface,"* and all he had said was swim to the other side, so I'll swim it over, but underwater. Well Bishop was back, and he handed me the belt, I took a deep breath and with 25 pounds sank right to the bottom, once there I laid the belt over the small of my back and using the drain screen like a ladder pulled my self over to the other side. I just held the belt and pushed straight up along the wall and with one hand threw the belt on deck. Bishop was there and he smiled and said,

"Barton, that's using your head instead of trying to drown yourself."

We then played the quarter game, followed by a theory session and then day two was done. Well with day two done I was wondering what was so different from any other diving course such as NAWI or PADI (National Association of Underwater Instructors and Professional Association of Diving Instructors) or for that matter, any recognized diving course. All I could see was that we were all cops and what was so special about us being working divers, as Bishop liked to refer to all other divers as, 'sport divers and weekend warriors etc.'

The third day was identical to the first two except in the pool we had scuba gear and spent 4 hours on ditching and recovery of equipment.

To those of you who have use scuba gear and taken a certified diving course you know that you had to ditch and don your equipment once or twice to pass the course and become a certified diver. This to a new diver is kind of terrifying and a moment of truth type situation, but once it's completed it's a tremendous ego and confidence builder.

Now Bishop was quick to point out that we were ditching and donning in a swimming pool and the water was clear, calm and no obstructions and only 9 feet deep and that as working divers we would be in rivers, lakes, canals, or the ocean, and that in some of the places the water is completely black and if an emergency arose where your equipment had to be ditched the chance of its recovery wouldn't be like a swimming pool. Well with that statement I began to view the course with a more serious attitude rather than just fun diving. In all the diving I had done so far it was calm and clear conditions.

For those not familiar with diving, the art, or method of ditching

and donning of equipment, the procedure is to dive to the bottom of the pool and to take shallow breaths while doing this, so as not to float up to the surface, get into a seated position, unbuckle your weight belt and put it across your upper legs or thighs. it's important to breath shallow as a body has a tendency to float up if you take too much air into your lungs. Next you unbuckle your scuba tank harness straps from your waist and chest, all straps are secured with what is called quick release, so that in releasing any equipment it just takes a simple pull and it's released from your body. Once this is completed you pull the tank over your head, the regulator still in your mouth, and put the tank between your legs, it's just like pulling a t-shirt off. Once the tank is over your head and between your legs you replace the weight belt so that it is now over the scuba tank and your legs, now you still have your mouthpiece in and your mask and fins on but remember to breath shallow. You then reach down your body and remove your fins and place them inside your legs next to the tank. Now the moment of truth for you, you take your mask off and place it on the scuba tank. Breathing with the tank and regulator below your lungs is very easy as most all regulators are what is called DEMAND and so your regulator is in what's called a free air state as it practically forces air into your lungs. The only remaining thing to do is to take one last breath and with one hand on the mouthpiece and the other on the tank or air valve, you turn off the air and place your mouthpiece under the valve and then you start up to the surface. IT'S MOST IMPORTANT THAT AS YOU ASCEND YOU CONTINUALLY EXHALE UNTIL ON THE SURFACE. It's important to know that your lungs are like a balloon and that water pressure increases .45 pounds for every foot in depth, so if you take a big breath of HP, (high pressure) air at depth and hold it as you assigned, the ambient, or surrounding pressure decreases while you are ascending, so having no way to vent itself, your lungs will explode, just like a balloon, now as little as four feet can do this so you see the importance of exhaling. Once on the surface and you're resting, all you've got to do is plan exactly how you'll don your equipment, it should be the exact reversal of your ditching it. You can take a deep breath before you dive down to your equipment as it's not HP air, and only air at sea level pressure, 14.7 pounds per square inch. Now I have done this many times, always in a swimming pool and I've even done it in the ocean on an extremely calm day where it was great visibility and was only around 12 or so feet in depth, so I just couldn't think of recovering it in black water no matter how shallow. I could see ditching my weight belt at the most but never leaving my tank and regulator on the bottom of some lake or canal, they cost too much and were too hard for me to leave or lose. I didn't make an issue of it and neither Bishop nor Haley brought it up.

The rest of the week was basically the same, but the pool work turned from physical exercises to stamina and search patterns for recoveries. They consisted of a search from a pier where a weighted line was sunk to a certain depth, anywhere from 5 feet on down and the diver descends and puts a snap ring on the descending line so that it will rotate and then he makes an arc from side to side, ever increasing till he finds what he was looking for.

In large lakes a boat is used, and a line is attached to several foundation blocks, or a very heavy object is dropped to the bottom, the diver descends and attaches a second line to it by a snap ring so it will rotate freely around the descending line and the diver searches in a circular pattern, letting out about 3 feet of line after every rotation.

Days 3 and 4 were spent in familiarization of these patterns while we still had the use of a clear water pool. Of course, this was after a 2-mile run followed by PTs. Now our theory sessions didn't deal with the dive tables but somehow focused on the recovery of bodies, victims of drowning, vehicle accidents, boating or aircraft mishaps involving water. Now I saw why Bishop kept harping about sport and weekend warrior divers, there was to be no sport in finding a body underwater. On the 5th day of the course, we packed up and went out in the county boondocks, rural area, to a place called Cleary Brothers, it had numerous canals. All these canals were man-made, 25 to 35 feet wide and were made by a drag line, some were up to 12 or 15 feet deep. They were made to be used as fill for roadways, homes etc. and they were what is called shell rock. Visibility is good as they have long since settled. Well Bishop produced, out of the truck of his car, a weighted dummy that was to be the object of recovery and had all the troops hide their faces while he hid the dummy in some portion of the canal. Now this particular canal was about 300 feet long. An arc pattern was used, and each student got the opportunity to locate and recover the body. It was kind of eerie to find a body just lying there and to pick it up underwater where it had no weight. Bishop and Haley really empathized the buddy system while diving in canals due to the fact of the dangers of recovery diving especially in black water canals, due to sunken trees, cars, jagged metal and glass etc., and should you ever have to dive alone, you might not get assistance soon enough, so the need for a partner or buddy.

Well, I thought to myself. I'm an experienced diver and I've been diving in the ocean, and it was always clear, and the city of Riviera Beach had no canal of any size that was black water. So, Bo and I didn't have to worry about that kind of water. Little did I know what my future had in store. After everyone brought up the dummy, Bishop had us secure and told us to meet him at the Coast Guard dock at the Port of Palm Beach on Monday morning at 8:00 AM, that we'd have a Coast Guard instructor for the next week. 2nd week. Well at work the Chief told me that I would be off work due to us having night exercises.

My two days off I went diving in the ocean up at Salerno for lobster and fish.

Monday morning found me at the Port of Palm Beach. This is in the city were me and Bo are on the Police Department so it's like working at home. Haley and Bishop are there and introduce us to a Bob Cowart who is from the Coast Guard diving unit in Miami. He has his van with the Coast Guard Emblem on it and it's full of diving gear. it's parked on the dock right were the Port Pilot Boat docks. Now this is the boat that the Harbor Pilot takes out in the ocean to go aboard freighters or ships so he can guide them into the port and dock's.

Well Cowart has what looks like a compressor with several coils of hose and each has a triangular face mask attached. This Cowart tells us is a DESCO rig or a shallow water diving unit that has surface supplied air from the compressor and is good to around 35 to 40 feet. However, we would be using it at only 20 to 25-foot depths and only around the Coast Guard Dock. He went on to tell us that before we use the DESCOs that we had to do 1 1/2 hours of PTs but no running due to all the big equipment, cranes, trucks and forklifts in the pier area. We went through the pushups, sit-ups, squats etc. We were all sweating, and he says, *"let's do one arm pushups,"* and while we stood there, sweating and tired out, he proceeded to do 30 one arm pushups with each arm. I almost shit when I saw this. I don't think I could have done one, well at least I never could. Cowart says matter of fact that when he was in shape, he could do 75 with each arm. I think he was yanking our chain, kidding us. I should be in as bad a shape as him. Well, I tried it and only got 1/2 of a pushup done. I made it from the up position and went down and that's it.

Anyway, I was picked first to use the DESCO rig. it's a triangular mask and fits over your chin and is pulled up over your head. It has 5 straps that you pull tight once you have the mask seated or on your head. The hose and safety line are the air supply and it's attached to the upper right side of the mask and a simple lever opens the air flow, it's cool air blowing down on your face. The exhaust valve is a venturi valve, one-way valve, it's located on the lower left side of your chin. Once the diver is ready, all he has to do is hold the mask with one hand and jump in the water, the jump from the pilot dock was only about three and so it was no problem.

Anyway, I got squared away as far as putting the rig on and Cowart put the other rig on. He signaled he was ready, and we both jumped in the water, we both had weight belts on, and we sank immediately to the bottom, it was right round 25 feet deep. Now I was fortunate that I dove so much that my ears cleared automatically to the pressure change, so I had no problems with my ears as we descended. Others who weren't used to diving had to go down a piling and give their ears time to adjust.

Well, the water was clear, and the tide was in. The bottom around the dock had a lot of cans, bottles and trash. We were weighted heavily for working on the bottom and not for swimming, so it was kind of like hard hat diving without the suit and helmet and shoes. We both had 50 feet of hose, and each had a line tender on the surface. I started walking from the boat dock to the pier, now this is where the tourist ship docks that goes to the Bahamas, it wasn't in port at this time. I found a whole stack of dinner plates that had a British crown emblem on them, and they were all intact, so I picked them up and walked back to Cowart and showed him my find.

He gave me a roger with his hand and pushed me towards the Coast Guard dock and several foundation blocks in the sand. Well, I got about three feet away from the blocks when up pops this green moray eel, he's about 5 feet long and looking like he wanted to bite my bod so I jerked back, I could hear Cowart laughing in his mask. You could talk to someone if you were close as there's room in the mask to talk so I got close to him and called him a prick. He laughed and signed for us to surface. We both signaled our dive tenders to surface us, that's keeping the lines tight while we come up. Now all signals are worked out between the diver and tender before so there's no mistakes made. We had one long pull for the tender to play out more line and, two long pulls for the tender to surface the diver as it was the tender's responsibility to keep the line taunt all the time. On surfacing the diver could see if the line was straight up and not at an angle so he could get right under the tender, you can see that a tender's job is very important when a man is underwater, and he can't be doing anything else or be distracted. This also applies to hard hat divers. The air hose is attached to the mask at the upper right-hand corner, and it also serves as a lifeline, the diver has it looped under his right arm so that it doesn't get pulled off his face.

Once in position, and the pull-up signal is given, we both held onto our lines and got up to the surface. It was quite an experience using a DESCO rig for the first time and Cowart said I did really good for a first-time user. I told him I liked it but that I wouldn't use it in any recovery in any black water because I didn't want to be tied to the surface with a hose, that I'd use scuba gear.

Well, I give a plate to everybody as a souvenir. All of the students got to use the DESCO rig, some had great difficulty as they got chocked up, by that I mean they over oxygenated themselves by breathing to heavy and fast as though they weren't getting enough air when in fact they were getting too much. You can relate to this as on the surface, a simple remedy is to breath into a paper bag, this lowers the oxygen content and the person calms down, unfortunately under water the paper bag doesn't work to well and all the diver has to do is calm down, relax, talking to yourself helps a lot. Diving with a DESCO rig is a mind game and you got to psychic yourself.

Well, Rivenbark and Baker were two who had problems and after a lot of drinking salt water from ripping the masks off, ditching their weight belts and getting punched in their stomachs by Cowart to make sure they didn't hold their breath on the way to the surface, they never did get used to a DESCO rig.

Well, we started on projects such as a submerged tank that had a dozen different holes that were colored, each hole had bolts and nuts colored the same, with fittings to go into that particular hole. The object was to fit the right bolts, nuts and fittings with the right colored hole. When all this was done an air, hose was attached, and the tank was purged of water, and it floated to the surface. Now this was done in teams of two and was timed against a clock. Well, the first day of the second week ended with Bishop telling us to be back at 9:00 PM for our first night dive. The department had given me off this week, but my wife Claire wasn't all that choked up about my making night swims and dives, but

I figured that as long as I was off work, I would have more time at home with her and Heidi.

Well at 9:00 PM I was at the dock along with everyone else, the night was clear and warm and an almost full moon, so it glittered across the inter-coastal waterway. Bishop, Haley and Cowart were in the Harbor Patrol boat and told us students to grab out masks and fins and climb aboard, with that we crossed the inter coastal, past the Peanut Island Coast Guard Station and out the Palm Beach Inlet into the Atlantic Ocean, and we continued east. I looked back at the Florida Power & Light Company smokestack and the town of Palm Beach. It all looked a hell of a way off and we were still east bound. Bishop killed the boat engine and says, *"this is your first night swim and its roughly 1500 to 2000 yards to the beach, make sure you swim in pairs."* With that he told us to gear up. He then gave each of us a battery powered light to attach to our mask straps, the kind used on bicycles, so that we could be followed into shore, and they could keep track of all 6 swimmers. Now we were directly west of the inlet, and I had dived here many times so I knew the water was about 75 to 80 feet deep and I had seen lots of big sharks, turtles and manta rays, schools of barracuda and sting rays so I could just envision all sorts of beasties waiting to take a bite.

Well, we got the word to get in the water and so myself and Bo slipped in over the transom, rear of boat, so as not to submerge our lights. the water was warm, calm and the tide was running toward the inlet, our destination. It was an easy swim, so we started toward the beach. We didn't talk much, but every once in a while, we kind of checked on each other and I know Bo was thinking the same I was, that some shark was just waiting to bite us, but nothing happened. We all made it to the beach okay, it took about an hour to pick up everyone and secure back at the boat dock. Well one swim down and two to go, and besides no fins showed up, shark's that is, and no beasties seen.

The second day was much like the first, with PTs and under water construction projects conducted by teams of two and timed for speed and coordination. I felt this was good experience, however I felt that projects like this were conducted in clear water and would have no bearing in black water or recovery work. All we were doing is putting in under water time. We used both DESCO and scuba gear in these dives and projects.

Cowart had us all get out of the water and while standing on the dock told us that our next exercise would be a free dive to the DESCO rig while it was on the bottom, 25 feet down. The air compressor was on, and the air was just turned off at the valve on the mask and all you had to do was free dive 25 feet to the mask with your fins on, put the mask on your face and tighten the 5 straps and turn the air on. Now all this was hard until you turned the air on, the air pressure would clear the mask and you could breathe, simple. *"Just to show you how easy it is I'll show you,"* with that Cowart throws one of the DESCO rigs off the dock into the water and lets it sink to the bottom, then he free dives with no fins on and in a minute or so he surfaces, mask on, air on, and he's breathing easy. Well out of the water he comes, takes the mask off with the air turned off and throws it back into the water. I figured he'd just ask who wants to try it as it didn't look all that hard, but he pointed to Tom Murray, a deputy sheriff and told him to go in and get it on, meaning the mask.

Now I know everyone taking the course and the only two I thought who could do it was myself and Bo Wells, not because we were such good divers but we had been diving awhile and were more used to it and besides, free diving meant just the use of mask and fins and I don't think that the others were comfortable in the water, as they had done little if any diving at all. Going after a mask with something to breath in 25 feet of saltwater is a whole lot different ball game than diving in 9 feet of clear water in a swimming pool. I told Bo, *"Five bucks he don't make it."* I bet he didn't get down 12 feet when he came back on the surface gasping for air. Cowart asks Murray if he wants to try again, *"NO."*

Cowart picked another student and then another and then he picked Bo. I was sure Bo would do it with no problems because he dove and stayed down a lot longer than the others, but then he to surfaced with no mask on. He was calm and told Cowart that he'd try again and so he hyperventilated, took deep breaths, jackknifed and dove again, he didn't make it to the bottom, and he had to give up. He got out of the water, and I guess that only left me and Rivenbark. So, Cowart points to me and says, *"okay your turn,"* I stood-up, hyperventilated and dove for the mask. I opened my eyes and followed the hose down through the blurry water and I could see the mask, next thing I know I had it and was standing on the bottom. Now water is about 900 times as dense as air and I had trouble getting the straps out of the way so I could put my chin in and pull it into place, by now my lungs are burning and I'm still trying to get it on right and I can't wait any more, I need air, so I rip the mask off my face and push off for the surface and air. Now I still got 25 feet to go and that's a long way to go. Well, I must have come out of the water 3 feet when I broke the surface, just like a whale breaching, only I was smaller, it seemed I couldn't breathe for several seconds, but I was really gulping air. I finally caught my breath and slowed down and told Cowart, *"I'll try it again."* I looked at Bishop and Haley and they had the look that a bet was made that I wouldn't or couldn't do it. Well, I figured I'd drown or the next time I broke surface I'd be wearing that dam mask.

I lay in the water, resting and hyperventilating and thinking of the best way to put the mask on, and then I knew. Turn the air on first so that I had something to breath. I took a few more breaths, jack knifed and dove down and pulled down along the hose, got the mask with no problem and pulled the straps out of the way and pushed them back, stuck my chin in and put it against my face. By now my lungs hurt, but instead of screwing with straps, I tilted my head up toward the surface and I held it in place with my left hand and with my right I turned the air on. Immediately the air pressure pushed the water out of the non-return valve and the mask was clear of water. After this I was sucking air like crazy and I knew I had to settle into a normal breathing rhythm, so now I had something to breath anyway. Still holding the mask in place. I started adjusting and tightening the straps. I first got the one on top of my head in the center, and then the two on either side of the center one. The last two were easy as I didn't have to look up anymore. Now the mask was on, and I was breathing a normal cycle pattern.

I walked to a piling and started up and broke the surface, and I heard Bo holler, *"yea hamburger!"* Hamburger is a euphemism coined by Bishop to anyone who can't do the impossible like he can, you know, like 100 pushups, free dive 100 feet etc., or one who is soft. Well, I know that Bo didn't mean it that way. Haley, Bishop nor Cowart said anything and so I was sure a bet was made. I didn't feel that I was any better diver than the rest of the students, but I figured that's the way Cowart did it. Under water your first concern is for something to breath, once you got that, you had all the time to screw around with straps or whatever. Well, that was the end of this day's session and we had to hose off all the gear with fresh water, coil the DESCO hose, secure all the diving gear in Cowart's van and the Harbor Patrol Car. Bishop told us to be back at 9:00 PM and then we would have a night compass course swim to the Peanut Island Coast Guard Station.

Well, we all met again around 8:30 PM and again, like south Florida is famous for, it was calm and a moonlit night. Now only Cowart and Bishop were there, Haley was a detective and involved in a murder investigation. Cowart got us all together and told us, *"We're going to scuba dive to just west of the Coast Guard dock on Peanut Island."* and he pointed out 3 pilings jutting out of the water about 150 to 200 feet from the dock. It was about 1/8 to 1/4 mile away from where we stood, and he went on with. *"No lights will be used, and we'll all be roped together, me being in the middle and I'll have the only light and it will be from my compass,"* He produced a Sunato compass which was about 21/2 inches square and had a luminous dial and he told us, *"we'll take a fix on the center piling and come up there, okay saddle up."* It was determined that 5 troops were making the dive, no Rivenbark, and that with Cowart there would be 6 divers' total. Anyway, we put on our tanks and gear, and we had 2-foot lengths of rope with hoops on each end so when all troops were ready, we stood on the edge of the dock looped together. I was on the extreme right end, so no one was on my right side. Cowart took a fix on the center piling and said, *"ready, let's go,"* put his mouthpiece in and we all jumped in the water. The water was nice and cool, not cold, and the tide was coming in so the water was clear, not so as you could see anything anyway without a light, but at least there wasn't any junk in the water coming from the Ermine River or the inter coastal waterway. I guessed that Cowart was taking another fix on the piling as we settled on the bottom and weren't moving yet. We'll all of a sudden, I felt a jerk on my left hand, so I figured we were moving so I started swimming. We stayed close to the bottom, and I let my right hand drag down so I could feel the sand. I could hear boats in the area and some even went over our heads, but we had to be 20 to 25 feet down, so they were no problem. We swam for about 5 minutes and stopped so I figured Cowart was taking another fix or just checking his compass. It's very easy to get disoriented and swim in another direction so frequent compass checks are in order to maintain a straight line. it's got to be especially hard swimming with 6 guys and none swimming with the same force. Well, we started swimming again and all seemed okay when all of a sudden, I ran into something hard and my first thought was, *"hell some beasties gonna get me now,"* but all it was, was a big piece of coral rock and it had grass and algae on it. I had to feel my way around it from the bottom with my right hand. It was about 4 feet high and about 5 or 6 feet long so I just swam over the top of it while being pulled along, but I definitely figured that from here on I would keep my right hand out in front of me and not down. Now with my right hand out in front it had kind of exotic effect as my hand disturbed the phosphorus plankton, a type of marine plant/animal in the water and it illuminated around my hand like a sparkler would. The next thing I know my left hand is being dragged and so I pull my feet under me and hell, *"I can stand up"*, I'm out of the water to my waste and there's Cowart right beside the center piling, dam it was a good feeling to tell you the truth, I didn't think we would come close. Now it was just a short walk to the dock where Bishop was with the boat, and he took us back to the mainland. We all secured after washing all the gear off with fresh water

    The next day was just routine but still hard work and I know that all of us students were glad that the course was winding down and that we had only one day left, and no one had mentioned the 2500-yard swim, so it looked like it was forgotten.

It's Friday, the last day, yahoo!! First, it's 2 hours of PTs which are not bad now, no hurting or sore muscles anymore, I guess I must have been in some kind of shape. We spent the day just working search patterns and using the DESCO and scuba gear.

The DESCO gear belonged to the Coast Guard and Cowart said that now we were qualified and could borrow it any time to use and that it was always available. Well come 4:00 PM Bishop tells us to secure, wash the diving gear in fresh water and police up the dock area, clean up the surroundings.

Bishop called us all together and said beer and pizza were on him and Haley that night, also that Sheriff Martin Kellenburger would be present. Certificates the next day at 9:00 AM and to bring our families, also we had approved for us to wear diving pins and we all pitched in $5 for first class divers' pins that were bought at ship stores at the Naval Base in Key West, Florida.

That night we all met at an Italian restaurant, ate pizza and drank beer and told war stories, and like most cops having good intentions, saying how we would all get together again and do this every so often. But it never came to be. Well, I got about half tanked, drunk, along with everyone else and then Bishop and Haley told all of us that they would be proud to assist any of us on a diving detail should we, or our department ever need it cause we weren't hamburgers or sport divers anymore but working divers now.

Well, it's always nice when someone blows a little smoke. Now it's Saturday and the big day. I have a clean, starched,

Riviera Beach Police Uniform on, my shoes are shined, and I'm standing tall. I had my wife and baby daughter Heidi all ready in plenty of time so we arrived at the port at 8:30AM. Several of the troops were there already with their families.

At 9:00 AM sharp Bishop gets us in line and stands us at attention, Sheriff Kellenburger was there, and he presented each of us with a certificate of merit, he also gave us our first-class diving pins and congratulated us on the course completion. The formal ceremony didn't take but about 20 minutes and then we stripped to our swimsuits and put on a scuba and DESCO demonstration for the audience. We said goodbye and promised to go diving and spear fishing for some good times, and then we all went to our respective departments, never to do any of this except, 10 to 12 days later a prominent attorney and his wife. went into the ocean during a storm and both drown, so we got together for one last dive.

****

A follow up shows that Bishop left the department later on. Haley almost drowned in a charter fishing boat accident, "THE TWO GEORGE'S," boat had hit a sand bar out of Boynton Inlet and flipped over. I don't remember how many people drown but Haley got tangled up in a mooring line and he was unconscious when Bishop got him out. Haley never dove again that I know of. When this happened, I dove off the beach looking for fishing gear off of "THE TWO GEORGES" and was bitten by a moray eel on the ankle.

Murray and Chasteen, the two members of the Sheriff's Department who took the dive course dove one time and that was for the attorney and is wife. Bo Wells who was our Crime Scene Unit in Riviera Beach quit the department as he could make more money as an iron worker.

Me, well 20 months later I was to join the sheriff's Department and I soon learned about 'working dives' I recovered bikes, cars, motorcycles and check writers, safes, jewelry and 13 or so bodies, 5 of them in one two-week period. I dove in a canal where the harbor patrolman used a 12-gauge shotgun on water moccasins, I dove in a sewage outflow looking for guns, and I even got slapped by an alligator.

From all these dives I even got a fungus on my hands that filled my joints up with a puss type liquid and it took a lifetime to get rid of.

I got trapped under water by a caved-in fence in a black water canal. Yeah, I know all about working divers.

DIVING FOR $600,000 - F.B.I.

By now I had been on the sheriff's Department three or four years, and I had been a road sergeant about two years. Well, the one thing I did for recreation was SCUBA diving, self-contained underwater breathing apparatus, and I also free dove, that using only the mask, fins and snorkel also my spear gun and I used up to 20 to 25 jugs of air a week so that's a lot of carrying of scuba tanks.

Well, I got into free diving. That's just breath holding and a mask, fins, and snorkel, also my spear gun. I used a 7-pound weight belt, I got pretty good at it. I was able to free dive to 70 feet and work for fish at that depth. I liked spear fishing and had a homemade spear gun with a reel that had 100 feet of 600-pound test line on it, so I did pretty good getting fish. I mainly went after what we called Jew fish. Some are called black sea bass in other parts of the country, and some are called Warsaw grouper in other parts. Anyway, they don't stop growing and are good eating. The biggest one I got was right at 500 pounds and I needed a wrecker to get him out of the water. I still have a picture of him.

Now the sheriff's Department had its own Navy, and it was known

as the Harbor Patrol and at this time it only had one man, Bob Marks, a retired army airborne soldier but who had busted his ear drums during the Korean War and so he couldn't dive. So, the department didn't have a regular deputy to dive for body recovery, evidence etc. So as a result, when a diver was needed, they would call me.

It just so happened that the town of Palm Beach, yes, the rich folks, had a $600,000 robbery and it was all in cash, all in small bills, nothing bigger than a $20 bill and all was unmarked. Now I don't remember any BOLOs, (Be on the Lookout) or any information was given at any of the line ups, as far as any suspects or vehicles, so I didn't think any more about it. The sheriff's department had enough crime and corruption to combat. Besides I wasn't that choked up with the town of Palm Beach because I was always over there to go diving at Palm Beach Inlet, and back at this time they used to arrest people, men, for not having a shirt on. Now I'm talking actually taking a guy to jail if he was caught on the street topless. You can imagine that sheer terror struck in the hearts of Palm Beaches when confronted by a topless male jogger or a swimmer, and besides that, the police department was a joke that catered to the residence and treated any other people like some criminal element. Now if my true feelings show through its because I had a run-in with one of their patrolmen and who knew I was a sergeant on the sheriff's department, and I told him if he fornicated with me that he would have the biggest RAWV, (Resisting Arrest with Violence) that he ever had seen in his young life. Now when I empathized the violence, he didn't say anything, but he reported me to the city manager, a man by the name of Greg Forester who wrote a letter to the Sheriff, as a result I was given a 3-day suspension. You might say that Greg frosted my balls. Anyway, I didn't care about crime and corruption in the town of Palm Beach. We had robberies all the time in the county and so far, as I was concerned the only thing different was the amount stolen, one thing I have to say for their town of Palm Beach, when they had a robbery, they had a ROBBERY.

Now it had to be professional robbers as it certainly wasn't nickel and dimes. Well on a crime involving so much money the F.B.I. got involved in the investigation at the request of the police department and maybe the fact that JFKs family lived there, John Fitzgerald Kennedy, now you all know who he was. There was also a lot of other very prominent and wealthy people who lived there and that just have had some bearing on it.

Well, the AIC (Agent in Charge) of the West Palm Beach office was a man named Kliner, and no, I don't think he was related to who you think, but I'll bet he did eat corn flakes. I guess combined with diligence and stealth, Kliner worked up a stinger, informant/snitch, or an arrest was made, and the suspect was playing let's make a deal for a reduced or lighter sentence, that if the money was turned over to the F.B.I.

Now the robbery took place in the town of Palm Beach and so the agent, Kliner, should have requested assistance from the Palm Beach Police Department but none of the PDs in the county did any of their own diving, they always asked the sheriff's department for any diving assistance that had to be done in their cities.

Now Kliner's suspect/stinger had advised him that the money was in a sea bag, military type, and that it was just thrown into a canal that runs parallel to state road #7 or U.S. 441. Now this canal is about 25 to 35 feet wide, and it runs 20 or so miles that I know of, and its black and scummy water. Well, Kliner went to our Sheriff and requested the services of a diver and so enter Watashi.

I know some police officers from Palm Beach Police Department, and I knew they could dive, but I think that Kliner didn't even bother to ask and besides the FBI agents don't do this type of detail and so the request from the Sheriff.

The diving target area was narrowed down to state road #98, Southern Blvd and Forest Hill Blvd as far as the north and south boundaries. Now it a distance of about 2 1/2 miles. The date was June 18, 1971, a Friday morning, and I had just gotten off work as I was on the night shift, I had checked my troops paperwork and was just getting ready to secure when I heard Captain Sanchez on the speaker in the sergeants office advising the dispatcher to call road patrol and have Sergeant Barton 10-23, wait for him. The phone rang right away, and I answered," *yep, I heard him and thanks."* I didn't even give the dispatcher a chance to deliver Sanchez's message. Now all I can think of, *"what did I do or what didn't do now."* Well while I'm waiting at road patrol for *'God'* I'm thinking it's a nice day with no wind. I'll go over to Palm Beach Inlet and do some diving. Then I hear the captain go, *"200 Palm beach 10-6 at road patrol,"* now 200 is his ID or call sign, and 10-6 is *busy*. Of course, this was done in his 5-octave voice below middle C. I walked outside to the parking area and ask him in a firm and polite voice, hoping I'm not showing my uncertainly since when Captain Sanchez talks to you he always makes you feel like you did something wrong. *"What did you want me to wait for Captain." "You're going diving today,"* he tells me, *"Shit"*. I thought to myself with a relieved feeling, this man has got to be psychic knowing that I'm going over to Palm Beach Inlet, but Sanchez isn't thinking of a fun filled day at Palm Beach Inlet, no the bastard don't even take into consideration that I just got finished working the night shift. Then he tells me about Kliner and the 600K robbery saying," *look at it this way Pollack,* he used to like to refer to me by my native heritage, *today you'll be rich."* Now at first, I was all chocked up about helping the FBI and even the town of Palm Beach and their PD, at this time in my career I had about as much respect for both agencies as mammary glands on a boar hog. But he tells me about 60K reward just for recovering the money, a sort of finder's fee. I figured I could get off of tube steak and ground round for a long time and so I said okay, and besides you don't say no to Captain Sanchez. Well, we outlined the game plan. Agent Kliner would meet us at road patrol in about an hour or 0900, that's 9 AM, so will Sergeant Marks, Admiral of our Harbor Patrol and a Deputy Biff Werner who will dive with me. Well, I call my wife Claire, and tell her about the detail and how rich were gonna be when I get home with 30 grand. At first, she has no comment and then says, *"why don't you just move your clothes to road patrol?"* Now Claire always did have a soft spot in her heart for the sheriff's department and all the diving details they gave me. Anyway, I already had all my diving gear in the trunk of my car, so I just changed out of my uniform and into my cutoffs and zorys, flip-flops. At this time Werner pulls up with Sergeant Marks and we load up all our diving gear into the harbor patrol car.

Agent Kliner arrives, and to me he looked like a retired old man in a business suit and says hello to the captain and that he's anxious to start. So, the three deputies saddle up and follow Kliner's car west on Southern Blvd. all the way to state road #7. Kliner pulls off right at the Palm Beach canal, it runs east & west. We're at its intersection with the south bound canal and on state rod #7. Now there's flood gates right at this junction of these two canals and all the canals drain off from lake Okeechobee. The canal that goes south parallels state road #7 and goes all the way to Broward County that's 18 to 20 miles away. Well, we get out of our cars just over a bridge on state road #7. Then Kliner tells us about the 600K in a sea bag and it was thrown in the canal between where we stood and Forest Hill Blvd, a distance of about 2 miles, now that a long way to swim underwater folks. The canal at the flood gates, our starting point, was about 35 to 40 feet wide and it tapers down to about 25 feet in width and stays about the same width all the way to Broward County.

I told Werner that I'd just check on the depth and the visibility, so I put on my knife, mask, fins and snorkel. The water looked calm and warm, I jumped in looked down, and I can just see my fins, so visibility is about 5 or 6 feet at most. So, I dive down. The bottom is about 10 or 12 feet deep so I come up and tell Werner this so we will just free dive, no tanks, that way we can cover the canal a lot faster. Now about 50 feet south of the flood gates are several sections of a floating dock and these sections are attached to a cable that just under the surface of the water. Now this dock goes from the east side to the west side of the canal, and the cable, and floating dock have a lot of water hyacinths that are growing or caught on both. While I'm busy checking the visibility and depth, Sergeant Mark walks south toward the dock, then I see him walking back as I was getting out of the water to talk to Kliner. Well, I don't pay any attention to Marks, and he don't say anything, but I see him go to his patrol car, open the trunk and take out a shotgun, then he turns around and walks south again toward the dock and cable area. I still don't pay him much attention cause I'm still talking with Kliner about the money when all of a sudden, BAM! BAM! BAM! Marks had cranked off three rounds in a hurry. So, I holler at him," *hey Marks, What the hell you doin?"* Marks comes back with," *I just shot three water moccasins and I don't see any more. You must have pissed them off when you jumped in and sent waves up the canal towards them. I'm going to walk 25 to 30 feet south of you guys while you're swimming."* Now I got to say that my sphincter muscle puckered some with that remark. I don't mind snakes, and I've caught lots of diamondback rattlers, but I was in no way chocked up about moccasins at eye level as they bite at anything near, and I was near.

Well, me and Werner spent about a half an hour checking out the widest part of the canal around the flood gates and right up to the dock to see if there were any more snakes, we checked for ourselves, and we were pretty systematic. We both had swam under the cable, dock, and undergrowth and we started to swim south in the canal with Sergeant Marks about 30 feet south of us with his shotgun looking for snakes

Now me and Werner swam about 5 to 7 feet apart, we both dove at the same time, and we tried to stay in sight of each other. By now we had covered a mile of the canal when it shallowed up to about 6, or 8 feet so it got easier to cover. I dove down and all of a sudden, my left thigh got a hell of a whack and I thought," *damn you Werner, get away from me!"* I surfaced to chew him out and I see him, Werner, a good 15 or so feet away from me, so I looked back towards the northeast and saw a gator about 7 feet or so long swimming on the surface away from me. He must have been on the bottom of the canal and when I dove down and disturbed him, he had slapped me with his tail when he took off. Now I couldn't believe this shit, first snakes and now a gator. Now I could see our agent Kliner walking the canal bank about even with me and Werner and wishing he was in the water too, also if that dam gator was any bigger, he would have probably attacked me. Now the thought also crossed my mind, what it would be like to spear a gator cause that is some fine eating.

Well, we continued diving and going south on the canal and still no sea bag. I got to admit that swimming down the canal, as I'm sure it's in the mind of Werner. If I do spot the sea bag, why not come up and get a landmark and just continue to swim and maybe come back in a couple of days and pick it up. Hell, small bills, and unmarked and insured, I'm sure. Now wasn't 600K ten times gooder than 60K?

Well by now we had swum all the way to Forest Hill Blvd bridge, and we didn't find any sea bag, so that took care of any thoughts of larceny on my part. Agent Kliner thanked us for the assistance and took off. I thought, *"yea, our FBI in peace and war and in action, ADIOS."* Sergeant Marks took Werner in his car to go back to road patrol and now my buddy Steve, who owns a wrecker service in the county, and Ralph Long another Deputy Sheriff had met us on the bridge of Forest Hill and state road #7.

I had told Ralph that I had seen something shiny beside the bridge and I'd come out of the water as soon as I checked it out. Now Ralph and Steve had been looking for me at road patrol as they wanted to go diving up at Salerno, a good reef about 45 miles north. I swam back to the north side of the bridge in about 8 or 10 feet of water and dove down. Now here it shallowed up to about 7 or 8 feet and I checked in the bottom grass and found a brand-new claw hammer. I swam around and found 5 more hammers and also a large battery charger, the kind with 2 wheels and used in a gas station, fruits of some crime. Well it was around 1300, 1:00 PM, so I told Ralph and Steve that I'd have to pass on Salerno and diving. So, they took me back to Road Patrol for my car. Now Steve asked me about the big red welt on my left thigh and I told him about the gator.

****

Now the 600K was recovered in Boston Mass, so Kliner's stinger was just jerking his chain to cop a deal. Agent Kliner retired from the bureau, FBI, after 25 years of service. In 1976 he ran with the incumbent Sheriff, Roger Ways who was successful in becoming the new Sheriff of Palm Beach County and chose retired agent Kliner to be his new Chief Deputy as 2nd in command of the department. Sergeant Marks left the harbor patrol to take charge of the departments school female crossing guards' division. Me, I wonder to this day what I'd have done if I had spotted a sea bag that I knew had 600K in it. Well folks, I never found out.

ELRICO CONSITNO LATINO BAR

This a story about a bar. Now Elrico Consitno Latino is a bar, and one that is used by migrant labors. They are mostly Mexican and Puerto Ricans. I never saw any blacks as they had their own bar, but that's another story. There's was called Koetters Juke or the Night Owl Bar.

Now ERCL was used by Mexicans and Puerto Ricans from south Florida labor camps, and it wasn't the kind of bar you would take your wife or girlfriend to for a quiet romantic evening out. It was Latin and loud, and I don't think the board of health cared to much, or even dared check on it as it was out in farmland Florida.

This bar was run by a Mexican named Paco who I think made a lot of money fueling and fleecing the patrons of his bar. You can be sure there was always some to serve whiskey and beer to.

Paco was easy to ID, identify, as he always wore his shirt open to the waist and he wore a large, I mean LARGE, solid gold medallion. It had to be 4 inches in diameter. I don't know what it weighed but you can bet it was heavy. Wellbeing the owner Paco had to make some enemies in his daily dealings. Now people, the males, who frequented Paco's bar didn't waste time, nor had the time, to go see a lawyer and settle things in a court of law, they just took matters or any disagreements into their own hands and settled any differences they might have.

Now this time it was no different, but the sheriff's department was called.

The time was early evening on a 3-11, a PM shift and the dispatcher came on the air with, *"Palm Beach to zone 7, signal*

33, shooting, at ERCL and unknown injuries." This bar is in the patrol area of zone 7 and he responded that he got the call and was enroute. Me being the shift sergeant also acknowledged that I was also on the way. ERCL is on Boynton Road on the north side just west of Smith Sunday Road and it has a porch which is part of the building so you can look into the bar from the outside as it has a large bay window that's about 4 by 6 feet square and it's right at bar height.

The bar itself is about 35 feet long and you can see the entire bar and all that are inside at the time through this bay window. Now zone 7 and I arrived about the same time and all radio goes on 10-33 traffic, emergency only, for the both of us, and we ran in, guns in hand to find Paco down and all bloody in his upper body but he was still alive.

Well, we called the dispatcher right away for a 10-71, ambulance, At the time there were several males in the bar, a bartender, and Paco, also called were the detectives from the Delray substation and a crime scene unit.

Me as the sergeant know that any reports, witness statements, and all zone 7 had to do was a supplemental report so I had him seat what patrons were in the bar we also closed it to anyone else as it was now a crime scene. We did see that the big bay window was broken, shot out. Now the ambulance arrived along with EMTs. and they advised that Paco was going to Bethesda hospital, the closest one.

While waiting for the detectives and the crime scene unit, myself and zone 7 found out that Paco was standing at the far north end of the bar, and someone, a disgruntled male, had stuck a shotgun through the bay window, pulled the trigger and hit Paco in the chest.

Whoever it was that shot Paco, shot down the length of the

bar and he didn't care about anyone along the bar when he pulled the trigger, just as long as he got Paco. Fortunately, the patrons who were standing and also seated at the bar only had minor injuries. However, one Mexican male who was seated on a stool about halfway up the bar, had his elbows up on the bar, leaning over drinking his drink and minding his own business. He had a cigarette in his mouth at the time, it was shot right out of his mouth, and it was laying on the bar and he never got hit. Talk about luck and innocent victims.

The detectives and the crime scene unit showed up and after filling them in on what happened, the whole scene was TOT, (Turned Over To) them, and the dispatcher was advised to lift 10-33, traffic, so normal radio transmission could resume. So, zone 7 and I went back to routine patrol. Investigation showed that whoever used the shotgun had loaded it with number 6 or 7 buckshot, so the pellets were very small and many.

****

Paco who was shot in the chest lived. The patron, lucky patron, who had the cigarette shot out of his mouth never did realize just how lucky he was. I had the cigarette with a hole in it for a long time, but time finally took its toll and it just fell apart, just another warning that smoking can be bad for your health. I believe an arrest was made in the case.

FRANK NARDONE

This is a story about Frank Nardone, I always called him friendly Frank as he always had a shit eaten grin on his face whenever he saw a green and white sheriff's department car. Now Frank liked his sauce, booze, and you could always find him out in the county on some lonely road sleeping off a drunk and he was always in his old brown Chrysler. I don't ever remember seeing Frank driving while he was under the influence, or for that matter remember any of my troops busting him for DWI, driving while intoxicated.

Now Frank liked to beat on his wife pretty regularly but nothing I can remember as serious enough to call the sheriff's office, so it wasn't reported that often. When Frank worked it was painting houses. He was about 5'10" tall, around 170 pounds, and maybe 40 to 45 years old.

I was soon to find out that Frank really wasn't all that friendly as he made out to be.

He lived in Westgate, now that's a large section of low-income houses and had a lot of criminals, redneck, type people. Now to be fair and unbiased, there are a lot of good people who also live there, unfortunately I don't know his name.

When I started on the sheriff's department it was in 1967, I worked in Westgate regularly and made several felony arrests a shift, and I had a lot of violence calls, and as a member of the department you seldom ran into the nice folks and just the asshole.

Well, I was sergeant at the time, it was about the mid 70's, and I had the 3 to 11 PM shift, At the time it was the responsibility of the sift sergeant to hand out capiases, arrest warrants, to the troops for people who lived in their assigned zones or patrol area. Back then the warrants section of the department was very small and so the road deputies got felony as well as misdemeanor warrants to try and execute. Now attached to the front of each capias was a work sheet and it contained the capias number, charge and description of the person to be arrested along with his address and a vehicle type and color if available.

Once received it was the responsibility of that deputy to take some action toward executing it if he could, and to write down on the work sheet the date and time and who he interviewed at the residence or neighborhood, and any action taken if it was executed. Then the capias went to the jail with the with the prisoner and just the work sheet was turned in with the deputy's paperwork at the end of the shift. Now if no action was taken, the capias was turned over to the oncoming shift for possible action.

Well, I'm reading the capiases and giving them out to whatever zone they're in when I come across one for a Frank Nardone and it's for GL, grand larceny, now that's a felony, the bond is set at $2,000.

Like I said, I know Fred personally and the deputy working in zone 2 is Jack Stacy, a new troop, and he's also big and aggressive in his law enforcement attitude. Now Jack was in the army airborne and was a Vietnam veteran. Well, I gave him the capias on Nardone and told him to see me at the end of line up in reference to that capias, then I finish up the rest of line up, that's giving out the rest of the capiases, any BOLOs or any patrol requests and then I tell the troops to go 10-8, in service. Well, I see Stacy waiting for me, so I fill him in on friendly Frank and I also tell him about the brownish Chrysler that he drives and that he lives in the first house on the north side of Westgate Avenue just west of Congress Avenue, I even remembered the number, it was 2345, and was a duplex.

I tell Jack that Nardone has a lot of tattoos and a mustache that is pencil thin and that he shouldn't be any trouble, famous last words. When I hear you check out 10-49, busy attempting to execute a capias, I'll come by and assist.

Well Stacy went 10-8 along with the rest of the shift and the calls were just routine. Now Stacy as zone 2 comes on the air to talk with me and to advise that the Chrysler wasn't at the residence, he didn't have to tell me that, but I guess he just wanted me to know that he was checking when able. Well about 1700, 5:00 PM, I hear zone 2 tell the dispatcher that he would be 10-6 10-49 at 2345 Westgate Avenue, and I come right back to the dispatcher and tell her to tell zone 2 to 10-23, to wait, that I'd be with zone 2 in 2 minutes.

I had been in the area anyway as Westgate is always busy especially during rush hour because of all the main road arteries, but

I did go out with zone 2 to that address. Now Frank's duplex sits about 20 to 25 feet off of Westgate Avenue on the north side. We had pulled up facing the front door. Nardone's Chrysler is parked in the car port on the east side of the duplex.

Normally I don't assist troops with misdemeanor capiases as they're mostly for traffic violations anyway, and unless the troop asks for assistance, I let them handle it themselves. On a felony capias it's a little different, I want to be there first to protect my troop, and second in a felony arrest it always has the possibility, or the potential is there, for violence if something should go wrong. I'm the one who catches hell from Captain Sanchez for the actions taken, or not taken, so I want to be there. Not that I expected any problems with Frank. Well Jack and I walked up to a jalousie front door with Jack having the capias in his back pocket. A white female opens the door about 6 inches, and I say, *"hello, is Frank here, I got to talk to him."*, in my nicest, I got to arrest your husband voice) Well she looked scared and says, *"no,"* in a loud voice, but with her hand in front of her she points inside the house somewhere and she opens the door all the way. Now she did this to tell us that Frank was inside and since Frank couldn't see us or her, he couldn't blame her. Anyway, we went into the living room area and seated on the floor is a little boy about 5 or 6 years old, you could see that he was retarded, seated in a chair was a white male, not Frank, and he didn't say anything to us, so we didn't bother saying anything to him. At the time we had no interest in him. We walked through to a kitchen that had a door leading to another room and this door was ajar several inches. We didn't know it at the time, but this door led to the bedroom and guess who was in there. Now Stacy was a step-in front of me when he walked up to this door and all he said was Frank, and that's all he able to get out cause the door slammed shut and both me and Jack hit it at the same time. Door, hinges and lock split the frame on its way down, and there stood Frank Nardone, but not looking quite so friendly, he stood only long enough to let the door hit the floor. Now he jumped at both of us, and the fight was on. Stacy is about 215 pounds and in good shape and I'm around 210 pounds and in pretty good shape so it's just a brief scuffle and we get Frank on the floor. Now I didn't punch Frank I only helped get him on the floor as I didn't want to hurt him, and only held his left arm so we could get the handcuffs on. Now Stacy is siting astride on Frank's chest when he grabs Frank's right arm and then Frank pulls free and reaches up and grabs a handful of Stacy's hair and yanks, I hear Jack yell immediately and at the same time I see a big handful of hair in Frank's hand, and I know it's got to hurt Stacy like hell.

Now I know Jack is mad and ole Frank is lying flat on the deck, so Jack makes a fist, hits Frank on the jaw and out he goes, now I see blood on Jacks forehead, and I know that he's hurting bad. Well at this point we cuff Frank and now I smell something bad, I looked at Jack and we realize that ole Frank had shit his pants. I told Jack that we weren't picking him up and so I grabbed a cuffed wrist and Jack got the other one and so we dragged him out of the bedroom, into the kitchen and through the living room where Frank's wife and kid were, the little boy didn't even look up and just kept playing. I stop and tell Frank's wife that he's under arrest and going to jail. I looked at the guy sitting in the chair and say to him," well *you got anything to say?"*, this time I don't think my voice was as pleasant, and he says no and looks away. Now looking at Frank's wife she looks almost happy, and I'll bet she was to see Frank get it for a change instead of her.

Well, we dragged ole Frank down the two front steps and over to Jack's patrol car and by now Frank is really ripe. Jack opens up both back doors of his patrol car and Frank is still out and limp as piece of fecal matter and so I reach from the far side and pull Frank into the car by the handcuffs while Jack pushes from the other side until we got him in the car.

Frank is a little bloody around the face and I know that the jail won't book him in looking like that and so I tell Jack, *"Take him to Good Sam Hospital, Good Samaritan and I'll follow you."* I got in my car and told the dispatcher that we had a 10-15, prisoner, and that we were on our way to Good Sam Hospital. I followed Jack to the hospital and instead of the emergency entrance he pulls up to an entrance about 100 feet away from emergency. We parked our cars and I tell Jack that we're dragging him in cause ole Frank is really stinking now. Well

Nurses, Doctors and people all stop as these two deputy sheriff's drag this unconscious man through the hallways down to the ER. Down at the ER, we lifted ole limp Frank, I think he was faking it, and took the handcuff off one hand and re-cuffed him to the table railing. Now that things settled ole Frank woke up, he's moaning and we tell the ER nurse what happened and that Frank shouldn't be too bad and that he also defecated, now she figured that out for herself.

Well, the ER doctor comes in and checks Frank out and I don't think he's all chocked up, happy, because of the aroma emitting from him. The doctor tells Frank he's okay and that he can leave. I think he just wanted Frank out of the ER in a hurry. Well Frank could walk and was awake so we uncuffed him from the rail and re-cuffed him again, then walked him to Jack's patrol car. He went to jail and got booked, and I went back on the road with the rest of my troops.

Well, it's the next day and I'm in road patrol early, like always, to make the lineup for the day when I hear, *"Sergeant Barton. my office."* Well, I wonder what the hell I did now. I go into Captain Sanchez's office, and he says, *"Sergeant Barton, what's this shit about you dragging someone through the halls at Good Sam. Hospital, a couple of doctors called the Sheriff to protest the brutal way two of his men conducted themselves at Good Sam Hospital by dragging and unconscious, handcuffed man through a hallway,"* I told the captain that Nardone had shit himself and I wasn't about to carry him. Well, the captain didn't say anything else but at least he had the whole story and could tell the Sheriff why we acted like we did.

Well about 4 or 5 months later me and Jack Stacy were subpoenaed to go to court on ole Frank Nardone. Well, his defense attorney was from the public defender's office, they defend indigent people, and I was called to testify first. The states attorney, or prosecutor, only ask me several questions pertaining to the case, and then the public defender, Nardone's attorney, got me on cross examination. They had invoked the witness rule before the trial began, meaning that Stacy had to sit in the hallway outside the courtroom while I testified so he couldn't hear what I said.

Now ole Frank sat at the defense table, dressed in a suit and a tie, and hell, he looked like Valentino on trial with that pencil thin mustache and his hair slicked back. Now I wasn't that close to him, but I bet he didn't smell like shit. Well after the preliminary questions as to my name, rank, length of service and was I on duty the day of the arrest. He then wanted to know my version of what happened, and I told him stopping short of Frank's bowel movement. The public defender then crossed the floor to be in front of me as he had been away at the beginning of my testimony and he wanted to know if Mr. Nardone had been advised of his constitutional rights, Mirada warnings, and again I explained that he, Nardone, never gave us the opportunity to advise him of anything as the fight started right after the word Frank. He then wanted to know if Deputy Stacy and myself used nightsticks or flashlights, (he was referring to what's called K-lights or B-lights to beat Mr. Nardone into submission. I explained, looking at the jury that we didn't use any flashlights or nightsticks and that they hadn't been taken out of either patrol car, that it was Mr. Nardone who initiated the violence. I was then excused, and Jack Stacy was called to testify.

Mr. Nardone got convicted of the original felony that the warrant had charged, and it had been plea bargained down to a 1st degree misdemeanor and also a felony conviction for RAVV, (resisting arrest with violence) but this charge was also plea bargained down and ole Frank got 8 months in the slammer, jail time. He was put on probation once he got out.

Well, I was always busy, so I didn't follow Frank's career, or for that matter, I didn't much give a bowel movement, when lo and behold, one day at line up I got a capias for who else but Frank Nardone. it's for VOP, (Violation of Probation) Now a VOP warrant carries a no bond, and guess whose working zone 2, ole Jack Stacy who by now realized that ole Frank was not so friendly. I tell Jack that I'd help him again, just to let me know when he sees Frank's car. Well lineup is over and about 2 hours into the shift zone 2 advises that Nardone's Chrysler is at home, so I acknowledged him and told him to wait until I can get there and park east on the street north, Congress Avenue, of Frank's residence so that I can come up from behind the backside. Well Stacy gave me about 3 or 4 minutes after I went 10-6, busy, assisting zone 2 on a capias. Stacy parked in front of the house like we originally did and knocked on the front door and when he did, I saw ole Frank sneak out the back door. He was trying to work his way to a little shed that was in the back yard when I walked up and said, *"Hi Frank, you're under arrest."* Well, he turned and smiled and put both his hands out for the cuffs. Stacy comes out the back door of the residence. Well, we cuff ole Frank and Stacy take him off to jail.

****

The last I heard of ole Frank Nardone he still lived in Westgate but at a different residence. Jack Stacy left the sheriff's department after a few years.

FROGS

It's the night shift an all's quiet, no action in any of the zones and since we all have digital computers, what few calls there are, are dispatched over the digital so no voice traffic. Hell, the only voice communication is a time check from every zone starting with zone 1 through 9 and it's done every hour on the hour when it's slow, so all you hear is the zone number, and a 10-4, okay. Now I always thought that time checks were to make sure that the troops were awake, and you could tell by the way they answered the radio if they were awake or sleepy or if they didn't answer at all when called, even after being called several times. Then it was my job as sergeant to ask the dispatcher if that zone was busy, on a call, or out for a 10-40, meal, if not, then I had to get my car rolling in that direction and try and locate him. If no valid excuse was given when he was found, or some other legitimate police function was given, then it was my job to enlighten the lad and make sure it didn't happen again.

Now I was pretty fortunate that I had a way of getting any infractions across to the troop so that it never happened again, or at least don't get caught.

it's right around 4:30 AM and I'm kind of getting heavy of the eye myself when I hear a sharp report on the radio and the dispatcher sounds the alarm 3 times to denote 10-33 traffic, emergency, it's immediately followed by the dispatcher calling zone 3 and not waiting for a reply but just advising him of a signal 4, accident, with injuries at the intersection of Belvedere and Haverhill Roads and that a 10-70, ambulance, is already enroute. At the end of her transmission zone 3 acknowledged and advised 10-4, 10-5, meaning he got the message and was enroute. I immediately called the dispatcher and advised that I was enroute.

Now zone 3 is located approximately in the exact center of the east coast of our county and though it's a small zone it is highly populated and very busy on days and evening shift and so when the signal 4 was given out I was in the close proximity of the call. I was only about 1/4 mile away and driving 90 to 100 mph and with no traffic at that time of the AM it doesn't take long to get to point B from point A.

Tonight zone 3 was Ralph Long, one of the best deputies we had and also a close personal friend of mine. Well both zone 3 and I got to the intersection at the same time and the whole intersection was a mass of metal and glass. I told Ralph to put out his flares and I'd check on the injured. Now what we had was 2 pickup trucks, and both had airboats in tow. From the point of vehicle(s) rest showed that one truck was east bound on Belvedere Road, a 4-lane divided roadway, and the 2nd truck was south bound on Haverhill Road, a 2-lane road and the trucks had apparently been racing to catch the green light at the intersection.

Unfortunately, the race ended violently at the intersection. I checked the first truck, and the driver was dead, he had been hit broadside in his door and never had a chance. His airboat had jumped off the trailer and it looked like it went completely over the truck and landed in the far corner of the intersection. A strong aroma of alcohol was evident from the driver. As I finished checking him there was really nothing, I could do for him anyway. The ambulance arrived at that time and also Ralph finished putting his flares throughout the intersection. I filled him and the ambulance driver and his attendant in and we moved quickly to check on the driver of truck number 2. Well, he was all busted up with 2 broken legs and some facial cuts and probably some internal injuries, and he wasn't talking. He was unconscious and you could also smell booze on him. Well, the four of us managed to get him out of the truck and put inflatable splints on his legs and some bandages on his head wounds, then we assisted the ambulance driver and his assistant in lifting the victim into the ambulance and securing the stretcher, so it was secure on the floor.

Well, I took some pictures with the camera that's in the sergeant's car of the entire scene and of the dead victim still in his truck and then we extracted him and put him into a second ambulance, as the first was already enroute to the hospital. Fortunately, at this time of morning we had no trouble with traffic control. Now that the victims had been cleaned from the scene, we had to clean the intersection of all the glass and metal, trucks and the airboats. Now zone 3 had previously told the dispatcher that 2 wreckers would be needed, and both had been dispatched and one was Steve's, Ralph's request. Deputies weren't supposed to request any special wrecker when a wrecker or two was needed, (unless a certain one was requested) the deputy would just ask the dispatcher for wreckers off the rotation list and she in turn would send whatever was needed and then put their names on the bottom of the rotation list. Well in this case, one of the drivers was dead and the other was unconscious and so Ralph just slipped in the request for Steve's.

Now a word about Steve's Wrecker service. Steve had been a police officer in the city of West Palm Beach years ago, he had hurt his back on a police motorcycle, and he had surgery to remove a disc, so he was on a disability pension and so the wrecker service. He was like a father to all cops, and he would come out at all hours to pull deputies/police officers out of the soft sand or whatever the problem was that they needed a wrecker for, and it was always free of charge. He never complained and he was always fixing some police officers patrol car or deputies personal car at his home. He had a 21-foot boat and was always taking a bunch of cops out diving and he never ask for gas money. He was just an honest guy that liked the law enforcement community, so anytime we were able to throw some business his way we were only too happy to do so.

I also advised the dispatcher to notify the night shift detective that a signal 4 and 7, traffic accident & death, was enroute to the hospital and for him to respond for the death investigation report and that zone 3 would do the accident report.

Well with all that taken care of I went back to check on the airboat that was still attached to a truck, because a detailed inventory had to be taken. Both trucks and airboats had to go to a storage yard, so I was going to help zone 3 by doing the storage report on the trunk and airboat. Well, I was going to start with the airboat when I saw a large burlap sack, the kind you might see a 100 pound of potatoes come in, but this bag had the St. Vitus dance, it moved. The end was tied so I undid it and, lo and behold, the dam bag was full of frogs. A quick glance around the airboat showed 2 long bamboo poles about 12 or 15 feet long and each had a 3-pronged brass gig on the end. Besides the driver's seat and close to the footrest was a long funnel tube made from a rain spout, and it went down to the bottom of the boat where the bag had been tied to, so a frog, after he was gigged, was pushed down the tube and he went right into the sack. The victims had been out in the swamp probably all weekend gigging frogs and now they had a whole sack of them. Well one driver was dead, and the other was close to it. There was no problem with the storage of the trucks, airboats and all the personnel belongings but what was I going to do with a big bag of frogs.

I went to my car and contacted the dispatcher by digital and told her to call Fish and Game, tell them about the accident and also about the bag of frogs and what we should do with them, or what they advise? She acknowledged me and told me to standby while she called. Well, she finally came back to me on digital saying that Fish & Game wasn't too choked up, about being wakened at 5:00 AM especially about a bag of frogs. Well anyway they wanted to know if the frogs had. Holes in them from being gigged. I told her to advise them in the affirmative, yes. Back she came right away with, *"it's your problem."* I thought to myself, it's like hell my problem, anyway I acknowledged her.

Well, it so happened that zone 3, Ralph, just happened to live

about 7 or 8 blocks away from the accident scene, so I told zone 3 to check on the driver that was alive and maybe he could advise of some disposition of the frogs. He gets the dispatcher by digital and in a while, she replies also by digital, that the driver brought into the hospital was still unconscious. So now I tell Ralph that we just acquired a big bag of frogs and that were taking them to his house. Well Ralph is all smiles because he has an airboat and he knows how long it takes to get a sack of frogs, so he says, *"that's good pollack."* Well, I try to pick the bag of frogs up from the bottom of the airboat, but it doesn't budge. Now I can lift over 250 pounds from the ground, but this bag was all soft and pliable, so I had Ralph help me lift it, and I know that it had to weigh around 300 pounds. We loaded the bag of frogs into the trunk of Ralph's patrol car. Now by this time both wreckers are on the scene and hooking up the trucks and securing the airboats, Steve is there with his son-in- law Mike, we tell them what we had and to meet us at Ralph's at 8:30 AM for some frog cleaning. Well by now it's 6:00 AM, and the accident scene is all secure. The wrecker drivers have swept up all the glass and metal junk from the intersection and we secure and take the frogs over to Ralph's carport and unload them from his car. Well, I tell Ralph to go to the hospital and finish his report, and me, well I get a cup of coffee and clean up somewhat, the rest of the shift went by without any incident. Ralph and I are at his house by 8:20 AM and in comes Steve and Mike. We start cleaning frogs by 9:00 AM with Ralph just holding them by their legs and hitting them on a foundation block with the other 3 of us cleaning them. We didn't get done until 1400, 2:00 PM, and that's with no breaks. Now we weren't able to weigh the bag of frogs before we started but we did weigh them when we were done, and we had exactly 60 pounds of frog legs. That's 15 pounds apiece.

****

Up to this point I have never indulged in frog legs but let me tell you. I couldn't wait for the next passing airboat. The rewards for being a Deputy Sheriff are small, well most of the time.

GUN SAFETY

It was in the early 70's, and I was the shift sergeant and I guess the acting Lt. We happened to be on the evening shift and at this time of night it was really quiet with no wild calls and just an easy evening. Thank God, as it rained the whole shift, and when it rains it usually means lots of accidents, but somehow this evening there was none. I carried a Smith & Wesson model 28 with a 6-inch barrel, it was a 357-caliber weapon, I also carried a nasty little High Standard Derringer, 22 Magnum in my pocket. Now I was always preaching gun safety to the troops at lineups when there aren't that many things to cover like BOLOs, (Be on the Lookout) and directives from God, in this case the captain, etc.

Gun safety is a good subject to keep bringing up. Anyway, the shift was ending so I went to road patrol to the sergeant's office to brief the oncoming sergeant of any happenings on our shift that he should be aware of, as I didn't even have to make out a log entry such as accidents, deaths or murders or anything serious that the captain could review in the morning. Well at my desk, I take my gun belt off, wipe the gun off and spray it with WD-40, wipe the gun till it's dry and put it all away. I check my troops paperwork as they come in, reports, citations, trip sheets, and finish up early. Now this doesn't happen very often. In my desk I keep a 'Colt Commander' it's a 45 caliber, satin finished automatic, and I carry this to and from work. I just put it in my belt on the left side. Now I always carried the gun with a round in the chamber and the safety on. Cocked and Locked, just the way the military teaches. Well anyway it's still raining like hell, and I get soaked going from road patrol to my car that's in the lot. Then I get soaked again when I get home going from my car to the house. Inside the house I see the gun is soaked along with me, so I take it out and put it on a chair, I take my uniform off and leave it on the floor as it's soaking wet. So now all I got on are my skivvies, under shorts, Claire, my wife is long asleep as well as my two little girls, Heidi and Wendy, Now I usually watch TV for a while and drink a cup of coffee, so I get a cup of 'joe' and also my gun cleaning kit out and sit down.

The first thing I do is take the clip out of the gun, release the safety and pull back the slide which ejects the live round from the chamber. I break the gun down and spray it with WD-40, wipe it off and then put it back together. Next, I take the clip and insert it in the gun. All cops and most people know that the slide on a 45, well for that matter on all automatics, have vertical groves on each side just behind the ejection port. Well I grabbed these groves with my thumb and index finger and pull the slide to the rear of the weapon and this action lets a live round come from the clip into the chamber as you let the slide come forward, now the hammer is cocked, so what you should do now is put the safety on, but instead of doing this I put the clip in the weapon, thank God it was pointed up toward the ceiling, and I didn't realize that my finger was on the trigger as I was watching TV and I held the weapon in my right hand, and with my left hand, using my 2 fingers held the hammer, not tight enough, cause when I squeezed the trigger the rear safety on the grip, it's the bar that's got to be depressed, I pulled the trigger and it went BOOM!

It's about 0100, 1 AM, all quiet in the neighborhood and everyone is asleep by now. Now that ole 240 grain hollow point made just about the loudest noise this old polish boy ever heard. I think I almost had a bowel movement. I just sat still for a couple of minutes and calmed down. Then I took the clip out of the weapon and also the live round that got chambered and I just sat there. Well in about 5 or so minutes I hear a meek voice say," *Hon, Hon, you okay,"* but Claire still didn't stick her head out so I could see her. I answer, *"I'm okay"*, and she runs out and puts her arms around me and hugs me. She had thought for sure that I had accidentally shot myself and she was afraid to look.

Well, I tell her what had happened, and the kids didn't even wake up from the noise. I went and looked at the ceiling and saw a small hole, now my house is just one story tall and has a tapered crawl space but I'm hoping that the round hit a joist or something that stopped the round, anyway I'd check it in the morning.

Well, the next morning I got a ladder and went up on to the roof and shit., there's a 4-inch hole. Well, I never told the troops about this incident, and I kept on them about gun safety.

****

This is the second time I had and accidental gun discharge in my house. I eventually got to be safe with guns.

THE CARBINE HALEY

The time was in the mid 70's, and the shift was a 4-12 PM. I had already been a sergeant for some time by now. The sheriff's department had the responsibility to answer all water related calls within the county, even though they occurred in a city's jurisdiction, and believe me, there were lots of cities. They were also responsible to answer all calls that may involve explosives, bombs, etc. and anyway, they were the only one with a bomb truck in the county.

The bomb truck was patterned after the one they used in Dade County. Once a bomb, or explosive device was found, the dispatcher had to go 10-6, busy, on the intercity radio channel of which all cities had, It was then the responsibility of their patrolman to block traffic until the bomb truck had passed by them. Now not only was this time

consuming, but you can understand, it held up traffic in the numerous towns as U.S. #1, a major highway, ran through all of them. You can also see that it was a major task to coordinate all this with so many people. This is not to say that each city also had other traffic outlets in their city in addition to the one used by the bomb truck. The straits of Florida, also called the Gulf Stream, was a broad current that ran northward all the way to Newfoundland, as all countries in the world used it for ships going north as it was a place to get fuel and was a time saver. Palm Beach County was the closest it ever came to U.S. land, and it came within 3 miles of the county. Now along with all its shipping benefits, the Atlantic Ocean also had its share of storms. That's were wind and waves and rain occur and as these great ships ply steadily northward and get caught, they routinely lose cargo off their decks, just washed overboard.

The ships that lose cargo, never stop and turn around to pick up what was lost overboard, so they just continued on their way as time, I'm sure, was money and schedules had to be kept. Besides anything lost could be written off as they all carry insurance to cover such events.

One such ship must have lost a number of 55-gallon drums that had to be lashed to its deck during such a storm. Well time and tide taking its course, one of the drums washed up on the beach in Palm Beach County and just sit there in the sand at the high tide mark. Now Palm Beach County has so much water area to cover, and things are always washing up on its beaches and people forever beach comb, so in no time someone reported some strange drum on the beach.

All cities cover their beaches but if something strange appears, they call the sheriff's department to check it out and if, in fact, it is an explosive device in nature, the sheriff's department had to recover it and dispose of it. This is where the dispatcher and the inter -city radio come in as she had to change radio channels, advising that an explosive device was to be moved through their city so that they had ample time to reroute and block traffic. Of course, while the dispatcher was on intercity channel, the road units were in the blind, meaning they had no communication with the dispatcher at all. Any city had the right to refuse the sheriff's department access through their city when they found out a bomb or explosive was to be moved through it. The counties shoreline went from Boca Raton in the south to all the way to Jupiter Inlet to the north, and all flotsam, items, finally ended up on the beach somewhere. Reports of flares, marijuana and even bodies are constantly called in to their respective cities who in turn, call the SO if it warrants it.

The beaches, also known as the Gold Coast of Florida, always have hundreds of bathers, lovers and beachcomber, so someone is always reporting something found.

Now it just so happened that the 55-gallon drum had washed up in the north end of the county. It was dark and a long way from any inlet, and there was no foot traffic at all, or very little there. The drum had foreign writing on it, but it also had a chemical name printed on it which after checking with the dispatcher, the contents were found to be a very volatile substance. Well, all this was reported to the sheriff's office who now had to go through the proper channels to recover and dispose of it.

Well, the call was given to zone 1 as the drum was reported to be in the north county area, and that was his patrol zone. At this time the sheriff's department had what is called, CONVERACOM, for radio communications. Simply it's where your police radio is in a unit in your patrol car and constantly being charged, the minute a deputy goes 10-6, busy, he simply hits a button and he has a fully charged walkie talkie that he takes with him and so he's in constant communication with the dispatcher, and she knows exactly where he is at all times and can get him help right away should he ask. If he's on a call and taking an undue amount of time, she can get a periodic check as to his wellbeing. I, being the shift sergeant and hearing the call, advised zone 1 to 10-22, disregard, that I would check it out first to see if I had to go through the whole-time consuming procedure. A Lt. Vince Haley, a vice unit, also heard the call and told me that he would go with me. This just goes to show that you never know who's listening on the radio, and it could be anyone with a police radio, we had detectives, vice units, and even administrative units who were on the air, so you never knew who was listening or heard you. All I was ever concerned with was the uniform units as that was my charge.

Now Haley was the Lt. in charge of vice operations, when I first met him, he was just a sergeant when I had taken a diving course sponsored by the SO I was still on Riviera Beach Police Department at the time, so I see he had received a promotion. He apparently didn't have anything pending at the time as he wanted to go with me. Well, I told the Lt. to meet me on Singer Island. We met and parked our cars off the road and our dispatcher knew what type of call we were checking out. Now all I took was my radio and flashlight with me. The radio for constant communication, but here come the Lt., a flashlight and a folding stock military carbine that had a 15-round clip in it. Now I didn't say anything as he's a Lt. and can carry anything he wants. He knew what type of call we were on, but vice cops always carry some sort of weapon. We walked to the beach and started north walking in the soft sand looking for this 55-gallon drum. So, there we were, a uniform sergeant and a civilian looking guy with a flashlight in one hand and carbine in the other. Although there were people on the beach, they could see us walking north, and didn't pay us any mind, as one was in uniform, ME, and they continued on their stroll. It was a starry night; the ocean was calm with waves just barely lapping the shore.

We had walked about a mile through the sand and by now tourists and lovers had long since passed, when lo, there was the drum, just standing in the sand where the last high tide left it. Not a soul was around and off in the far distance were condominiums where affluent people lived, but none was even close to us, so I went over and checked the drum and sure enough, it had foreign writing on it and also had what looked like printing on it in English. I copied it down and advised our dispatcher who checked it out and sure enough, the contents of the drum were explosive, and it could blow up.

Now that it was confirmed, I had to get the bomb truck, then have the dispatcher notify the cities it would have to pass through, and then try to move a 55-gallon drum off the beach through soft sand. You know that drum had to weigh a good several hundred pounds and the truck dam sure couldn't come through the sand, it only went on hard surfaces like roads.

Well, I was just about ready to tell the dispatcher to notify Marco to get is bomb truck ready when Haley said wait, *"why not blow it up right where it is."* I got to thinking that it would certainly element a lot of problems, no bomb truck, no cities to call, and best of all, none around to get injured nor anything to sustain damage.

The sheriff's department had no need of the chemical contents, and we would have had to dispose of it and so I told Haley, *"Yeah. That's a good idea,"* with that Haley handed me the carbine he carried and I took the safety off, we moved away from the drum and I pulled the trigger, holding it hip high and pointed in the direction of the drum and crack, I saw the round hit and kick up sand about 10 feet in front of it so I just walked the rounds right up to the drum and BOOM!, up goes the drum in a big fireball and then nothing. The drum and all its contents were gone, all that was left was a blackened hole in the sand where the drum was.

I told Haley that, *"we had ignition,"* and I said thanks, put the safety back on, and gave him his carbine. I told the dispatcher that we had disposed of any problems and that we were enroute back to our cars.

****

Lt. Haley went on to become commander of the Delray Beach substation. The drum was never reported as missing, or any ownership was confirmed. The department still got calls of flares, bales of marijuana etc., and we still responded.

JOHN I LEONARD HIGH SCHOOL STUN GUN

The time was early 70's, I was the shift sergeant, and we had a newly made Lt., who had been a detective, but he got promoted to a Lt., so he was put on as a uniform Lt. He was now a commander of a shift, my shift. Now they had separated me from Lt. Begley as they felt that some sort of click had been formed, 'oh really?' when our shift competed against the other two shifts, as we regularly had choir practices, made more arrests and criminal cases than the other two combined. Now it was true that we had to straighten out some mistakes or take some action where they didn't. This all goes back to what is known as aggressive patrol, also known as Begley's Bas,

anyway, Decker had been a Lt. on another shift, brand X, and now he was on mine.

Back at this time Palm Beach County experienced a lot of racial unrest, just like the rest of the country, at the schools, due to bussing schedules etc. Unfortunately, the County sheriff's department handled any complaints, and some were classified as signal 28, riots.

We were on the 3 to 11 shift and had been advised by our intelligence, vice unit, that there would be trouble at JILHS, (John I Leonard High School) right after the school day was finished, and where the school busses lined up to wait for the lil darlings to take them home. Well, the day shift had been held over and so I took my troops, about 10, right to JILHS after a hurried line up, and sure enough trouble had already begun. The black students were fighting with the whites and when they saw the sheriff's green and whites, they stopped fighting and ran to their assigned busses. Now there were about 8 busses, and they were almost loaded with students, so they were about ready to go. To add to the confusion a lot of parents were standing and milling about in the parking lot, and the school bus area as their children had told them about expected trouble, so they were all pretty vocal. As I saw it, the best way to defuse the situation seemed to be to get the busses moving. Just then Lt. Decker pulls up, gets out of his car, and he's carrying a stun gun.

Now the stun gun is just what it sounds to be. It will stun the dog shit out of you if you are the stunee. To describe it, it's a black plastic tube on the bottom half and is probably about 37 millimeters in diameter, or about the same as a federal tear gas gun. The top half is smaller in diameter and is machined, not smooth, in design and is made of the same plastic material. The whole thing is about 30 inches long. The gun breaks in half by swinging the lower half sideways and it's loaded with what looks like a federal cartridge about 6 inches long. These casings can be loaded with a variety of goodies such as a 6-ounce bean bag or with 5 oaken wedges that splinter on contact with a hard surface, also a bag when it strikes a person leaves a highly visible color on that person so that he can be readily identified for some time. The oaken wedges when they splinter into the shins of a hostile crowd help greatly in removing any hostility in anyone. Now the propelling charge behind the stun gun is just a large primer and the bag(s) are also recoverable, and the casing itself can be recharged/reloaded by the sheriff's department armorer. The gun is fired from the hip position and two hands are needed. The trigger is a spring-loaded mechanism.

Decker is an expert on the stun gun as when he was in pursuit of his Lt's. bars he volunteered to be the dummy when the department was thinking about its purchase as it was billed as a non-lethal weapon. It was to be demonstrated at the Road Patrol in front of the Sheriff, Chief Deputy and several other department heads. Now as Marice Chaviiller and Hermaine Gingold sang in, *"Gigi, ah yes, I remember it well,"*

Decker stood about 50 feet away when he got hit with the bean bag and it took his lil, soon to be Lt.'s ass, up off his feet, and he spent the next two weeks in traction cause it screwed up his back. I often wonder what he would have done for Captains bars.

Well back to JILHS where I was about to get the busses moving when a teacher, I think it was the boy's counselor, came out of the school shouting that one of the b/m students in the back of the bus number 2 was the instigator of most of the trouble and he wants him off the bus and taken away. I take a deputy named James Kilborn with me onto bus number 2 and it's loaded with blacks. We make our way to the rear, to this big black juvenile male that the counselor is pointing to from outside the bus, and we just told him to follow us. He gets up and walks out with us, and he's no problem. We ran the kid over to a patrol car and get him moving toward the juvenile detention center. Now we're ready to move the busses out of the school area. So instead of him, Dacker, just going to the first driver's window and telling him to move out, he instead takes the butt end of the stun gun and hits the bus. Well, there's a loud bang, I look up and see some guy fall and he's hollering in pain. The busses are moving out and away. I ran over to the guy on the ground and he's still hollering. The bean bag caught him in the thigh, and it just missed his nuts. I figured, *"you dumb shitt Decker,"* now this is really going to start a riot and the poor guy is going to own a good part of Palm Beach County, or at least have a vested interest after the lawsuit is over. Well, the main thing at this point was to get the injured guy out of there and I wasn't going to wait for any ambulance, so I reached down and picked him up I in my arms like you would a kid and took him to the nearest patrol car. I then put him in the front seat, moving the deputy's things over. I wasn't about to stick him in no cage, and I told the troop to take him to John F. Kennedy Hospital 10-18, blue lights and siren, I told the guy, victim, he would be all right and they left. Boy! at this stage I could really see a lawsuit coming. Well by now the busses had left the school grounds with no further incidents, the crowd dispersed, and we went back to regular duty, and I stayed away from the hospital, DGI! (Don't Get Involved!)

Next day I'm standing at the counter getting my line up ready when this guy comes in the front door, and I know right away that he's the one Decker shot so I put my head down and shied away. I didn't want NO part of what was about to happen. Well, I snuck back to the sergeant's office when I hear, *"Sergeant Barton, come to Captain Sanchez office please."*

Please, now that's new, well I go out and down the hall to the captains office and he's talking with the guy who he introduced me to, and he grabs my hand and shakes it. Now this takes me off guard as I had been thinking bad thoughts when this guy up and says,*" sergeant, I just wanted to see the deputy that picked me up and put me in that car the way you did. I weigh 205 pounds and you picked me up like I was a kid. I want to thank you for your prompt attention to me, and thank you all for a fine job,"* He shakes my hand again. SOB, Decker aces out again! No lawsuit. The guy said he realized it was just an unfortunate accident.

****

The paper that day had a picture of me and Kilborn taking the black male to a patrol car. The stun gun was sent back to the factory as having a faulty release. Decker stayed with the department for about 8 more years till his golden hook, cops will know what a hook is, straightened out, and he became the victim of political musical chairs, He is now the Chief of Police in the town of Juno Beach Florida. Because of Decker, I had gotten a three-day suspension at a time when he wasn't even my Lt. Ah hell, but that's another story. I still have a cartridge and a bean bag.

KARMEN GHIA RECOVERY

I had been on the Sheriff's Department only about 4 months and I dived with the Harbor Patrol deputy Larry Jobes just once and that was when we had recovered the little 7-year-old boy in North Palm Beach. I had never seen Jobes much prior to that dive as he seldom came to the Road Patrol. He kept the Harbor Patrol car and took it home with him then used it to get the sheriff's department boat at whatever dock they used. Now he alone comprised our Navy Harbor Patrol along with several other auxiliary deputies who road with him mostly on the weekends. Now Jobes never went to court or attended any CHOIR PRACTICES, that's beer, pizza and war story time. After the recovery of the boy, he had ask me to bring my wife and kids to visit him and his wife sometime. I had told my wife and she thought it would be a great idea, so I told Jobes that we'd be over on my next day that I got off.

Well, we drove to Lantana, found his house and met his wife. We sat around and shot

the breeze and I told some war stories. From the conversation, I took it that Jobes had never spent any time on the road as a policeman, that he had been hired by the department just to dive and run our Harbor Patrol. Well, the conversation was mostly about diving when Larry up and says, *"Hey, let me tell you about a couple of dreams I keep having, one is that I'm called to go dive in a canal for a car. It still has people inside. Rand its black water. I finally find the car, open the door, and go inside. The water is black, and I can't see inside, so I got to feel for them. Well, I find 2 people in the back seat and when I go to get out with a body the door had closed again. So, I try to open it, but it won't open, and then all of a sudden, I realize that I'm trapped in the car with 2 signal 7's, dead bodies. Nice dream huh."*

He didn't say anything like I wake up sweating and hollering so I said, *"hell, that's a peach of a dream."* Then he tells me about his second dream where he's asleep in bed and his hand falls down off the bed and it wakes him up and he naturally looks over the side of the bed and his hand is on the face of a dead female; she's dressed in a gossamer night gown. I get out of bed and push her back under the bed, get back in bed myself and go back to sleep. It's not 5 minutes and I hear a movement under me, I look, and this female is back out from under the bed again.

I broke in at this time and said, *"Hell, that's no dream, that's a nightmare,"* Well we stayed a little while longer and then left. Driving home my wife said,*" those dreams that Larry had kind of gave me the creeps." "Eh,"* I said, but I didn't pay much attention. I guess I should have though, if I had thought about it any, I'd have seen that Larry was getting the lump, or spooked about diving in black water canals for bodies and things.

Canal diving is nothing like sport diving for fish, lobster, shells in clear water in the ocean, or in lakes where it's clear and you can see. I was soon to find out about Jobes.

I don't think it was a week later, it was my day off. The weather was cloudy, and it looked like rain, so I didn't go diving in the ocean as I usually do but stayed home with my wife and girls. Well, the phone rings and it's the communication sergeant, he tells me about a car in the Palm Beach Canal on Southern Blvd, and Captain Sanchez says that I was to respond and that the Harbor Patrol unit was 10-51, enroute. I said, *"shit, it's my day off, what about Murray and Chasteen they're divers."* The sergeant says, *"don't ask me, I'm just relaying the message," "okay I'm 10-*

51," enroute. Now my wife hears all this so she asks if she and the kids can come and watch. Sure, it's okay with me, so I grab my wet suit from the den. Canal diving is altogether different than diving in the ocean, so I take the suit along just in case I need it. The rest of my diving gear was already in my car and my tank was filled, so I got my cut offs and my flip flops, now I'm ready to go. I get Claire and the kids and start south on Haverhill Road. Southern Blvd. is about 10 miles from home, so it takes a good 20 minutes to get to Haverhill and Southern Blvd. intersection, and sure enough there's a deputy directing traffic. He sees my car and he yells, *"hey Bob, they are waiting for you,"* and with that he stops traffic so I can pull across the road, Southern Blvd., and onto the small berm. Now besides all the vehicular traffic there are a large group of people lined up along the berm watching toward the canal. The Harbor Patrol unit, Jobes, is already on the scene and he's got his wet suit on. The zone man, zone 3, Steve, and his wrecker are there. I find a place to park my little VW, Volkswagen square back, I tell my wife to stay in the car and I walk over to the zone man, Steve, and Jobes. Also standing with them is a young white female, she's holding a little baby and both of them are soaking wet and the baby's crying. They all say hello and Jobes asks me if I'm ready to get wet, *"sure am, but what do we have?"* Jobes explains that the wet female was east bound on Southern Blvd. State Road #80, or else U.S. 98, in her Karmen Ghia when a vehicle pulled out from a dirt road and cut her off. Now although she had the right of way, she had turned to the right to avoid a collision and had crossed the berm and it just so happened that there was no guard rail there, and as a result went over the embankment, which was about 30 degrees, and traveled through some brush for about another 70 feet and then just went off the canal bank into the canal.

Fortunately, a VW is pretty airtight, and it floated for several minutes, and the woman was able to get out of the car window with her baby and swim to shore. She was extremely lucky that all she got was a bloody nose from the steering wheel and a heck of a scare for her and her baby.

The car then sank out of sight as she got to shore and a passing motorist had seen the accident, stopped, and I then called the sheriff's department. The zone man was given the call and, on his arrival, called for a wrecker.

A word about Palm Beach County Canal, it's a large canal that is the main source of water for the city of West Palm Beach, in addition to several other cities in the county. Its width varies from 40 to 50 feet wide, and its depth varies from 7 to 35 feet deep. It originates in Lake Okeechobee and in its eastward flow junctions at a place called 20 Mile Bend where the south bound fork is known as the Miami Canal. The east fork becomes the Palm Beach Canal. Now about 2 miles east is the world's largest low-level pump station which gives the normally slow-moving canal a drastic eastward push when the flood gates are open, and the pumps are in operation. This is a method of flood control used to regulate Lake Okeechobee and also meet water demands on the various cities using its water. When the gates are open, and the pumps are on, the water moves with such force that there isn't anyway a person could swim against it, because of this it stirs up the bottom and there's no visibility and it's completely muddy on the surface. Right under the surface a foot or so, it becomes completely black, also in its eastward movement it pulls trees and branches from the banks.

Unfortunately, that was the condition it was in this day. This was to be my baptism of canal diving and from the looks of the water there was no doubt I'd be using my wet suit this day. I don't mind telling you I was kind of apprehensive about diving in that canal as I

had never been diving before in completely black water and as the saying goes, my sphincter muscle tightened considerably. Hell, with all these people standing and watching, the woman and her baby, Steve and zone 3 standing by, and they all seemed to be just waiting for the divers, me and Jobes, to do something, Anyway I was going to help Jobes, or so I thought. So, I got busy with Steve, the wrecker driver,

Now we had no idea where the car was as it was underwater, and there was no gas or oil or bubbles, this was due to the fast current. All we had for sure was where the car went into the canal, and we knew it floated several minutes and traveled east before sinking out of sight. Now I didn't pay any attention to Jobes who was with zone 3 and the victim(s).

I told Steve, the wrecker driver, that a search pattern from our side of the canal, north, wouldn't be any good as the current would just sweep me back to the bank. So, there wasn't even any way that I could get out to the middle of the canal which was a good 50 feet wide at this point.

Now Steve was an ex-policeman from the city of West Palm Beach and was retired on a disability. He had started a wrecker service, and he said, *"I got a Jon boat back at the house, I'll get my other driver to go over to the house and pick it up with the motor and bring it here."*

While this is going on, I put on my wet suit and carried my tank, weight belt, mask and fins down to the water's edge so that I'd be all ready. Well, it was no more than 25 minutes when the wrecker driver showed up with the Jon boat, so Jobes, Steve, me and the wrecker driver carried the 12-foot-long boat and motor down to the water's edge.

I said, *"Steve, I want you to secure a line straight across to the south bank and one on our side, north side, so that the boat will be about in the middle of the canal and I'll use it as a work platform"*, meaning I'd follow the line from the north bank to the boat, and from the boat I'd take a line and start making an arc, north to south, then I'd surface and Steve could give me more line and I'd do it all over again until I found the car. I told Steve to give me about 3 or 4 feet on each sweep as there was no visibility.

Now Jobes started to bring his diving gear down to the water's edge. We launched the boat and Steve took it to the south bank and threw a line to a spectator who attached it to a tree on that side of the bank. He then slowly backed the boat to the center of the canal as we already had a line on the north side. Now both lines were pulled taunt, and the boat was in the center of the canal

All I had to do was tank up, put my weight belt, mask and fins on. I got into the water and put my snorkel in my mouth as I had to pull myself to the boat first by the line. I first made sure my mouthpiece was in front of me and my air was on, So I started to pull myself toward the boat. As I was doing this, I saw Jobes get into the water and stand in about 3 feet and he didn't even have his tank on, nor did he make any attempt to swim out to me as I was swimming to the boat. Well, I got to the boat and hung my arms over the gunnel, side of the boat, in this case it was over the front. I spit out my snorkel and told Steve to give me a line, that the car had floated a few minutes before sinking so it had to be east of us. I couldn't estimate how far so I told him I'd swim east on the surface about 25 or 30 feet and submerge, make an arc while holding the rope in my left hand with my right hand out in front of me feeling for whatever. As I said before, the water was completely black just under the surface and it was like diving in an ink well. I told Steve that after I surfaced to play out another 3 or 4 feet of rope and I'd do the same thing, make another arc. He nodded that he understood and said, *"be careful Yash"*. He always called me that. I put my mouthpiece in and looped the rope around my left hand and started swimming away from the boat. Now it's a lot harder swimming on the surface with a SCUBA tank and an 18-pound weight belt, holding and pulling taunt a rope from their boat. I had on all this gear with a snorkel in my mouth, but I had a taunt line from the shore to the boat. and now there was no platform anyway I got about 25 feet on the surface, east of the boat and Steve stopped the line from playing out, well this was my moment of truth, my first dive in a canal that was black, *"I mean BLACK."* I was scared as hell and wondered what the hell happened to Jobes; it was like he wasn't even here. I was to assist him, and he just gets in the water and that's it. No tank on or even mask or fins. I figured with all those people lined up and standing on both banks I can't quit now. Hell, as long as I got air and my mouthpiece, I should be all right.

So, I dove, now I had been looking down while I was swimming on the surface and I could see my hand at about 6 inches, but the second I was under water it got completely black. I felt like I was never going to see light again and no one would find me in this absolute darkness. There wasn't any sound except for my exhaling in the mouthpiece and my regulator letting out the exhaust air. I kept going down with my right hand outstretched in front of me. I had on a pair of cotton gloves when all of a sudden, I realized I was in the mud, it was so soft and gooey, I didn't even realize it. Well, I stopped descending, brought my feet down and pulled my hand out of the soft mud. It was unbelievable how lonely it was, and being all covered with a wet suit, rubber booties, fins and gloves I didn't realize that I had dove into the mud. Well,

I tried to get my bearings and I had to keep talking to myself trying to rationalize things when I realized that I was breathing very fast and hard which is bad for a SCUBA diver, so I kept talking to myself to take it easy and breath slow and even, and that I was all right at this moment. I had air to breath and a line to the surface, so I wasn't completely alone, and I had a way back from this blackness.

I probably stayed this way for about 5 minutes and had managed to slow my breathing down to an even rhythm, then I got to wondering how a diver could tell if he was up or down when in black water, no one ever told me, and it was never brought up at dive school. As I sat there on my knees and fins in the mud all I could hear was my exhaust bubbles from my regulator as I exhaled, and then I knew, hell, just reach my hand back over my regulator and as air always rises, I would at least know which way was up.

Well by now I felt a little more confident and I judged my depth to be about 12 to 15 feet from the surface, so I had to be closer to the boats. I had about 20 some feet of rope as I dove and kept the line taunt. I thought I'd swim in an arc. I figured with rope wrapped around my left hand, and pulled tightly, that the boat was directly behind me, and up, so if I swim/crawl to my left I'd be going toward the north bank, the bank where the car went in. So, I started to move in that direction with my right hand out in front of me and waving in a circular motion and feeling for trees, branches or whatever. Now all of a sudden it got hard going and I was going against the current so I knew that I had gone as far as I could on this sweep to the north, so I stopped, wrapped the rope around my right hand, and, keeping the rope tight, used my left hand as I had done with my right to feel my way. I swam/crawled south to the extent of the arc feeling for anything but black water. I swam to the surface; I was close to the south bank and Steve in his boat saw me and he automatically let out 3 or 4 feet of rope, so I dove back down. The minute I got on bottom I changed hands again with the rope and swam/crawled and made sure the rope was always taunt as this was my only way of telling direction. I must have gone 15 to 20 feet when I ran into a tree. I stopped right away and used my right hand in a much larger arc not wanting to get tied up in any branches or get my regulator hose ripped or my mouthpiece ripped out of my mouth. Keeping the line taunt, I swam along the tree, and I ran across the stump. I knew then that it was a coconut tree as the roots are in a tight ball, so I just felt my way over the top of the roots which was about 3 or 4 feet and I kept swimming my arc.

I got back to the north bank, surfaced and Steve played out another 3 or 4 feet of line and I changed hands again with the line. Now all the time I'm down and telling myself to be calm and breathe easy as it was easy to conjure up a beastie, namely an alligator, and I wonder what the hell I would do cause I'd never know what it was until I touched the dam thing, but a gaiter would know as it could hear my breathing and the exhaust from my regulator. I wondered how aggressive it would be. I figured it would depend on how big it was. Anyway, all this is going through my mind when all of a sudden, I slammed into something and all most spit my mouthpiece out, I'm so scared, but I feel like it's a wall. It's smooth and definitely metal, then I feel a tire. Hell, it's the Karman Ghia, I found the car.

It's laying on the passenger side facing north and south, and I ran into the paneled bottom of it. Dam I was happy and felt good finding it. It sure calmed me down. I swam/pulled myself up to the passenger door and stood up. I was still holding the rope tightly in my left hand and I got up on the tips of my fins. When I did my head was just out of the water up to my chin. So, with my free hand I took out my mouthpiece and hollered, *"I found it!"* Then I got a fix, landmark, on how far I was from the boat. I was about 10 or 15 feet from the north bank. I then had Steve pull me back and I pulled myself to the north bank along the rope.

Jobes was still standing in the water when I got to shore and said, *"good find Bob,"* so I stayed in the shallow water about 4 feet deep and took a break.

It was good to get back to life and people again. Now while I was taking a break Steve freed the Jon boat, beached it and was giving orders to the wrecker driver to release his hook and bring it down to the water's edge. Well, he pulled it down all right, it must have weighed 10 pounds. The cable was 3/4 inch, so it was a hell of a lot of weight I was gonna have to drag out to the car. I could see that there would be no swimming, just dragging along the bottom. Well by now I was rested up and I told Steve just how the car was laying, and he said, *"just hook to anything you can find to hook onto, once we get it up close to shore, we can re-hook it."*

I put my mask back on, put my mouthpiece back in, grabbed the hook and went under water. The hook and the cable just pulled me down into the mud. After I moved it, I'd have to get out on the mud, but anyway I finally got back to the car and felt over it. I found the left front tire which was up in the air and just looped the cable around the axle, right behind the wheel. I surfaced and told Steve to take up the slack. When he had taken the slack up, he advised me that it was holding as the wrecker was straining against the heavy load. When the car finally came up close to shore, I re-hooked the cable, it was no problem.

The wrecker pulled the Karmen Ghia slowly out of the water so that the water in it would drain out. The young woman with the baby came over and thanked me for getting the car out. The deputy, zone 3, got the rest of his information for a report. Steve the wrecker owner, by this time had the car out of the water, drained, and said, *"thanks Yash,"* and he took the car back to his salvage yard.

****

Jobes never did offer any explanation as to why he didn't help me recover the car, but a very short time later he quit the Sheriff's Department. My wife, who had been standing with the zone deputy thought it was just great to recover something from a canal.

My Captain knew that I had to dive on my day off, and that the car was recovered, but he never said, *"Good job Pollack,"* or," *take a comp day."* Well, I guess it just went with the job. I dove many times in my years with the sheriff's department and it never got any easier diving in black water canals for bodies, evidence etc. I finally understood why Jobes had those dreams and finally quit the department.

I saw Jobes again about 10 years after that dive. Now I was a sergeant and Jobes had gotten a big rig, tractor and trailer, and took his wife on all his trips. He was doing great and told me he sure didn't miss diving anymore. He never had those 2 dreams anymore that he had told me about so long ago.

RIOT KENNEDY SUGAR MILL

The time was around early 1968 and I had been on the sheriff's department just over four months, I had already been involved in several shootings, fights etc. and had made more felony arrests than all of my time I spent on police departments. This was prior to joining the sheriff's department. In fact, I was just getting over my shooting incident with Deke Tanner, who was the president of the Outlaws motorcycle club. I even got national media coverage on it and several years later someone gave me a copy of a detective magazine and it had the story and all about the Outlaws M/C gang. Then I read it and remembered what happened and that I was just doing my job and trying not to get my head knocked off with a chain belt.

Well, it's January 2nd and a nice day, and my day off. I think I'll go diving over at Palm Beach Inlet. I was just getting ready to load up my diving gear when the phone rings and my wife answers it and its someone from road patrol for me and I mumble," *awe heck!"* I take the phone and it's the night shift sergeant. *"Barton! were on 10-100 (stand by alert) "get to road patrol as soon as you can."* I ask where it's at, the emergency, and he tells me *"It's Belle Glade." * I thank him and hang up. I tell Claire, my wife, that there's no diving today and that I got to go to road patrol right away and I also tell her about the alert status we're in. I change out of my cutoffs and flip flops and skivvy shirt, t-shirt, and put on my uniform pants, shirt and boots, black cowboy, and just grab my gun belt. Now back in 1968 that was just about all the riot uniform that the sheriff's department had. I didn't even bother with my Stetson as I would probably get a riot helmet when I got to road patrol. I kiss my daughters Heidi, age four years old, and Wendy age four months old, I kiss Claire my wife goodbye and tell her not to worry and that I'd call her as soon as I could leave. From where I lived, I was only about 15 minutes away. Road patrol headquarters located off Southern Blvd., and access to palm Beach International Airport. As I pull in, I can see the parking lot is full of personal cars of deputies from all 3 shifts. So that means the night shift never got to go home. The day shift was on the road and lots of deputies who were off, or from the 3-11 shift where already there. Now road patrol is shaped like the letter 'L', and it doesn't have any hallways connecting any of the rooms, so you had to go outside to go to another room. All the buildings at the airport were vintage World War II when it was a military base there. Well, I first went to the squad room where a bunch of deputies where in the process of checking out their issued riot gear they had drawn from the arms room, armory, and were putting on gas masks and adjusting the straps and also checking the canisters on the bottom of the masks for tape, duct. It was taped, so you removed it, if not taped there was a good chance it was no good and so you drew another canister, filter, because it was expired. Some of the deputies were blousing their boots. Walking over to the arms room I could see Lt. Sanchez and Sgt. Bendick were in with Captain Herron, the officer in charge of the uniform division, talking to the Belle Glade substation and also with the sheriff who was still in his office in West Palm Beach, the city.

Well, I got to the arms room and signed for my riot gear. I was given a riot helmet made by *"Bucco"*, painted green just like our uniforms and heavily padded inside to protect your ears and neck. It also had a heavy Plexiglas shield to cover your face. A pair of jump boots with two elastic snaps so I could blouse them, a pair of black gauntlet type gloves and a riot shotgun. Before you left the arms room, they made sure that you knew you were responsible for all the gear you signed for. I left and went to the squad room, put on all my gear and adjusted it to fit, checking the mask and filter. Just then Lt. Sanchez came into the room and in his pleasant voice said, Sanchez was retired from West Palm police department, so they didn't call him *"hollering Hank for nothing."* Hurry up, were going to Belle Glade substation in about 5 minutes. One of the sergeants passed out military surplus pouches, the kind you could put a box of 25 shotgun shells into, and he also gave out boxes of 00 buck shot or #4's, that's the only type shells used other than slugs. Sergeant Weaver was busy checking on the patrol cars, making sure that all the additional gear we would take along was in the trunks, and that they/we gassed up ready to go. They had federal gas guns, 37-millimeter, gas grenades, both CS and CN type and also first aid gear etc. It was decided to take 7 patrol cars plus Lt. Sanchez's Ford. I don't know how many detective cars were going as our detective bureau was downtown in West Palm Beach where the jail was and so was the sheriff's office. That's where the D-bureau would draw their riot gear from.

Anyway, they would just be a backup unit for the uniformed division. We loaded up, 4 to a car, because of all the gear we each had. I saw Sanchez take his M1 carbine with a folding stock, Sergeant Bendick had a Thompson sub machine gun with a clip in the weapon and 4 more in a pouch. He also had another Thompson with clips for it and he put it all in Sanchez's trunk. I was just a deputy and didn't have any contact with anyone in Belle Glade, but the situation must have been bad cause Sanchez is hollering like hell for us to saddle up and get moving. Well, we take off code 3, lights and sirens, all 8 cars and with Lt. Sanchez in the lead. Now Belle Glade is straight west on state road #80.

Southern Blvd. State Road #80 is only 4 lanes divided for about 1 1/2 miles from road patrol and the rest is just 2 lane and busy.

Well, a convoy of sheriff's department cars with lights and sirens on and pushing close to 100 mph must have been something to behold to the taxpayers of Palm Beach County that day. People were pulling out of the way east and west bound, driving over curbs to get out of the way. Now that I look back at it, we were probably more of a hazard than where we were going. Sanchez never let up on the gas and traffic finally eased up around Lion Country Safari, just east of 20-mile bend and into that area of Palm Beach County where Belle Glade starts patrolling that part of the county. Now right at 20-mile bend is a large canal that brings water into west Palm Beach, all cities, and it goes all the way to Miami, that's fresh water from lake Okeechobee. Right, there is the world's largest low-level pump station, what the sign says anyway. We pass the bridge and continue on state road #80, still speeding and screaming along. We were running eight alongside the canal that's a good 25 to 30 feet wide and a good 12 to feet deep. We pass three nice white crosses, in Florida, white crosses designate a death, where someone went in the canal and drown or was killed in a traffic accident.

Anyway, they were dead. At that point there are no guard rails to stop you. It kind of makes you think, especially when you're in the back seat of a cage car with no window or door cranks and doing 100 mph. With no guard rails to stop you. If you get off the road 10 to 12 feet, you're in deep water already. Now out here in Belle Glade it's all farmland and cattle country and if you look at the dirt its almost purer black. Hell, it's so rich you can almost watch sugar cane and corn grow, but not too good at a 100 mph. We cross a bridge and head north going through cane fields on both sides, we still have the blue lights on as well as the sirens, but now on manual operation off the horn button. The road is dirt and roughly 2 lanes wide, no berm as I remember. We turn west and still cane fields on both sides. I see Sanchez run some farmer off the road and I almost shit, I laughed so hard. The farmer had a flatbed truck, and it was loaded with crates of vegetables stacked 5 crates high, so it was a good 10 to 11 feet off the ground to the top crates. Now they were tied down but when Sanchez went around hitting his siren the farmer jerked the wheel hard to the right and I could see 2 rows of crates stacked 5 crates high fall off and I could just imagine what the farmer had to say. I'll bet it wasn't pro-law enforcement.

Well, we came to the Belle Glade airport and turned right or north. The substation was only about a mile beyond. We pulled into the parking lot behind the substation. I'll bet it take 25 minutes for the whole trip. Well, the uniform troops, slick sleeves, stayed in the parking lot area going inside only to use the head, bathroom, get coffee or a soft drink. We finally found out from a Belle Glade deputy that the trouble was in a place called Kennedy sugar mill and that it probably involves 200 to 300 Jamaicans in a dispute over wages. Now I don't know much about sugar cane, other than that sugar comes out of a bag. I know less about sugar mills and the workers. I do know that the mills can't get native Americans to burn, cut and harvest sugar cane so they import Jamaicans on a contract basis. I guess the companies pay them room, board and a salary.

Well, our Lt. Sanchez has been inside the substation with Captain Claud Tindal, the officer in charge of the station. Now they all came outside to the lot and Sanchez advises us to saddle up that were going to Kennedy sugar mill camp. Now there are about 25 to 30 uniform deputies getting into patrol cars, there are also several deputies from the substation. There's also a lot of unmarked cars and detectives, so we have a lot all told. We take off with Tindal and Sanchez in the lead car, and this time no lights and sirens, but fast. We headed north. Then Sanchez pulls into what looks like an abandon warehouse and stops, gets out of the car, gets his sergeants together. That's Weaver, Bendick and Steidley. I guess he was giving last minute orders and then I hear him holler, *"Barton up front",* so I run up from near the end of the line and he says, *"gimmie your shotgun!"* Now I don't question his order, he turns around puts it in his trunk and gives me the other Thompson submachine gun plus 5 stick clips and says, *"you ride with me and Bendick."* So, I get in the back seat of his Ford. Now this really took me by surprise as I figured that Bendick had one of the Thompsons, and the other would go to a Sgt. or a Lt. I was just a slick sleeve and only on the department about 4 months. Well, we take off again just as fast as we could on a dirt road and in about 5 minutes, we turn into a shell rock road, and we could see that we were all 10-97, arrived. What we saw off to the right as we approached was a small, shed type office, and right behind it were two, two story barracks buildings. From where we were facing the ends of both barracks' buildings. From where we were facing the ends of both barracks. The second story had like a porch with a railing and there were Jamaicans standing shoulder to shoulder watching us. On the ground floor were also a lot of Jamaicans watching us. They were also hollering and shouting at us as we pulled up. I rough guessed that there were 200 to 250 Jamaicans in all. A few were standing in the vicinity of the office. All got out of the patrol cars and formed two lines.

At this point captain Herron, our officer in charge already on the scene advised that only Sanchez, Bendick and me would advance toward the office and the rest of the troops would remain in formation to the rear of us. Now there was nothing in the way such, as other buildings close by. It was all open and flat land. I saw Sanchez and Bendick their gas masks in the car and so I left mine there too. I put a clip in the weapon and raised it to the port position and then the three of us advanced toward the office about 25 feet away. The time was mid-morning, so the sun was up, and it was hot already. Well as we walked forward all the Jamaicans started toward us and to me it looked like the shooting was going to start any minute now, but that was all they did, just holler at us. I never did see any of them make an antagonistic move.

Well, I could just see into the office, several people moving about and also Bendick who said it was company officers and representatives and also the Jamaicans who had negotiators. The sheriff and chief deputy Bennett where now on the scene and I heard the riot act read over a bull horn. In Florida a gathering of 2 or more people is an unlawful assembly, a misdemeanor crime. It has to be announced as an unlawful assembly and now it became a riotous situation, and a felony and they must disperse. Of course, this is read by the sheriff himself or a law enforcement officer who must ID himself as a representative of the state of Florida. Once read it becomes a felony and if it becomes necessary, deadly force can be used. Out of all the Jamaicans I don't see any sort of weapons displayed. Now they use machetes to cut sugar cane, using the kind with a hook on the end and the blade is about 18 inches long. I don't see a one in sight, but I know they can't be far away.

I hated to think of me and Bendick standing closest to the Jamaicans having to use those Thompsons and Sanchez with his carbine with 30 round clips taped back-to-back. Captain Herron only had his service revolver, a 357, but behind us were two rows of uniform deputies, each with a 12-gauge shotgun. Up the road were the unmarked cars, the detectives, and I know most, if not all, had shotguns. All department personal also had a service revolver. The detectives were just standing by as needed. It would have been a slaughter. I say one thing for the Jamaicans, they didn't show any sign of fear at our show of force with all those weapons, they just kept right on hollering and shouting at us, those in front and those still at the barracks.

Well, we stood and stood, and I couldn't see any head way and now the morning turned into afternoon and the sun still got hotter and hotter it seems, as it always does. Well at least no one got shot yet. Now we have our canteens full of water and that's all we had. There was nothing to sit or lean on and no shade. We didn't even have slings for the Thompsons. So, for all this time we were holding them at high port. I held mine while Bendick took a drink of water and vice versa. My arms and wrists were stiff from holding the weapon so long. Well, I heard the riot act read aloud for the second time. So, I figure that things are going bad in the office and it's probably going to start for sure. I look back at our squad and up the shell rock road where we entered and I see it lined not only with our detectives and uniform units, but also F.H.P. had some troops there, Florida Highway Patrol, some Pahokee PD officers, and some from Belle Glade PD units. Well, the negotiations are still going on so at least they're still talking and that's a good sign. I guess it's around 4:00 PM and I'm hot and tired from standing, I got bad feet anyway, and I'm tired of holding the Thompson when all of a sudden, the Jamaicans on the ground floor move to within 20 feet of me and Bendick, and I guess this is it for sure. I bring my hand back on the bolt to get ready to charge the weapon, a round in the chamber, I see a couple of pop bottles on the ground and figure they'll throw them first, but instead they take those damn bottles, stand them up and make a game of grabbing one foot and pulling it up behind them and then bending down to pick up the bottle with their teeth, hell I hurt just watching. The crowd kept hollering but now it was directed at the bottle game participants.

Well, this goes on for a while and now it's after 6:00 PM. Off to the side I see 4 school buses pull up on the shell rock road. These buses are used strictly for transportation of migrant workers. Someone from the department gets on the bull horn and advises that anyone who wants to leave can get his belongings and get on one of the buses. Well, our crime scene personal move forward and set up a table and they get their cameras out and set up. There's Lt. Gimpel, Jimmy Drake and Benny Green. Well, we all stand easy and pretty soon the Jamaicans that got suitcases start filing toward us. Captain Herron wanted a deputy's picture taken with each and every Jamaican after he was printed then they entered the bus through the rear door, emergency door. Well, all this took some time, so when the 4 buses were loaded up with Jamaicans. Sanchez had me take 4 uniform troops from they're squad behind me, and Bendick take the other barracks along with 4 men and clear both of them of all peoples inside. We found very few inside but what we did find as we entered was a wooden barrel completely full of sharp machetes. Walking through to the other end there was another barrel with just one or two machetes. What had happened was that at the beginning of the day the workers took a sharpened machete as they left the barracks for work. When they returned at the end of the day, they put the dulled machetes in the other wooden barrel so someone would sharpen them. There had to be a good 225 to 250 sharpened machetes in the two barrels.

Well, the buses finally took off for Miami International to be taken back to Jamaica. It was dark when we finally secured and when I finally got to sit down in the car with Bendick, both my arms got muscle spasms from carrying the Thompson for well over 7 hours. Needless to say, the ride back to road patrol on the east coast was a lot slower. We returned all our assigned gear to the armory, and I called my wife and told her I was on the way home. She had already heard about the riot; it had been on the radio and TV. Going home I thought that I probably wouldn't have gotten any fish anyway if I had a gone diving.

****

Later a group representing the Jamaican Sugar Cane Cutters at Kennedy Camp brought a $12,000,000 lawsuit against the sheriff's department and Sheriff Heidtman in the U.S. District court. Alleging that they were illegally deported. On July 15,1969, a year and seven months after the incident at Kennedy Camp, I gave a sworn statement as to my knowledge and participation of the matter. The suit was dismissed by the federal court.

KOOTERS JUKE NIGHT OWL BAR

Kooters Juke is strictly a black, mostly migrant bar, and it's located on Boynton Road at U.S. #441, or a Tee intersection. Now when Kooters really jumped, and was really busy, was on a Saturday night. The roadway was jammed with cars so they parked wherever they could. This bar catered to black migrants. These are people who follow, pick and pack vegetables in the whole country as they ripen.

The bar is not the type of bar you would want to take a date too, unless you had a death wish or just a low regard for your date. It was also known formally as the Night Owl Bar. It catered to black migrants and Palm Beach County had lots of them. At peak season, the county had around 100,00 to 125,000 migrants who followed the crops of vegetables, flowers and sugar cane. Of this number a large percentage were black, and they were strung out through the county in various camps that they called home while working. Now all migrants worked hard, and partied just as hard, so once Saturday came, and they just got paid, most went off to Kooters Juke to unwind and have a good time. It just so happened that I had to work zone 7 this Saturday night and Kooters fell into my zone. I was just a slick sleeve deputy and worked where I was told to. Beside the sergeant knew I liked to work in the south end of the county with all the migrants and labor camps. I got my assigned zone and was cleared to have a 10-12, passenger, who after filling out the proper forms, was given the okay to ride with me. My passenger was none other than Bo Wells, an experienced police officer, he was still on the force in Riviera Beach, and he had attended dive school with me. He was also a close friend and wanted to see how the Sheriff's

Department operated, especially in the south end of the county with all the labor camps, packing houses, bars, so he wanted to ride with me. It's Saturday night, a 3-11 PM shift, and I got Bo as a passenger and I'm west bound on Boynton Road not far from the Range Line, another name for U.S. 441. We had just passed El Rico Consito Latino Bar, another bar used by migrants, Mexicans, I had also written about it in a precious story. The two bars are about 2 miles apart and you can believe me blacks don't go to Mexican bars and vice versa.

Anyway, as I approached the vicinity of Kooters I see the cars parked all over the place, not on the road itself, but all over. The bar's hopping, lots of people as they've got live entertainment inside, and it's pretty lively outside too. I know people are making out or trying to make out and just about all are drinking. Well driving real slow, those outside see me in a green and white and they know that I'm, *"the man"*. I'm driving slowly and this black female who had been in front of me just runs up to my car as the windows were down and says, *"that S...O...B... just tried to shoot me,"* and she points at a Mustang that's ahead of me. I can see the car and it's got two black males in it. Well right off I can see that a felony had been committed, and it was a good, aggravated assault case, migrant or not. Right away I put the blue lights on and hit the siren and put my search light on the driver. The car pulled off the road and stopped right away. I got out and went towards it, gun in one hand and my k-light flashlight in the other. Bo came up on the passenger side, he also had a gun and flashlight in hand. The driver handed me his DL, driver's license, gave me his name and DOB, (Date of Birth). Holding both the driver and his passenger at gun point I found out that he was an ex-boyfriend of the female, they just happened to meet at Kooters and he had had an argument with her. He then put a gun in her face and pulled the trigger, but nothing happened.

Well, when nothing happened, and the gun didn't go off, he just drove away, never seeing me in his rearview mirror. That's when I stopped him. I got a 22 caliber pistol off him and arrested him for aggravated assault. In searching his car, I also got a 32 caliber Rossi pistol, it was 7 shot and loaded, the 22 was also loaded. It was the gun he used, or tried to use, on the female. Bo didn't find anything on the passenger side and after a 10-29, check on an individual, he had no warrants on him from, NCIC, FCIC and Palms. These are computer checks on a subject to see if he has any wants or holds on him.

Well, the passenger was scared and pleaded that he was just picked up and not involved in any way, so he was released by me. The 22 he put in the females face and pulled the trigger and nothing happened, showed, when I broke the gun open, that it had a live round in the tube and the firing pin had fallen when he pulled the trigger, but the round didn't go off. The female never did realize how lucky she was, or how close she came to dying. She didn't seem to care too much that her ex was arrested for aggravated assault and not murder, just as long as he was arrested.

****

Bo Wells was glad when the shift was over, and he never rode with me again. The Rossi, 32 caliber gun scared me as it's a cheap gun and we were always taught to count 6 shots from a wheel gun, revolver, and then it was empty. Now I know that with a Rossi that's not the case. The female, well, she was lucky. AMEN.

LEE BROTHERS

This occurred in the 70's. I was the shift sergeant, and the shift was 12-8 AM. This story hadn't been written down as the others and is being written from memory many years later. It concerns a snake, and some gamblers.

The shift was the night shift and was very early Monday morning. So far none of the zones had any calls of any consequence. The troops had been on the road about hour to an hour and a half, I my self was already on the road and was south bound on Military Trail and had just turned west on Lantana Road. Now there are very few houses on west Lantana Road, and it's mostly rural and farms.

Palm Beach County gets about 100,000 to 125,000 migrant workers a year as they follow the crops and flowers, so farming is a big business. The migrants stayed in camps spread out through the south county and Belle Glade. Now as I was going west on Lantana Road, I passed Lee Brothers camp, a large camp that held maybe 200 migrants. Lee Brothers is located on the north side of the road and on its western end is a commissary, store, where they sold everything to migrants from food, clothing and rot gut whiskey.

Now at 0100 in the morning all the lights are off as I'm driving west on Lantana Road. Most all are in bed, but as I drive past the commissary, I see a bare light bulb in front that's on and about 12 to 15 migrants hunched over shooting crap, dice. It was a dark night so I knew that if they saw a marked patrol car even slowdown that they would all split before I could even catch one, if any at all, so I just kept driving west at the same speed right on past them. Now what I did was to go past them to Haverhill Road, turn around, and head east on Lantana Road. Again, I saw them gambling in front of the commissary and they paid no mind to me as I went by. Well, I drove east to Military Trail and turned south on the Trail thinking all the while that I got to break up their crap game if only, I could get close enough without being seen.

Military Trail south of Lantana Road is very rural and has very little traffic, especially at this time of the morning, if any at all. Now one thing that Florida has is lots of snakes, and as they are cold blooded, meaning they lose their body heat, so you can be sure that as the sun goes down you will find one or more laying in the road, on the macadam as it retains heat when the sun goes down. Now as I'm south bound on the Trail, I see a coiled object in my head lights and as I got closer, I saw that it was a snake, and it looked pretty big, maybe 6 feet or so I guessed as it was coiled up. Well, I stopped my car, and the snake didn't move. I got out of the car and saw that it was a corn snake.

A word about corn snakes, first off, they're not poisonous but they are constrictors meaning that they squeeze to death whatever they catch and eat it. Now corn snakes are real colorful having lots of browns, reds, etc. I went back to my car and got my night stick that was on the door and then approached the snake who still hadn't moved. I put it right behind its head and pinned it down to the road grabbing it right behind the head with my left hand. Well, the snake uncoiled right away and then coiled up again around my arm. When it did this, I could see that it was a good 6 feet or so long. Well, I got back to my car and carefully got back in with the snake wrapped around my arm and me holding it just behind its head with the fingers of my hand. Now my left hand was hanging out the car as the window was down, so the arm and snake were outside. I slowly turned around and drove back to Lantana Road, Lee Brothers was just a short distance west from the Trail.

There's a dirt road in front of the camp and it runs parallel to Lantana Road. Now it might be a dirt road, but it was hole and rock free, and as I remembered, it ran right in front of the commissary where they were gambling, so I took the dirt road, turning my lights out and driving real slow. Even though it's dark, and having no lights, I could see the gamblers in the light from the store. I must have driven to within 150 feet from them and stopped with no lights showing, brake lights, I stepped on the emergency pedal to stop the car and the gamblers never even heard or saw me. I guess it must have been a good game. I opened the door by holding the outside of it with my left elbow and raised the handle inside with my right hand. I got out, left the door ajar, and quietly walked up behind the group of gamblers. I unwound the snake off my arm, but still held its head with my fingers and coiled it up with my right hand.

Now the game had to be pretty good as no one paid me any mind, so I just heaved the snake and it hit the store front and fell right on the crap game. Now all 12 or so participants ran in all directions, leaving dice, money and a pouch just lying there.

Needless to say, I didn't catch any one as they were long gone, but I did pick up the dice, money and pouch, I guess someone used the pouch to carry the dice in.

****

Well, I don't know what happened to the snake as it was gone in the dark, but I did get 3 pair of dice and a pouch to put them in, and also enough lunch money for several days. Best of all I never even got a case number from the complaint desk.

MARIJUANA

This is an account of just how marijuana was handled by the sheriff's department, a bunch of legals, that's us, and the illegals, that's the dopers and how they operated, and so follows a never-ending saga. Except for now days it's more sophisticated.

Speaking of marijuana, the sheriff's department was charged with the gathering, and disposal of it within Palm Beach County. Now since the county had miles of beaches that bordered the Atlantic Ocean, it stands to reason that bales of the illegal weed would wash up on someone's beach. Not only on our beaches but I'm sure on beaches everywhere. That's probably one reason why they called it the gold coast. A bale of marijuana was usually about 80 to 100 pounds, it was packed in several black garbage bags and then sealed with duct tape. Now all this croup of weed started its life somewhere in south America, loaded into what I call a tramp steamer destined for the USA...

Now these ships/tramp steamers come up the straits of Florida, also called the Gulf Stream, as the stream came within 3 miles of the county. These ships were met by boats called cigarettes, meaning they were long, powerful and very fast. The gold coast of Florida had numerous inlets that these fast boats could come out of, from Government Cut in Dade County, Broward County, or in Palm Beach County which had 3 alone. There was Lake Worth Inlet, Boynton Inlet and Jupiter Inlet, so they could come out from anywhere.

Now these cigarette boats would meet a ship that stopped in the Gulf Stream, and they would load up with bales of weed and run back

into some Inlet. The ship would keep its engines neutral while unloading its illegal cargo, and the continue north. Now during all this unloading in the open ocean, any number of bales were bound to go overboard and fall in the drink, or ocean. This was probably due to choppy seas or sloppy, hurried handling.

At this time the sheriff's department had only one helicopter and so if 3 or 4 cigarettes loaded up with bales of marijuana it stands to reason that trying to catch a boat with its illegal cargo, was a stroke of luck. We also had the Coast Guard Station on Peanut Island and south Florida had the Cape Fox, a coast guard ship, but I never recall them catching any dopers.

I was a road sergeant and not involved in dope on such a large scale. I did however pick up several bales of marijuana during my career that had made it to shore and were reported to the SO. What I would do is pick it up and TOT, (Turn Over To) the departments vice units, that way I was rid of it and no accounting for it on my part. Now after so many bales of weed, marijuana, had been gathered, it was decided by someone high above me to dispose of it. The sheriff's department had a pistol range that ran south off Okeechobee Road and was west of Military Trail, both being a major highway. Now the pistol range was out in the boondocks, wooded area, gunfire was a constant there and they certainly didn't want anyone shot or injured in anyway. That's why they isolated it in the first place.

The sheriff's department being the largest law enforcement agency in the county was self-insured as far as its cars. They also did repairs on patrol and detective cars, replacing wiper blades, oil changes etc. They also replaced automotive tires. They got tires at cost and went through so many that they needed to be replaced regularly. Now tires are not so big but changing so many so often the pile can grow to something really big. These tires might be good for Joe average citizen but certainly not on a patrol car. They were subject to constant high-speed chases and rigorous wear and tear so the need for good tires was evident.

It was decided again, by someone in authority, to take the tires to the gun range and burn them. the range being isolated away from people, homes and businesses, it was ideal. Now why not kill two birds with one stone, burn the tires and the marijuana at the same time. Believe you me, it would make one hell of a bonfire. The department would be rid of a lot of used tires and they could burn lots of dope.

I wasn't there but I know what happened, besides I was just a road sergeant, tires and dope disposal wasn't in my job description. Well after the proper paperwork was filled out on all the dope, and I'm sure pictures were taken of it, as one picture is worth, well you know the rest. The dope, probably all handled by the vice units was brought to the gun range and mixed in with this big pile of used tires and the whole thing was soaked with gasoline and used oil. Now the day was nice and sunny and bright, a typical day in the Palm Beaches so this bon fire, I mean BIG bonfire lit up right away from all the gas and oil. One thing about burning tires, when fired up they emit a very heavy toxic black smoke. Now this is usually no problem, but all this thick black smoke laced with marijuana and whatever other dope that was burned rose straight up in the air, well away from people, but all of a sudden, mother nature decided to intervene. Just at this time the wind started to blow eastward, and it pushed this cloud over an inhabited area, and then over the city of West Palm Beach. Now the fire is big, and, well, there was no way of stopping it.

Only God knows how many people it effected that day. There was the city, it had a large black cloud hanging over it and to boot, it stank with the dope in it. It was so big that the local newspaper, 'The Palm Beach Post Times', wrote a revealing article about it.

****

I know the Sheriff's Department finally fessed up to it. How could they deny it, they were the culprits? Accidental of course. The black smoke was bad enough from the tires alone but mixed with hundreds of pounds of marijuana and whatever dope they got rid of, made a lot of people sick or else just high.

SNAFU'S happen, just like bowl movements.

MURDER LOUNGE BAR

Here we go again, the 4-12 PM shift. it's usually always busy so this shift is no exception with lots of domestics, signal 38, but none are really serious, so there's lots of action and that's what I like. It makes a shift go fast. Like they say, *"time flies when you're having fun."* Well, we had made it up to about 10:00 PM and I was just going to the gas pump at road patrol, then in early to catch up on reports and to brief the night shift on any information that needed to be passed on. When off goes the emergency buzzer three times and we all wait for whatever from the dispatcher. Now the dispatcher doesn't call any zone by number, but just advises that she's on 10-33 traffic for a signal 33, shooting, at the Lounge Bar. She knew that the Lounge Bar was in Baker 3's area and that he was busy or 10-6 on another call and that by putting the call out in that manner that it would be picked up by the sergeant and that he should know that his troop, Baker 3, was busy and he also was supposed to be aware of where and what his troops were doing at all times and to pick right up on the situation and have a cover car or TAC squad (Tactual) take it.

Now being right on top of the situation I told the dispatcher to send Ethan, a senior deputy who was a cover car at this time. Cover cars were deputies in uniform that drove marked units. TAC units wore civilian clothes and drove unmarked cars. D/S Ethan answered in the affirmative that he was enroute and I also advised that I was also was on the way.

A few words about the Lounge Bar. At this time, it was located on Southern Blvd., State Road #80 a major highway just west of an overpass. On the east side of the overpass is the corporate city of West Palm Beach, where I often wished the Lounge Bar was, but unfortunately it wasn't. It was actually located in the town of Cloud Lake, a small, ONLY residential community, that just had one bar, guess which one. The town had a major, town council, and they even had a town marshal who I always figured should handle calls within his city limits and just use the sheriff's department as backup. Well, he never responded to any calls of any type that I can remember of. The bar was a typical redneck, good ole boy bar and there was never a 4-12 PM shift go by that the sheriff's department didn't respond to the bar over some type of disturbance. Mostly fights, but sometimes guns or knives etc. Now on the weekends when they had live entertainment, we had to just about keep a car there or in the immediate area.

Now the Lounge bar always kept two bouncers, the kind of guys that could give Hulk Hogan some serious concern for his safety. A lot of times the sheriff's department would respond and when they arrived ole Lurch and Mungo had already neutralized the situation or altercation and some poor guy would be all busted up, like his nose was trying to look into his ear or something to that effect, and always the same old story, *"He was creating a disturbance and we tried to get him to leave, and he resisted our efforts to go outside, and he tried swinging at us."* In all the years I responded to the Lounge, i never saw any resistors to be of any great size physically and that none of the bouncers were under 240 pounds.

The guys who resisted were dumb shit, but they didn't deserve all the pain and suffering for what they might have done. We finally put a stop to this by convincing them to go to the hospital and get treatment, most of the time a drunk wouldn't get treated at the hospital and also refused medical aid at the scene, so we just took some colored pictures of their faces and wounds and a copy of the report and try and convince the states attorney to file a charge. Then, and only then, would we arrest someone. Now several times we arrested a bouncer on the spot as the wounds/injury were so bad that we would charge them with aggravated assault, a felony. Anyway, the brutality incidents dropped dramatically. In our own small way, we helped the FBI lower the statistic for aggravated assaults down to a lesser significance to just a disturbance or investigation.

Well back to the present. D/S Ethan arrived at the bar about the same time we did.

We parked in front of the front door and left our blue lights on, the front door being just off the highway. We ran in, guns out and in hand, once inside we see the victim on the floor by the bar. He's a white male, alive and a quick look shows him to be gut shot. Now there's about 15 to 18 people in the bar and mostly all males so I had them all sit down at the bar and numerous tables and advised the dispatcher that I needed a 10-71, ambulance, 10-18, red lights & siren, I tried to make the victim as comfortable as possible. I raised his head and in doing so saw that he had been shot through his belt buckle. We got the story from the bartender about the victim at the bar. He got into an argument with his buddy and a big gun came out during the argument and one shot was fired. The bartender pointed out the suspect and we made an apprehension with no problem. At this point it was an aggravated assault, a felony, I took a Ruger Blackhawk, 44 magnum off him. At this time the ambulance showed up and loaded up the victim to take to the hospital. I told D/S Ethan to stay with the victim for any statements he might make. I didn't see how he could last long being shot with a 44 mag plus belt buckle fragments. By this time the detectives were on the scene and the prisoner was TOT them, and I'd let them get any witness statements from the bartender and the patrons.

I secured from the bar and went back to road patrol to fill in the oncoming sergeant on what happened and to tell him I didn't have time to gas up the sergeant's car. Now the shooting was bad enough but to hear the news that the car wasn't gassed up really choked up the new sergeant as the first thing he had to do was gas the car. I had lots of work to do, check reports from my shift, it was a standing order that no one goes home until all paperwork is done. The only report a troop could hold over was an accident report. I had to read all reports and classify them according to NCIC code. All citations checked for proper state statutes and court date, also daily trip sheets. I had to do this for 12 deputies, so this took some time, and it was only after shift ended.

I was sitting at my desk doing paperwork and the radio in the sergeant's room was on and I hear, 213, my ID number, the signal 33 victim just went signal 7", he died. Well with that I immediately called the complaint desk by land line to verify that the OD (Officer of the Day) not to overdose, everyone had been notified and that all bases were covered, and I wanted my troop D/S Ethan to get to road patrol as it long after shift change by now and the sheriff's department didn't pay overtime back then. The complaint desk acknowledged that D/S Ethan was 10-51, enroute, to road patrol and that a detective had relieved him at the hospital. I figured I'd get done and home at a decent time when I hear Ethan go, 10-7, 10-58, out of service & at road patrol.

He came in my office, and I ask him what happened at the hospital and he tells me he stayed right with the victim while they worked on him in the ER, and all of a sudden he, the victim, makes a noise and he bent over him to see if he was going to say something like who shot him or what they call a dying declaration, which is good in a courtroom, but it was the victims last exhilaration and he died without saying anything.

He had lived about 45 minutes which is pretty good considering that he was shot with a 240-grain bullet from a 44 mag, from a distance of only 4 or 5 feet at the most and the bullet went through his belt buckle, defecting off it and went in an upward angle toward his shoulder and head area and never exited his body, so his insides had to be tore up pretty badly.

****

Years later I left the sheriff's department because of a rare affection known as job burn out, going to Alaska looking for some impossible dream. I finally left Alaska and returned to Florida and of all places to go, returned to the sheriff's department, not as a sergeant or Lt., but as a 44-year-old slick sleeve rookie.

Ethan by now had been out of uniform and into the vice squad, then back into uniform as a K-9 unit and now he was a detective. No more was he that, Ball of Fire, or hotshot, but I was sure I could detect my old affliction in his tone. The Lounge Bar was still there but it wasn't the Lounge Bar anymore, it now had a name out of the Arabian Nights, and the customers weren't rednecks or good ole boys but ones who ran around in gay apparel and spoke with a lisp and a sigh. Hell, even the bouncers were like the customers but now they were called attendants. Well kiss my Ass.

MURDER/SUICIDE JAWS

Another 4 to 12 shift, I had just gotten my troops on the road, and had advised the communication sergeant of the shift lineup, and even spent a couple of minutes with the shift Lt. Mathias, and so I went on the road myself.

Now road patrol headquarters was kind of centrally located, at the approximate center of the east coast of Palm Beach County and was on the south side of Palm Beach airport. When I left road patrol, I headed south toward the labor camps, this was the time of year when they were all filled up with migrant workers. The south zones being 7 and 8. If we were lucky, we had a cover car also. Now these zones were always busy with disturbance or assault calls or calls generally involving violence because that was the normal way of life for most migrant workers when they were not in the fields or some packing house.

Now back at this time in early 1970's the department thought it best to maintain a car full time to go to the labor camps and check various stores and bars to let the residents know that the sheriff was always at hand, that old cliché, (OMNI PRESENCE OF THE LAW). Aah, but labor camps are another story.

I was about 10 minutes out of road patrol when the dispatcher advised zone 5 that Doctors Hospital had a white female shooting victim in the ER and as of now no determination could be made as to her condition. I ask the dispatcher just where the victim had been brought in from, and she advised a housing development right down the street from where I was and also 5 to 7 blocks from the hospital. I told baker 5 to stay with the victim should as she might expire, die, so that he could get a statement or dying declaration. I then told the dispatcher to notify the detective bureau and to have a detective respond to the hospital ASAP. She acknowledged in her mechanical tone, giving the impression, I know what to do and you don't have to tell me. I then I told her I was responding to the scene or at least attempt to find it. There was some confusion at this point as to just where the scene was, or where it occurred. So now the dispatcher in a more concerned and interested voice answered that the victim was just brought in by an ambulance and also that shift Lt. Mathias was in the immediate area and that he would assist or try to locate the scene or place of occurrence. I told her to get on the horn, land line, to baker 5 who was already at the hospital with the victim, to check for any identification that could be made at this point and a possible street address on the victim or the repartee. I also told her to have the complaint desk call the ambulance service who brought her in and at least get the address of where they picked the victim up. She confirmed my transmission and I advised her that I was in the housing development in the baker 5 area. It was a housing area of about 5 square blocks and had about 10 streets in it and would be looking for any sort of scene or possible contact with anyone who saw the slow-moving patrol car. I saw the Lt.'s car a few streets over and I knew that he was concerned because of all the vague information we had so far, besides that, he lived in that development with his mother.

I had been traversing the streets running north and south and was about on the 3rd street when the dispatcher advised me that baker 5 was unable to locate any personal effects of the victim so he was yet to establish any identity on her or any residential address. The dispatcher did advise that a detective was presently with baker 5 and was assisting him. The dispatcher then advised that the complaint desk had made contact with the ambulance service, and I got an exact location just were the victim had been picked up. I was only 2 blocks away from the address and by the time she gave me the street number, I told her that I was 10-17, out for investigation, the Lt. checked out with me also. We were at a neat one-story residence that looked like it had just been painted and the lawn was well cared for. I knocked on the door and an elderly white female answered and in a very excited and emotional state. I calmed her down as best I could as she was crying and I assured her that all was okay, at least with us, and could she help us with the identity of the woman who had been picked up from this residence by the ambulance and could she help us in any way!

At this point I couldn't understand how the victim who I hadn't seen could have suffered such a massive wound, her jaw was missing, and she had been picked up at this residence by the ambulance and yet there was no indication of any violence, blood or any evidence would indicate that such a violent assault or possible accident had taken place. The elderly woman was in her early 70's sat down and nervously advised me and the Lt. that right north of her property, north residence, that all she knew was that there was a knock at the front door and upon opening it saw her neighbor bleeding heavily and not having much face left and she couldn't talk, and she collapsed on her porch. I felt sorry for the old lady as it must have been a hell of a shock for anyone to witness. The woman then said she called the ambulance and also closed the door because she didn't want to get blood in the house, because by now there was blood all over her newly painted gray porch and then she sat down and waited for the ambulance, which came within minutes and took the victim away. I then asked her what happened to all the blood that should have been obvious from such a massive wound, and she replied, *"well we just painted the porch and my husband said we better wash off all the blood before it dries and stains the porch, so I put the hose on and washed it all off into the grass."* I thought, oh hell, there goes a good part of the accident scene. I then ask her as she went back into hysterics if the victim had a husband, and if so where I reach him, He was a mechanic at one of the new car agencies. I thanked her and she was still crying as I ask if I could use her telephone. I called the dispatcher and told her to give the victim's name and address to no one except baker 5 and to try and make contact with the victim's husband at his place of employment and to have him contact the detective at Doctors Hospital in reference to an accident, but not to say anything else. She acknowledged and I told her that the Lt. and myself were going next door to check on the victim's residence and I would keep her posted. She asked if we needed a crime scene unit to respond and I told her that we didn't have any scene left, not bothering to tell her it got washed away.

The Lt. and I then left and went next door to the victims residence. It was located about 50 feet north of the house we just left and also looked just like it. It was a one-story CBS block house, but this one had a carport on the immediate north side of it having a doorway leading into a storage area. A common setup used in Florida homes where the weather is mild and so no need for an enclosed garage, it is attached to the house by a roof so at least it covers you when it rains. A try at the jalousie front door showed it to be locked,

and we were able to observe the inside of a living room and dining area through a large picture window. Nothing seemed disturbed. We then went to the north side of the house, that's between the house and carport, there was a northeast door that opened to the kitchen area, and it was unlocked so we entered and found all to be in order. We checked the rest of the residence, there were two bedrooms and one bathroom. All were neat and clean, no indication of any violent scene. I was the first one to leave exciting the kitchen door when I saw yet another door into what appeared to be area entrance to the storage area excess able also from the carport. I went over and turned the knob and opened the jalousie door and was hit with the smell of stale air. The windows had been cranked shut and being frosted I couldn't see in from outside. I had just stepped inside but didn't have to go any further as the room was only about 10 feet by 12 feet. Lying on the floor on his stomach, I won't say face down because there wasn't any face, just a bloody stump where his head had been, a 12-gauge shotgun lay close by. The north, west and south walls of the room were covered with bits if globs of hair, flesh and bone that used to be a head, I stepped back outside and closed the door just as the Lt. was exiting the kitchen door and I told him that I found a white male who was probably the victim's husband and now I was going back in the house to call for a crime scene unit as we definitely had a crime scene now. The Lt. said he would stand by for it and I could secure as I had other zones to worry about. I went 10-8 and advised the dispatcher to tell baker 5 to secure and go 10-8 as the case was now a signal 5 and 32 and that the on-scene detective would handle it.

A signal 5 was a murder and a signal 32 was a suicide, all baker 5 had to do was a supplemental report.

Nothing else was outstanding and so I went to supper.

****

Long after shooting her husband from behind, the woman recovered somewhat from the self-inflicted wound, and she then put the shotgun muzzle in her mouth and at the last second pulled it out and turned her head just as she pulled the trigger, and the shot blew her jaw away. She was convicted of murder 2 after having reconstructive surgery on her jaw. And also had a psychiatric evaluation.

MURDER, DELRAY ROAD

Well, it might sound repetitious but here goes, another 4 to 12 shift and I was working out of the Delray substation. This means I got to drive 27 miles one way just to get there from my house so now I got to leave by at least 2:30 PM so I can get there in time to make up the lineup or a shift schedule, also to review anything that needed to be passed on to the troops that wasn't on the hot sheet. I didn't want to take the Delray station but Captain Howe, the officer in charge, had ask me if I would take it as he knew I had worked in the labor camps as a slick sleeve for close to 3 years and now also as a sergeant. I'm sure he liked my supervision and judgment calls, and he knew that I never had any repercussions on any incidents I was involved with or responsible for none of my troops being involved in, well almost never. I thanked him and told him I appreciated his confidence in me and that I wouldn't even have minded the extra time that I would put in mostly for traveling but the gas use would have eaten me up. He said, *"Hell, if that's all then don't sweat it, just gas up at the Delray Police Department pump."* Now that's where the south end units, uniform, detective and civil units gas their cars up and the town of Delray just charges the county at the end of the month. With a proposition like that I couldn't refuse. That's how I got transferred to the Delray substation, besides it was my first choice anyway.

Now this gas arrangement lasted about 4 months or so until the Chief of administration happened to get a copy of the gas log for the substation as it was submitted from the town of Delray, and he kept seeing the name Barton and the number of gallons and the ending mileage. I, at the time, had an old Chevy Corvair and the speedometer was busted, and I never thought about it and just kept putting the same mileage down all the time as I thought the captain had squared it away with Chief Windsor about me and the gas use.

Well one day I was advised I was being transferred back to central substation or Baker units, now no reason was given to me, but the captain had gotten his rear end chewed out but good by the Sheriff himself for certain improprieties. Anyway, the shift was on the road about an hour when the emergency tone sounded from the dispatcher 3 times, meaning that all transmission was to cease and to await the dispatcher and the emergency call. Back she comes with a Palm Beach to zone 8, signal 33, shooting, on Delray Road just west of state road 809, Military Trail, she also named a small mom and pop grocery store. Now the south end zones are the only ones that I had to supervise and those being zones 6, 7, 8, and maybe a cover car, so all I had was 4 troops to worry about. Ah! progress is beautiful. Our department now had a north, central and south substations and all that I had to supervise was the south end troops in the area, no more did I have to supervise up to 10 to 15 troops on some shifts and no more running from one end of the county to the other.

Now they were all seasoned troops, no rookies, and they really needed little or no supervision, mostly just assistance in the way of backup on their calls.

Anyway, the call is acknowledged by zone 8 and he replies 10-4, 10-51, received and enroute. She knows that zone 8 understood and is enroute. I also do a repeat of zone 8's transmission so that she knows that I am also responding and also the speaker is on in the detective squad room, as well as the captain's office, so that they will also be listening as it was a 10-

33 call. Both zone 8 and I were already on Delray Road about 2 miles east of the shooting incident, in the parking lot of a store, it only took the both of us about 2 minutes to go 10-97, arrived. Now we weren't physically on the scene but looking at it so as not to have to come to a screeching halt at a supposed crime scene and just sit for a second or two with mikes in hand. Anyway, by this time we can see a group of 4 to 6 white males gathered around a fallen white male, and just as we got out of our cars one of the white males' spots us and runs over to us and shouts, *"that SOB shot him."* The male was crying and in hysterics and in a rage and it was all I could do to contain him and stop him from running into the back door of the store. A background description of the store, it was a small mom and pop type grocery store, sold pop, beer, sandwiches etc. The surrounding area being flat and grassy and out back to the south side, had several picnic tables and more parking area if needed.

Now the store was run by an old man at the time and also at this time a lot of condominium construction was going on in the south end of the county, and the store just happened to be located to a lot of these job sites. It was right on Delray Road, a main highway so lots of construction workers stopped in after work, got a few beers and went out back to the picnic tables in the shade to unwind and just shoot the breeze before going home. We never had any calls or any disturbances before. On this day a group of about 5 or so workers stopped, got their beers and went out back and were just fooling around when up drove a security guard, an older fella. He was probably from one of the numerous security details going on in the south and ironically, he was on his way to work at a new condominium project just up the road. Now the guard looked to be in his late 60's or early 70's. He was small and kind of meek looking. All he had was a uniform and no gun belt as he wasn't authorized to carry a gun. Well, the old guard went up to the store, bought his things and was standing by the back door, it was just a screen door, when one of the young construction workers said something to the guard, and the guard told him to just stay away and not bother him. Well, the young guy wasn't about to have an old man talk to him like that, so he started toward the back door of the store where the old man was. Now the old man reached into his front pocket of his uniform pants and came out with a 25-caliber automatic, raised it toward the oncoming construction worker and fired once, the single shot dropped the young man in his tracks, dead.

I took the weapon off the old guard who was now in hysterics. I shook him down for any other weapons or anything that could be used as a weapon, cuffed him and placed him in the rear of a patrol car. We then had the dispatcher lift 10-33, traffic, and to have a crime scene unit and a south end detective respond, and that we also had a 10-15, prisoner, and a signal 5, murder. She acknowledged the transmission and in 2 minutes the captain himself was on the scene in addition to a detective and he also advised that a crime scene unit was 1 to 2 minutes behind him. Well, myself and zone 8 got everyone's name, address and then loaded them up for the trip to the detective bureau at Delray substation for their statements. The guard had been arrested for murder and turned over to the detective on scene. I turned the chrome 25 automatic directly over to the crime scene unit. Further investigation on the victim showed that the bullet had hit a button on his shirt, deflected upward and penetrated his heart. He was only 25 years old and had just gotten married.

****

I often thought about the case and felt sorry for the old guard and wondered if he had been a retired cop and now that he was older was lucky to get a job as a security guard at $2.35 an hour, minimum wage, and sitting out in some mosquito infested construction site for a 12-hour shift and be dam glad he had that. I used to wonder if my time ever came, and I was in a similar situation if I would choke up like he did when someone said an unkind word to me. I would like to think that I'd just pass it off and walk away.

MURDER/SUICIDE HAVERHILL

Well, the 4-12 shift was a hot and busy one, it was really active so far but no serious calls. Now I was the north end sergeant, the department had by now grown into 3 substations, north, central and south, also known as able, baker and charlie and having their own dispatcher and channel, this night there was no baker sergeant and so me and the charlie sergeant split the baker area.

The time was around 8:00 PM and I was in the vicinity of what is called 4 points, I always tried to stay in this area when I had to cover baker's area as it seemed to have the most activity. Well sure enough the dispatcher hit the emergency button 3 times to let everyone on the baker channels know that an emergency call was about to be dispatched and not to use the radio unless it was of a most serious nature, so that time wasn't wasted. The dispatcher called, *"Palm Beach to Baker 3,"* he acknowledged and then the dispatcher advised him that a signal 33, shooting had occurred just north of Southern Blvd. and west off Haverhill Road, and that a female had been shot and an ambulance had been contacted and dispatched and there was no other information. At this time Baker 3 just happened to be in the extreme west end of his zone which was west about 12 or so miles out in the area of state road #7 and close to RPB (Royal Palm Beach), being a community by itself. Now when the call came out, I was already moving in that direction of the Haverhill Road area so that I would be close by to assist the zone man and besides I was the immediate supervisor and would be expected to respond anyway. Now hearing that Baker 3 was so far away I told the dispatcher that I was responding and that I was just a few streets away and would be 10-97, would have arrived on scene. I knew that Bakers 2 and 3 would be heading in my direction when I found the street running west off Haverhill Road and just 1 1/2 blocks long and was a dead-end street. Now towards the west end I saw a white male standing in a yard on the north side and seeing my patrol car started in my direction waving his arms to catch my attention, which he already had. I slammed on the brakes and hit the car key in one motion while opening my door with my left hand and had started running to meet him. He shouted, *"he shot her,"* and then pointed to a house on the south side of the road which I had passed by on my entrance of the street. He continued, *"he's still in there."* I didn't ask any questions but drew my gun out and ran toward the house he had pointed to. I had my radio in my left hand and my gun in the right. I slowed to a walk and moved away from the triple front window of the house as it faced the street and me. I could see several lights on in the living room as I peeked in from the extreme east window and I could see a white female lying on the floor on her back. She had on a white blouse, and I could see several red splotches on her torso from where I stood. at this point there was no indication of where the male was. I didn't see any further activity, so I went over to the front door, gun and radio still in hand. I tried the door but it was locked and also the door opened outwardly and not in so there was no kicking it in. I then ran to the carport located on the west side of the residence. That door opened to the kitchen area and opened inwardly but it was also locked so I could kick it open. I told the dispatcher I was going to force entry and also confirmed that a W/F, white female, victim was on the floor in the living room.

So, with my walkie-talkie in my left hand and my gun in my right hand I gave the door a hard kick right beside the doorknob, it flew open in what was the kitchen. The door jamb was splintered but I wasn't concerned at this point. I entered cautiously and started through the small kitchen toward the living room where I could see the female on the floor but still no sign of the male. I got all the way through the kitchen and into the living room area now from there I could see the male, he was on his knees, bent over with his head on the rug behind a large chair. That was why I couldn't see him from the front window. With the hammer cocked on my gun I slowly entered the room from behind him and saw a revolver in his open right hand, a closer look at the male showed a small hole behind his right ear so I just left him and put my gun away, I ran around the chair and checked the carotid artery of the female for any pulse, but I couldn't detect any. I counted 3 bullet holes in her upper torso and one in her upper left arm. The gun the guy had looked like a 32-caliber revolver. I told the dispatcher that it looked like a signal 5 and 32 a murder and suicide, and to lift emergency traffic, call the crime scene unit, and to notify the detective bureau and also the shift Lt., Lt. Marston, and to start notifying all those who needed to know, like the Baker Captain, Capt. Humbolt, who was off duty but who had to know when a crime of any importance was committed, also the Sheriff and Chief Deputy.

At this time the zone man, baker 3, showed up and so I advised him to secure the crime scene and to start a supplemental report as the responding detective would do a face sheet. I called the dispatcher by land line from the kitchen phone to verify that the detective bureau had been notified and were responding. I then told baker 3 to get a disposable blanket from his car and to cover up the female. I then drew the drapes shut in the living room as a large crowd had by now gathered in the street and front yard trying to look in. The crime scene unit and the assigned detective arrived together. It was an easy case, the kind you would call a smoking gun case. All that was left to do was wrap it up and that was the crime scene unit and detectives' job. The road units were done as far as I was concerned. I told baker 3 to stay and assist both units if he was needed. I wasn't needed anymore so I went out the side door through the crowd toward my patrol car. On the way out I found Lt. Marston and told him all the bases were covered and that the complaint desk had been contacted. He then told me that he had gone to the neighbors, the guy who waived me down, when I had already cleared 10-33 traffic. The guy who had shot and killed his wife and then himself had also taken a shot at his 12-year-old son, but he had missed. The boy had run across the street and had told the neighbor about the argument and shooting that his mom and dad where having. The bullet shot at the boy was found by the crime scene unit in the wood above the front door.

****

I left the sheriff's department 2 years later, moving to Alaska for a 3-year period and then I returned back again. This time I had to start as a slick sleeve deputy again. deputy baker 3 was now a road sergeant. The detective assigned used to work for me as a road deputy and he was now a detective sergeant. The baker captain at the time had since left the department after me, to run for sheriff in another Florida county. He did poorly and lost the election. He, like me, came back to the department and just like me, was a slick sleeve.

MURPHY & BEANS

This is a story that happened in the late 60's. I was just a slick sleeve deputy at the time. The shift was a 3-11 PM and I was working in zone 8, the southernmost zone. Now zone 8 covered from Boynton Road, its north boundary, all the way to Broward County, it's southernmost boundary. You can see that even once around the zone covered many miles.

Now within this large area of patrol were lots of labor camps, migrant bars, a large dance hall, and even several packing houses. The southern part of Palm Beach County had an influx of migrant workers each and every year, who followed the crops nationwide to pick and pack them. In addition to vegetables, fruit, and flowers were harvested.

The western most part of the county, Belle Glade, also had several big sugar companies that grew nothing but sugar cane. Sugar cane alone was a big dirty business to harvest, and the companies couldn't even get American workers to harvest their crop, so they contracted with the country of Jamaica for help. The workers were flown in from Jamaica under a work contract, and when the crop of cane was harvested, they were flown back home. I had written a story about the Kennedy sugar mill and its Jamaican workers.

Well Palm Beach County got around 100,000 to 125,000 migrants that came following the crops, this was every year. Normally the south county area is fairly quiet, but all that changed with the incoming migrants. The east coast, which I was part of, dealt with blacks, Puerto Ricans and Mexicans, all of whom lived a very harsh life, and so life consequently had very little meaning to them. They worked hard, played hard and so death was no big deal.

When the growing and picking season occurred in the county and all the labor camps were full, the sheriff's department had certain deputies on each shift they would put in the south end to work the camps. Now these deputies worked in all the zones, but when the season arrived for the migrants, these deputies always were assigned to the southern zones. They, being zone 7 and 8, and even zone 6 had a few camps.

To give some idea of just who worked there, on our shift that stayed together, we had Bob Bressmer. He was a big country bumpkin sort of fellow, worked exclusively in the camps when they were full, and the season was on. Though he was only a deputy, he always worked in the camps. Now Bressmer picked whomever he thought would work out with the migrants. Bressmer was about 6'1' and a good 240-250 pounds and he had that good ole boy personality. During the off season of no migrants, packing houses closed. He carried a 38-caliber revolver, but during the season and the county was full of migrants, he carried a model 25, that's a 45-caliber long Colt. It had a 6" barrel, and woe unto anyone on the wrong end of it. In addition to this he also carries a 12-gauge shotgun, I believe it was a double barrel. He also carried a gas billie. It's a small metallic club about 9" long that shoots a tear gas cartridge.

Well anyway the season was about to get into full swing with all the migrants pouring into the□° county. Now Bressmer needed help in the south county areas. It was just too busy for one man, so me and a deputy named Billy Provo were picked to work in the south end and see how we handled ourselves. I don't know what happened to Provo, but he was picked to work in the northern zones, I was never told the reason, but I guess he just didn't work out in the camps. He was a good reliable deputy, but he probably just didn't have the temperament to work in the migrant camps. It seems that I blended right in and worked in the camps right up until I made sergeant. Then my duties were county wide, and not just in the south end exclusively.

Once I made sergeant, I had to make decision and assist all the zones when I could. When I worked in the camps, I carried a 357-caliber wheel gun, a gas billie and a model 97 Winchester shot gun, it was a 12-gauge, and was chromed. I also carried an iron claw; it was a single handcuff that worked like a racket. If I didn't have the claw, I had a pair of nun-chucks. You definitely knew that public relations were not a big item back then. Back at this time the department had Motorola radios. The microphone was in the patrol car, the radio itself was bolted down in the trunk. Once a deputy checked out on a call, the radio turned off, and he had to be his own backup because if he ran into trouble, which happens, and he needed help right away, or even if he could make it back to his car, he had to wait for the radio to warm up before he could even transmit his dilemma to the dispatcher. To make matters worse, the county had no repeaters for the radio so only the dispatcher could hear the deputy calling for help, or at least describing his call. No one else heard his call for help or assistance He needed right away.

So, if it was a call that required immediate help, well, if he was lucky, he would get help within 25-30 minutes. So, you can understand why a deputy took so much armament with him when he checked out on a call, as he also had no radio, it was just him. At this time the road patrol had only one portable radio and it was a radio phone, and the shift Lt. took it with him. Once out of radio communication, the deputy was on his own.

Enough background on the migrants and labor camps in

the south county area. I had worked in the south county, zones 7 or 8 for quite some time by now and was used to it when I was advised by my sergeant that I would be breaking in a new deputy to work in the south end and his name was Harold Murphy. Now I was told that though Murphy was a new deputy sheriff, that he was a seasoned police officer. He was coming over from the city of West Palm Beach where he had been an officer for over 5 years and that he certainly was qualified. However, calls on the Sheriff's Department were very different from city police calls as they had the benefit of help right away, were as it was different on the S.O., especially in the south end of the county as it took time to get help or assistance should it be needed.

When A city cop had a call of violence, or the possibility of violence he had the benefit of multiple officers responding, meaning he wasn't alone. So, the chance of personal injury was greatly decreased, this was not the case on the SO.

Well anyway here comes Harold Murphy over to our department and it had already been decided that he would work in the south end with its migrants and labor camps, somewhat different than the city, even though he was 6'7" and around 240, he was impressive size wise and experienced to boot. All he needed was to get familiar with the many camps, bars and roads in zones 7 and 8. So guess who got the honors of showing him all this. None other than me.

Now to explain just how deputies operated at this time. The uniform division of our department was located on the south side of Palm Beach International Airport in what was some old military buildings, built in World War 11. This is where lineups were conducted. That's where we troops on the road and in patrol cars received BOLO's, (Be on the Lookout) stolen/lost cars, people, guns etc. and also the zone assignments. They could be zone 1 through 8. As far as myself, it was peak vegetable/fruit season and I would work zone 7 or, this day, it was 8.

What deputies did once line up was over and zone assignments made and they were released to go on the road, years later a popular TV show about cops used the phrase after line up," *Let's be careful out there"*. What the deputies did was drive their patrol cars over to their personal cars and load up with their shotguns, reports etc.

Now Murphy who was zone 7, was supposed to stay right next to me in zone 8 and his zone 7, learning the camps, roads etc. Well in loading up his patrol car from his personal car, I saw that he had a double-barreled shotgun, just like everyone else, but his double-barreled shotgun was pistol gripped and cut off to about 12 inches and that's pretty small for a 12-gauge. Now all shotguns are mean looking but one that looks like that, well you know it would take a big man to handle it when it went off, and I guess Murphy was big enough. Once loaded up with whatever gear the deputy would drive to his assigned zone.

To give some idea just how big the county was, it took zone 7 and 8 a good 15 minutes just to reach the north border of their zones, The same held true for zone 1, It took him a good 10-12 minutes just to reach the southern end of his zone. The road patrol was at the airport, so it was in zones 3 and 4. These two zones were combined into actually one zone as it was highly populated, and it was also centrally located. That made it very easy to cover and to get help fast, either from zone 2 who could come from the north to assist, or even zone 5 who could come up from the south. Well to get back to Murphy.

He had been new to our department and had been told that I would show him the labor camps, roads, etc. in the south county area, I was supposed to be his somewhat □ training office. Like I said, it took a good 10/12 minutes just to get into zone and I showed him Smith Sunday Road, 1 mile and 1/2-mile roads, that's their names, I showed him Green's Commissary on Smith Sunday Road, a very large camp and store that needed periodic checks, it had a large amount of migrants living there. I showed him Trevino's dance hall and store on Delray Road, and also pointed out Farmer's Motel on state road #7, a very large camp that mostly had black migrants and a definite stop each and every shift, and to be careful when he did. Farmers Motel had a very large commissary, liquor store, restaurant, and dance hall. I never counted them, but I would say a good 3-4 hundred migrants lived there during the season. I even introduced him to Monk. Now Monk was a big black male who worked at Farmers Motel. I guess Monk was a type of bouncer there, keeping order and he carried a large hog leg, (pistol) a 45 caliber, 6" barrel, model 25 weapon and a baseball bat. So, shame on anyone who started trouble. Monk was credited with stopping a lot on incidents before they got bad, and the sheriff's department was called.

I showed Murphy all the packing houses in both zones 7 and 8 and some of the many golf courses, a lot of them private. I even showed him some of the vegetable and flower farms/fields in the south county, so if he ever had to get there in a hurry, he would know just were to go. I even showed him Whites Dairy in zone 7, his assigned zone, and to be careful on any calls he might get there, as dairy workers can be dangerous, especially if he had to arrest someone.

Harold picked up the zone lay out pretty quick and I certainly didn't have to teach him law enforcement, just the departments way of handling cases and the paperwork we used.

Well after showing him around both zones 7 and 8 I took

him to a dirt road that ran west off Military Trail, a major highway. It was just north of Boca Raton Road. A road that ran into the city of Boca Raton and one that had a fine police department. but then again, they were city oriented.

Now just about a 1/4 mile north of Boca Road and west off Military Trail was a dirt road that had an opening at its end, meaning there were no trees or bushes, and sitting in the middle of it was a very large cylindrical shaped machine, and was on wheels, it was maybe 15 feet long and the cylinder was fluted so it was open and the whole thing was slanted, on an angle. When it was turned on, it ran on a gas-powered engine, and the whole cylinder spun/revolved. What they did is to load it up with green beans that were just picked from the adjacent field, and as the machine turned, it spit out all the stems, leaves and roots, so that all that was left in the machine were string beans. These were then loaded into peck baskets, which were about 32 quarts of nothing but beans

At this time of evening, it wasn't quite dark as the sun had just gone down and not one of the workers or bosses were around, just two deputies an□˜d two patrol cars, and we were off the traveled road, so no one saw us. The bean machine was full of beans, leaves and roots and I guess they just shut it down and went home. Well, all the beans etc. were still wet in the now silent machine and there were just the two of us checking it out. Well one thing led to another, I don't remember who threw the first handful of wet beans at the other, but pretty soon both patrol cars were covered with wet beans that stuck to them. The same can be said about the two deputies.

Now there was no one close by to check on us, namely the sergeant, as we most surely would have had a very serious talking to if not fired on the spot and no questions ask.

But as luck would have it, and we both had some luck that day. We both drove to a closed golf course that was just north of the bean field and no one was around. There was a coiled-up water hose, all hooked up ready to us. It didn't take any time at all to hose off both patrol cars. We both cleaned ourselves up from all the beans and resumed routine patrol.

****

I was grateful that while all this was going on, neither one of us got a call of any kind. And also, I was just glad it wasn't tomatoes.

OUTLAWS: THE MOTORCYCLE CLUB

Motorcycle clubs have always held a fascination for millions of Americans. Now I am referring to renegade clubs and not those clubs sanctioned by the American Motorcycle Association. The fascination seems to stem from there, *"the hell with the system attitude, we'll do our own thing and to hell with everyone else"* psychology. A good example of this was described rather well in the 1950's picture, *"The Wild One",* and it remains to this day a kind of motion picture classic.

However, by today's standards that depict renegade M/C clubs' actions, feats of daring or just plain criminal activity is what they consider fun at the expense or pain of others is now regarded as tame or even square. Unfortunately, South Florida, Palm Beach County in this instance, has an ideal climate and excellent drug connections for buying and trafficking, so consequently became the home of a M/C club known as the *"Outlaws".* The Outlaws can be compared in notoriety, but on a smaller scale to the *"Hells Angels"* of California fame or infamy, depending on your point of view. However, they share the same psychology for murder, pain and a good time.

The time was approximately late 1967 and this young deputy had just been on the sheriff's department around two months and definitely still a rookie even though I had 3 years police experience on two other police departments.

Well, the Outlaws rented a small house in Westgate, an old subdivision of mostly low-income families so it had lots of criminals

and bad guys living in it, and it was right across the street from the city limits of West Palm Beach. What I thought was ironic was that Palm Beach County encompassed about 2500 square miles, but the Outlaws were only about 1/4 mile away from the Sheriff's Department Road Patrol Headquarters. Now even though they were just outside of W.B. police departments limit, so they wouldn't respond to any calls unless it was to assist a deputy sheriff.

There was no missing the Outlaws when they rode on their hogs, all shiny and chromed and definitely not looking like your show room motorcycles. They flew their colors, wore their dirty Levi's, and black engineer boots. There Levi jackets were minus sleeves, all had inscribed on them a skull and cross bones with the word *"Outlaws"* in big letters on top. They had various patches denoting other clandestine activities such as the patch 13, meaning that they had smoked pot, by today's standards so do some people, when on the road they were always in a pack of no less than 10 and as many as 20 bikes and taking more than their share of the highway. It was a foolish motorist that failed to yield the road to them. The sheriff's department had documented numerous calls of assaults where motorists were beat up because they had been passed by the gang. It's a sad fact that arrests and responses were minimal in comparison to the amount of assaults that actually took place. The victims seemed to have second thoughts about naming assailants or were further intimidated with more violence against them or their families if any law enforcement agency was notified.

Now the sheriff's department had just acquired a new sheriff, not by election as is the normal way, but by appointment, and by the governor no less. Claud Kirk was the Governor or Florida at the time, and due to the fact that the present sheriff, Martin Kellinburger, had suffered a stroke and was permanently incapacitated and was not able to complete his official duties. The new sheriff, William R. Heidtman, had only been in office about 1 month longer than I had been on the department, or about 3 months. Hiedtman had been an insurance executive and I guess the extent of his law enforcement experience was probably gained by watching Jack Webb on *"Dragnet"*, and he was known as the Gray Fox because of his silver hair.

Well, the 2 months I had spent on the sheriff's department had been spent on the day shift, 7 to 3 PM, and it was supposed to be a breaking in period, getting used to types of reports and procedures of the department. Working the day shift gives a deputy the impression that maybe he should have gone to secretarial school first before pursuing a law enforcement career as it seemed that all he did was reports on breaking and entering, vandalism etc., and rarely did he have time for any traffic control, roadblocks for driver's license violations or obvious equipment failure like no inspection stickers, lights out, etc. On the day shift you got very little exposure to the Outlaws as they were night people and mostly never up, or at least on the road during the day shift hours. All the day shift ever got at lineup was the incidents and updates from the 3 to 11 PM and 11 to 7 AM shifts activities concerning the gang, such as assaults, traffic stops and occasionally an arrest where 4 or 5 deputies would stop the whole gang and check driver's licenses for possible equipment violations.

Now ID's and DL's were checked through NCIC, FCIC and Palms. These are National Crime Information Centers, and Florida Criminal Information Center and Palms being the local check, so the checks were pretty through. Now these checks, needless to say, were very time consuming especially when you were checking on so many individuals all at once. This is in addition to serial numbers, tags, license plates, etc. If any of the computers were down as they were known to do for one reason or another, these lengthy stops almost always antagonized someone or just plain p them off. One or more of the members would invariably commit some sort of incident, most likely FWD (Fooling with a Deputy) which meant an arrest or two. Now when someone was arrested a wrecker had to be called and a hog or two had to be towed and stored

In the mist of all this the Lt. tells me I'm off the day shift and going to the 3 to 11 shift. that I had been broken in long enough. The 3 to 11 shift had been short of troops and was always super busy. Up to this point I had never seen a member of the Outlaws or even any of their bikes. All I had was hear say. That's lawyer talk, from the other deputies, that included threats or implications of violence against them for what the Outlaws termed *"harassment"*. At times the threats went so far as to include a deputy's family. One deputy in particular, Rick Paulus, a short and feisty troop who worked the 11 to 7 AM shift in zone 2, home of the Outlaws, so it was only natural that he made traffic stops on different members as they came and went. Paulus was the deputy singled out by the Outlaws to vent their anger on. Now he carried a chrome 12-gauge pump shot gun that was cut, shall we say, below the standards of an 18-inch barrel, according to federal standards for a shotgun, so he had a 5-inch piece of chrome pipe welded on. Now this extension was larger in diameter than the barrel, so it brought lots of stares and questions. All inquiries were met with,*" it's a silencer."* Believe it or not, some folks actually believed him, but when it went off you got the truth.

It was my first lineup on the 3 to 11 shift and the sergeant, Dick Hall, tells me I'm assigned to zone 2 and no other instructions other than the current BOLOs and warrants for my zone. Now even though I had been a cop for 3 years before coming on the department I knew that by their standards, grunts, that I had yet to be tested in a stressful situation, such as a fight, shooting or domestic etc., Only one troop knew how I would react and that was Howard Wyatt. He had been my shift sergeant when I was on Riviera Beach Police Department and many times we had been involved in fights, assaults etc. He had quit RBPD and had joined the sheriff's department about a year now and he was a slick sleeve just like me and was assigned to zones 3 and 4, or just to my south so he would be my backup should I need one on any serious calls or if I got any calls of questionable circumstances. In addition to zone 3 and 4, we had zone 9, a cover car, who's duty it was to cover any serious calls in any zone that needed him. However as big as the county was if he happened to be in the extreme north or south end when a centrally located zone got a call, he would never get there in time to help. Anyway, the majority of the time it was an adjacent zone that covered you and that you most likely depended on anyway. Rarely did the sergeant cover a zone car on a call. Mostly he would tell the dispatcher who to send as a cover. It would most likely be the adjacent zone and so the dispatch acknowledged with a 10-4. This would cover him for being outside his zone boundary. Back then the sheriff's department was very strict about having an assigned deputy stay in his assigned zone. Surprisingly several of the department's hierarchy liked to report to the road commander when they caught a deputy out of his assigned zone, I think that was learned in morale building course sponsored by the German SS. Anyway, being caught out of zone might be good for a day's suspension or maybe painting, or some dirty job that had to be done at road patrol headquarters. At the very least you could expect a good gnawing of the keister. Lt.

Sanchez was an advocate of slave labor and intimidation and I found this out immediately in my short tenure on the department.

Back at this time the department had no repeater system in the county so consequently the dispatcher would be heard by all the cars on the frequency or channel. However, the radio signal from each car was only heard by the dispatcher and no one else. For instance, if zone 1 had a shooting and he was on the scene and he was advising the dispatcher of the condition of the victim, or if a suspect was in

custody, or if he was still at large, or if he was in any danger himself. The only one who heard any of zone 1's transmission was the dispatcher and she had to wait until he was done talking before, she could advise the sergeant, and it was only then that everyone knew what was going on. Also, at this time with communications we only had one walkie-talkie and the shift sergeant took that with him so he could keep in contact with communications and be appraised of the zone status while he might be away from his car radio. None of the zone cars had a walkie-talkie and so once 10-97 was on a call, regardless of what type, from a simple assist to a shooting, there was no one who knew what was happening until the deputy got back on his car radio or else called the complaint desk by a land line if one was available. You can see the danger factor is highly increased by the lack of communications. Once involved in a fight or shooting incident and not being able to report the status of the call has left many a deputies sphincter muscle in a puckered position until a cover zone, 10-94, arrived.

Anyway, my first 3 to 11 shift and I got a zone 2 assignment, and I got a patrol car. I drove over to my personal car and loaded up all my gear such as my report file, flashlight etc. Back at this time I didn't have a shotgun, and I couldn't afford to by one, so all I had was a 4-inch barrel Colt Python. I then reported to the dispatcher as, *"zone 2 Palm Beach"*. She responded to go ahead zone 2 and again I was 10-8, in service, and I gave her my ID number 223, so now I was on shift. All that had to be repeated by the road sergeant who had to call the complaint desk and who kept a log of the shift personal with name, zone assignment and ID's. I left road patrol and took the access road to Belvedere Road and was in zone 2 in 3 minutes.

Now zones like 1, 6, 7 and 8 took up to 40 minutes to get to especially if there was any traffic, and it was heavy. I started cruising the streets in Westgate, stopping in the parking lot of a convenience store to talk to a couple of drunks and send them on their way. I cruised Okeechobee Road and checked the Square Wheel Bar; I think it's the original red neck bar. It's got too have 2 or 3 assault cases a night. But now it's just around 4:00 PM and too early for the red necks to start. Going through the Square Wheel parking lot onto Shawnee Road, it's just a dirt street, but what do I see, 2 choppers parked on the porch of a little run-down house. Hell, this is the Outlaws place, it's just a 3-room house that was probably painted last when H.M. Flagler built the bridge over the Keys, a very long time ago, and it was all on one floor, and didn't have any foundation to it. It had beer cans and trash all over the yard, I see no Japanese gardener for them as they did their own yard work. The choppers, both Harleys', were on a porch that was no bigger than 8 by 10 feet, and they were parked so a quick entrance to the house would be difficult through the front door. As I was right in front of the porch, I saw a sign about 12 by 20 inches attached to the porch roof support and printed on the sign in large black letters was, "TRESPASSERS WILL BE BEAT ABOUT THE HEAD AND BODY WITH A MOTORCYCLE PRIMARY CHAIN." At the bottom of the sign was skull and crossbones and it said, "OUTLAWS".

Now Outlaws are free spirits, but I wasn't about to have that kind of sign hanging in my zone, so I stopped right there and told the dispatcher that I was 10-6, 10-17, out on an investigation, in the 2400 block of Shawnee. The dispatcher knew where I was as she recognized the address and location and if within 5 or 10 minutes, she didn't hear from me that she would automatically notify the sergeant and zone 3 to check on me and only at that time would they know where I was. There was no concern as I had not been dispatched to any type of call to that address and I was just 10-6, busy, so there was nothing important at this point. Now at the time I was up on the small porch and made my way between the 2 choppers to the front door and knocked. I figured that me and the Outlaws were going to have an early understanding that their sign was coming down. Well, the door starts to open, and I expect to see someone in colors but heck, there stood a beautiful blond in tight skin black jersey, tight black pants and black knee-high boots, I was always a sucker for basic black. I couldn't get over how pretty she was, but she saw the uniform and with a scowl said, *"Yea, what do you want?"* Now I didn't know her but scuttlebutt at lineups talked about some of the good-looking chicks that crashed with the gang. Now as far as I was concerned, she could have stepped right into a Vogue Ad and been in place. I found out later that she was the daughter of a very prominent lawyer up north who just liked motorcycle freaks, so she ran away from home to join them. Anyway, I gave her a corn ball smile say, *"Howdy ma'am, can you tell me who put that sign up on the porch."*

Well with that she must have thought I was fresh off the pork farm, and she answers, *"no, but it was probably one of the boys."* Now again with my pearl drop smile I say, *"ma'am, would you ask the boy to step outside, I'd like to talk to him."* She tells me, *"No one else is here,"* so I tell her, *"Tell the boys that I'm taking their sign down."* She slammed the door in my face, so I walked over to the sign and tore it down, got back in my car and went 10-8, back in service. The whole incident didn't take but 8 minutes.

The rest of the shift kept me busy, however I didn't see any Outlaws or any choppers or even have any calls concerning them.

The rest of the shift left me with 3 or 4 assault calls to do reports on. The sign I had taken from the Outlaws I had just put in my patrol car and kept it. Now the next day I went to road patrol about 2:45 PM and checked in with Lt. Sanchez on some of my report follow ups when the phone rang in his office. He answered and then gave it to me saying it was a Detective Schuler and he wanted to talk to me. I was kind of taken aback at first, wondering what Schuler wanted with me as he was no ordinary general assignment detective but one of only two detectives on the department who specialized in kind of intelligence or OCB only. At this time all detectives were on general assignment, and they worked all the crimes, be it against people or property. Now only the vice squad kept up on dope cases, along with the try-county intelligence, Dade, Broward, and Palm Beach Counties. So now I couldn't figure out just what I had worked that had gotten me involved with Schuler.

Anyway he says, *"hey Barton, you took a sign down yesterday from a house on Shawnee didn't you,"* I said, *"yea why."* Schuler back, *"how about stopping back over there and see Deke when you go 10-8."* Now me, *"who the hell is Deke?"* Schuler again, *"Oh he's the president of the club, he wants to talk to you."* Me again, *"Okay as soon as I go on the road, I'll do it."* I hung up the phone, finished with the Lt. and now it's time for lineup so it's off to the squad room. Lineup was a few minutes till 3 so I filled in Sergeant Hall about the sign I had taken down at the Outlaws and also about my talk with Detective Schuler and what he wanted me to do. Hall says, *"just watch yourself."* Well lineup is over, and I got zone 2 so I loaded up my patrol car and went 10-8. It wasn't 3 or 4 minutes, and I was in zone 2 and I went right to the Shawnee address on a 10-17. Now today there were 5 hogs parked on the west side of the house, none on the porch, but in the same spot as the day before was another sign with the same words.

Now if I had been smart at this point, I would have called the sergeant and let him know what was happening, but no I just went to the front door and knocked and it almost opened under my knock, those inside saw me pull up, they were waiting for me. There in the doorway stood a white male, Levi's, boots, and a lei jacket with no sleeves. He had a short beard that just covered his jawbone from ear to ear. He had on a large belt made from a motorcycle primary chain with a big square buckle with a small link, timing chain, welded to it and it was all chromed. He was about 5'9" to 5'10", around 170 pounds and slightly bald. Now he wasn't all that big but what caught your attention right away was the unnatural look in his eyes. They were recessed in his head and dark and had a piercing stare. Now my first impression was he looked like a zombie, so in a dead pan voice he says, *"yea, whaddya want."*, I could see he was going to be a fun person. I told him I wanted to see Deke, zombie back, *"see away".* Now the way he talked with that dead pan stare and monotone voice should have told me that the fecal matter was about to come in contact with the rotating blade, but I say, *"Schuler ask me to come by, that Deke wanted to talk with me."* Up to this point I never met Deke or any of the Outlaws. The zombie again, *"you're the 'MF' that took our sign down."* Well with that statement I became unglued, figuring here I am, representing the law in Palm Beach County, doing my job in taking down an intimidating sign and this zombie stands there calling me that. So back in a slow and deliberate voice I say, *"yea, and I'm the 'MF' that's taken it down today."*

Now at this point we're both standing on the porch about 6 or 7 feet apart, with me right at the sign, when Deke gives a short jump in my direction and while he's doing this, strips off his chain belt with the big buckle and he wraps it around his right hand with about 12 inches hanging with the buckle loose. Now I was about 5 or 6 feet from him, so I unstrapped my python took it out and said, *"sport you better drop that f'n chain,"* Deke back, *"you'll take that f'n sign down over my dead body,"* I smiled at him and said, "sport that's the easiest thing in the world," and so I aimed the ole python between his feet and pull the trigger. Now the sound surprised me as much as Deke, and now there was a neat little hole in the porch right between his boots and I could see that he wasn't in as much control as he was a while ago, I could see it in his eyes. I raised the barrel from the floor and pointed it around his gut and cocked the hammer. When he heard the click, I said, *" you just heard what it sounds like to die cause you won't even hear this one if you don't drop that f'n belt right now,"* Now with no hesitation it uncoils from his hand and drops at his feet, and then he made a quick turn to go back into the house and was in the doorway when I lunged forward and caught him by the neck. I still had my gun in my right hand and as my left hand slide off his neck, I grabbed a handful of his jacket and just ripped it off his back. He was scared and ran into the kitchen shouting for one of the old ladies, the blonde from the previous day, to call the sheriff's department and tell them that some crazy f'n deputy was shooting at him and trying to kill him.

Now while this is going on I'm still in the doorway and I hear him holler for the people to call, I figure he was doing me a favor in notifying the complaint desk cause they would darn sure get me some assistance or the sergeant would show up 10-18, blue lights and siren. I then picked up the belt and torn Levi jacket, walked to my car and threw them in. I still had my gun in my right hand, and I started back toward the house, got up on the porch and was about to go through the front door when this big clown in colors and a big bushy beard stands in my way. I didn't know him then but got to know of him later, he was the enforcer for the club, and they called him fat Frank. He was about 6'3" and around 265/275 lbs. and you could pinch fat all over him. Now he says in a cool voice, *"hey, what you want man?"*, just like he didn't know from nothing. Now directly across the room from the door was a bed in the living room and 3 more members, one was a female, so that made the total of 4 males and 3 females in the house at the time with Deke, and 2 females in the kitchen which was just off to my right. My gun was just hanging down by my side still in my hand and I hollered for everyone to get on the bed. Well again old pudgy says in a cool voice, *"who me!"* Before the last word is out of his mouth I had the muzzle of my gun in it, well now he went to pieces and must have jumped 7 feet onto the bed, at that moment in his life he would have been good competition for the flat-footed broad jump.

Now there's all four standing on the bed and they could see that I was pissed. Now Fluffo says in a meeker voice, *"hey man don't shoot, no need to get excited."*, if only he knew how excited I was. In the background I can hear the yelping of the 2 patrol cars so now I knew that help was just a minute away. I turned toward the front door, which was still open, and I see Wyatt, zones 3 and 4 pull up. Before Wyatt could come in, I look in the kitchen at Deke and told him, *"You threaten me or any member of my family like you did to Paulus and your dead.",* now this is not exactly the rapport I was supposed to have according to WPBPD instructors. I'm sure he knew the adrenaline was pumping in me just like him and his buddies and he just nodded but the scared look was gone, and the piercing stare was back.

Well Wyatt jumped out of his car, gun in hand and ran inside to find me with the four on the bed just standing and Deke and 2 chicks in the kitchen. The phone was still in the blonde's hand so now the complaint desk probably heard all or most of the conversations. Right then another patrol car pulls up and its Sergeant Hall. He runs inside and finds me and Wyatt standing with our guns out. He surveys the scene and tells us to put our guns away. He tells me to go outside on the porch and a minute later he comes out followed by Deke who now is excited and shouting at Hall, *"that crazy 'MF' was trying to kill me, I want something done."* Now Sergeant Hall has a special look when he got pissed off. It kind of reminded me of Howard Hawks, *THE THING*, look as he gave it to Deke and in a slow voice said, *"you say one more word",* and that was all he said but it was more than enough cause Deke didn't say another word. The detective Lt., OD arrived at the scene along with a detective named Tom Spate. They talked with Sergeant Hall and then Hall comes over to me and says, *"Bob, you go down to zone 3 and 4 and work."* I don't question his order and so I go and get in my patrol car and go 10-8 advising the dispatcher that I'm no longer zone 2 but zones 3/4 for the remainder of the shift. Now zones 3 and 4 are fairly quiet so I had time to reflect on what just happened at the

Outlaws house and once calmed down I got the shakes and started to tremble. Fortunately, I got a minor call to answer and it kind of took my mind of the incident, however I still had Dekes belt and colors on my front seat. later on in the shift I had to meet with detective Spate at road patrol as he wanted a statement from me. Now even though I would have to do a report on the whole incident I still had to give Spate the information. He had been assigned to do a follow up by the OD. Now Spate treated me like I was a bad guy, and he took the side of Deke Tanner; I thought, you SOB, just like an internal affairs unit, or headhunters. Well, I didn't hear any more about the incident during the shift and so at the end I went 10-7, out of service, at the road patrol and turned the car over to a night shift deputy. I went into the squad room where Sergeant Hall was talking with Sergeant Bendick, the night shift sergeant. Now Sgt. Hall sees me and starts laughing like hell and says *"Barton, you crazy SOB, ole Deke like to shit his pants."* Sgt. Bendick says, *"any time you want to work on my shift just say so."* I spent close to 3 hours doing paperwork.

Well at home the next day I get a call from road patrol for me to come in early to see captain Herron. Now he was the captain in charge of road patrol at this time, hell he already had my report on the whole incident and as far as I knew statements had been taken from all the Outlaws that were in the house by detective Spate. I came into road patrol about 2:00 PM, and I saw a Mrs. Kerr, now she's the captain's secretary who took me right on into his office. I could see my report and all the statements on his desk, but he says," *Bob, tell me what happened"*.

Well, I thought shit, here I go again, and so I started right from the sign to Schuler just casually asking me to stop by and talk to a Deke, and about the threat with the belt. Now at that point the captain says," *Why didn't you just leave,"* I couldn't believe what he was saying," *Captain, that SOB threatened me with that belt, and I figure here I am, a deputy sheriff and he thinks he's going to intimidate me, well he'll never see that day."* The captain lets me finish the story and then he says, *"Why didn't you arrest him?",* I told him I was going to bust him for aggravated assault, but my Sgt. told me to leave, and I did so. The captain then asked me if I had stuck a gun in the mouth of one of them. I told him that he was acting like he was going to be a threat to me and was acting this way, blocking my way into the house for the benefit of his friends, and besides I was all worked up and that the quickest way to get his attention was to stick my gun in his mouth. At this point the captain says, *"Bob, you got to be the craziest bastard in the world or the bravest, I don't know which."* He also told me that the sheriff wanted to see me, I figured oh hell, I do my job, don't take no guff from those maggots and now I guess I'll get suspended or even lose my job. Well the captain dismissed me and as I walked out of his office he hollered at me," Oh *Bob, make sure you take the belt and the jacket with you to the sheriff,"* "yes sir, will do."

Now I got to tell you I was nervous, on the sheriff's department only a few months and already I got to see the old man, hell road patrol deputies never see the sheriff unless its pink slip time but hell the captain could have let me go on the approval of the sheriff unless he wanted to do it personally. Next day I went into the city of West Palm Beach, that's where the sheriff's office was and sitting in the secretary's office, I could catch a glimpse of Sheriff Heidtman and his Chief Deputy, William Bennett. Finally, I'm told to go into the office.

Now I'm really nervous as I go in and the sheriff walks over to me and shakes my hand and says, *"I just want to commend you on your actions the other day, I feel you acted admirably, and your action was a credit to the department. I'm sure if I was put in the same position I would have acted differently."* I give a sigh of relief thinking well at least it's not goodbye time. I said in a relieved voice, *"thank you sir, Captain Herron ask me to bring you this belt and jacket that I got off of Deke,"* I handed them over to him and he excused me telling me to keep up the good work.

Well Deke and his troops tried to file charges against me with the county solicitor's office, states attorney, for shooting at him and ripping his jacket off and so did fat Frank, he also wanted to file as I had stuck a gun in his mouth. Well Marvin Mounts was the solicitor at the time and told them that if they thought any jury in Palm Beach County would consider or convict a deputy sheriff of such a charge after all the notoriety that they had caused in the county and for that matter in the whole of south Florida, to go ahead and try. Anyway, they stopped attempts to file on me. I got involved many more times with the Outlaws, but I never had any situations like my first experience with them.

They continued their activities in the county until finally it cumulated with their nailing one of their old ladies, 18 years old, to a tree for holding out $10.00 from her old man. Now Deke wasn't responsible for this particular incident, but the Sheriff and Captain Haley went all the way to Detroit, and in a raid on the Outlaw headquarters there got Fat Frank, Super Squirrel and Mangy. All 3 where extradited back to Palm Beach County and tried and convicted for the nailing to the tree. The raid and arrest got national coverage and a picture of Super Squirrel and Mangy kissing was taken and in all the papers. I even made it into a national detective magazine that did a story on the Palm Beach Outlaws, needless to say I nor my family ever got any threats from Deke or his band of merry men.

****

Deke was convicted of a conspiracy in a grand larceny and went to jail where I hear he became a born-again Christian. Sgt. Hall, Dec. Sgt. Spate, and Lt. Haley all got a 30-day suspension later on when it was discovered that they had been drinking and riding with the Outlaws. Later, Spate was charged by the county solicitors office for larceny as it was discovered he had been taking money from migrants and had been arrested. Deke never told anyone about my last statement to him as it was never mentioned by the detective, the captain, or even the county solicitor. The Outlaws finally moved out of Palm Beach County and in 1982 several members were indicted for murder in Broward County.

PLEDGE TO THE FLAG

I pledge allegiance to the flag of the United States of America and to the republic for which it stands; one nation under God, indivisible, with liberty and justice for all.

Graduation Exercises

of the

Police Recruit Class 45

DADE COUNTY PUBLIC SAFETY DEPARTMENT

POLICE ACADEMY

APRIL 25, 1968 at 11:00 A.M.
Auditorium, Museum of Natural History
and Science, Vizcaya

BASIC POLICE TRAINING CLASS
No. 45

DADE COUNTY PUBLIC SAFETY DEPARTMENT

Askew, Donald R.	Kaudner, Alan R.
Boyd, Norman D.	Lockhart, Robert A.
Boytell, Jean J.	Martin, Odessa R.
Carey, Ronald I.	McGroarty, Dennis J.
Cope, Gerald K.	Neuman, Gordon H.
Darrington, Clifford E.	Stark, Ellen M.
Devine, Luis J.	Turner, Joseph, Jr.
Dobson, John D.	Van Der Weid, Stephen J.
Hitchcock, Gerald H.	Wenner, Dorothy S.
	Winn, Roger B.

MIAMI BEACH POLICE DEPARTMENT

Acuna, Robert	Fajarczyk, John R.
	Kratzer, Benjamin

CORAL GABLES POLICE DEPARTMENT

Cabrera, Victor	Clark, Bobby C.
	Poor, Ronald F.

PALM BEACH COUNTY SHERIFF'S DEPARTMENT

Barton, Robert G.	Webb, Richard L.
Quackenbush, Stephen V.	Wiles, Ralph T., Jr.

ACADEMY STAFF

P. BOHARDT, SUPERVISOR

Lt. R. Senk	Lt. W. Rutledge
Sgt. J. Grant	Sgt. J. Ford
Sgt. H. Needler	Officer F. Kovacs
Mrs. C. Daye	Miss A. Cabota

PROGRAM

INVOCATION	Sgt. R. Kaye
PRESENTATION OF COLORS	Honor Guard
PLEDGE OF ALLEGIANCE	Paul Bohardt
WELCOME & INTRODUCTION OF GUESTS	Paul Bohardt
INTRODUCTION OF GUEST SPEAKERS	E. Wilson Purdy, Director, Public Safety Department
GRADUATION ADDRESS	Peter Masiko, Jr., President Miami-Dade Junior College
RESPONSE	Richard L. Webb, Class President
PRESENTATION OF AWARDS	Fraternal Order of Police, Police Benevolent Association
PRESENTATION OF CLASS	Lt. R. Senk
PRESENTATION OF DIPLOMAS AND BADGES	Police Officials
SWEARING IN CEREMONY	E. Wilson Purdy, Director, Public Safety Department
BADGE PINNING CEREMONY	Family Participation
BENEDICTION	Sgt. R. Kaye

POLICE OATH
STATE OF FLORIDA
COUNTY OF DADE

I do solemnly swear (or affirm) that I will obey the Constitution and laws of the United States and of the State of Florida and that I will in all respects observe and obey the provisions of the Home Rule Charter of Dade County, Florida, and all ordinances adopted thereunder, and all rules and regulations promulgated thereunder; and that I will well and faithfully discharge the duties of the office of Metropolitan Deputy Sheriff and Public Safety Officer.

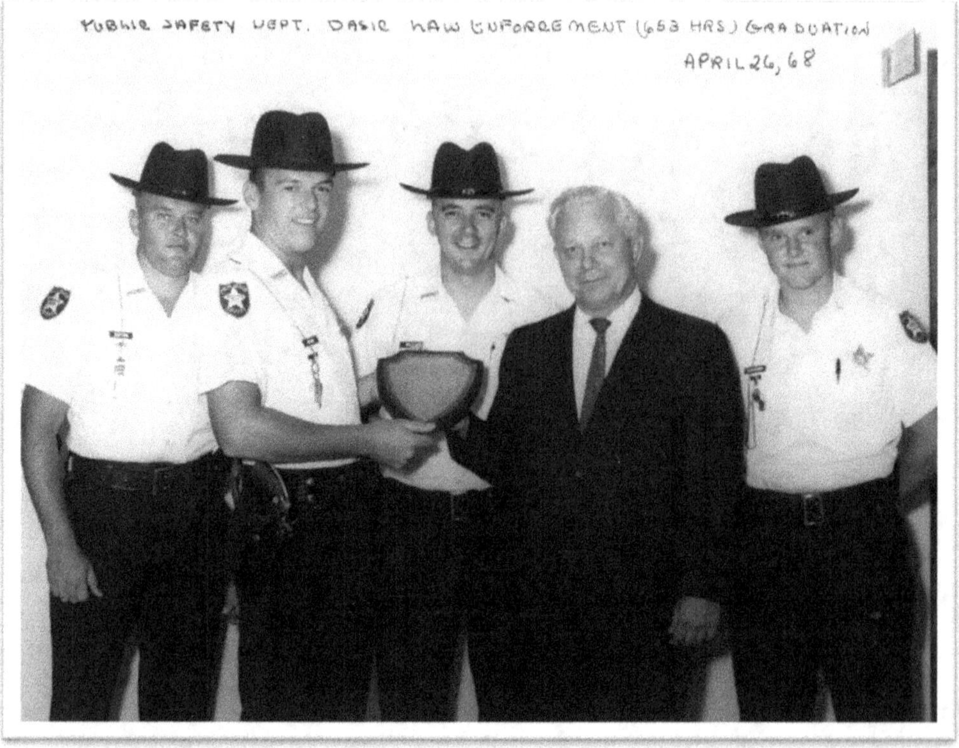

PUBLIC SAFETY DEPT. BASIC LAW ENFORCEMENT (653 HRS) GRADUATION
APRIL 26, 68

Photo by Joe Rickles

EMERGENCY RUN — Palm Beach County Deputy Sheriff Sgt. Robert Barton was on an emergency run to investigate an accident Monday night and wound up being involved in one. Barton swerved to avoid a car and ran into a power pole on Military Trail. He was treated and released at John F. Kennedy Memorial Hospital.

BOY RESCUED — A critically injured 12-year-old boy was taken by the Palm Beach County Sheriff's Department helicopter to John F. Kennedy Hospital yesterday, minutes after he stepped into the path of an eastbound car on Southern Boulevard in West Palm Beach. Larry Watson was given first aid by deputies and taken to the intensive care unit of the hospital suffering from severe head and leg injuries. The boy was staying with his family at the nearby Boulevard Motel. He was playing on the Palm Beach Canal Bridge when he stepped into the traffic shortly after 6 p.m.

Two RB Police Officers Complete Course

OFFICERS ROBERT BARTON AND RONALD WELLS, who have just completed diving course sponsored by the Sheriff's Department.

The Sheriff's Department recently sponsored a course in the use of scuba gear and diving equipment used to recover vehicles, bodies and evidence from different waters. Two men from the Riviera Beach Police Department, Officers Robert Barton and Ronald Wells participated in the course. Four other law enforcement officers also took the course, 2 from the Sheriff's Department, 1 from the Sheriff's Auxiliary and 1 from the Lake Worth Police Department.

Instructors for the 120 hour course were: Sgt. Bill Bishop and Sgt. Valgene Holly of the Sheriff's Department and Bob Cowart, Coast Guard diving instructor from Miami. All of the six students received certificates. The course consisted of running 5 miles, swimming in Palm Beach canal, pools, ocean and Lake Worth. The men swam from Peanut Island to the Port of Palm Beach, underwater day and night with a compass. They swam in the ocean for 1,225 yards day and night with and without swim aids on top of the water. A life saving course also was included in the program.

Chief Cottrell made this course possible for his men in keeping with his practice of having the men receive all available courses to be as versatile as possible.

3 Weeks In The Water, But They're Not Wet Behind The Ears

Wet but happy, six students in the Palm Beach Sheriff's Department Divers Unit will be presented with proficiency certificates Saturday by Sheriff Martin Kellenberger, winding up a vigorous three-week training period.

Under instruction of Det. Sgt. Val Haley, Sgt. Bill Bishop and Bob Cowart, who was borrowed from the U. S. Coast Guard Diving Unit, they are: Winston Wells and R. G. Barton from the Riviera Beach Police Dept.; R. C. Baker of the Lake Worth Police Dept.; Auxiliary Deputy Sheriff Tom Riverbank and Sheriff's Deputies Tom Murray and Dave Chasteen.

The Sheriff's Divers Unit began in September of 1962 after a series of water tragedies. At that time, Haley and Bishop free dived without the benefit of equipment. After discussion with Sheriff Kellenberger and Chief Deputy Ray Nunamaker, it was decided that funds would be alloted from the existing budget for enough equipment to start the two-man unit with Nunamaker in charge.

"The latter part of 1963," Haley said, "it became evident that the demand for divers was growing. We had to train divers to assist in the additional work load.

"For example, on one occasion Bishop and I had three automobiles in canals between West Palm Beach and Belle Glade within a 48 minute period, which also resulted in five deaths. On another occasion, we had to recover a drowning victim north of Canal Point and then had to travel 90 miles to the scene of another drowning in the Loxahatchee Game Reserve."

Bishop was sent to Miami to the Coast Guard diving school to acquire a better working knowledge of the mechanics of diving and to learn the medical aspects, and the department decided to train available men, since volunteer divers were found to be impractical.

"With the increase in air and water traffic," Haley said, "we are constantly faced with a possible mishap. This is another reason why the unit is vital."

Haley feels the six graduating students are well equipped to cope with any problem. They have been instructed and worked nearly to exhaustion. They are not "Sunday divers," as Haley calls people who engage in the activity as a sport.

Basically, the school consisted of training with desco and scuba gear. Two weeks of physical training to tone muscles and varied medical lectures were also included.

The conditions the sheriff's divers find include sewage, dirty, brackish canal water and spoil ditches for local sugar mills. They work with such objects as demolished vehicles, which increase hazards, and search for drowning victims and crime evidence.

To pass the course, the men must complete four 1,100-yard swims, two with swim aids such as fins and face masks and two without. There are two night time swims and two are conducted in the daylight.

They must also complete four 500-yard swims under the same conditions.

They must also be able to complete a five-mile run on foot.

The men were given practical problems in the Palm Beach Port, which included placing numerous fittings and connections on a submerged tank, 30 feet under water, filling it with air and bringing it to the surface. "This teaches the use of tools and equipment under water," Haley said.

Training is required in various search patterns which allows a complete area to be fully searched during the day or night. They are taught to swim by a compass and life saving techniques.

The first two weeks of the training program were conducted with the cooperation of the Knights of Columbus, which allowed use of their pool. The last week was completed in the Port of Palm Beach.

The Sheriff's Divers Unit will be set through its paces to demonstrate what they have learned Saturday, and Haley said the public is invited so that it might gain an insight into the aspects of the program. County commissioners are also expected to attend.

Ceremonies will be held at 10 a.m. in front of the Port Authority and U.S. Immigration and Customs buildings.

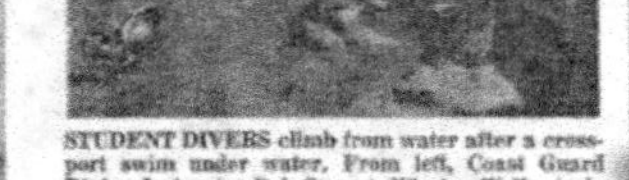

STUDENT DIVERS climb from water after a cross-port swim under water. From left, Coast Guard Diving Instructor Bob Cowart, Winston Wells, (submerged), Instructor Bill Bishop and Tom Murray. Proficiency certificates will be presented by Sheriff Martin Kellenberger.

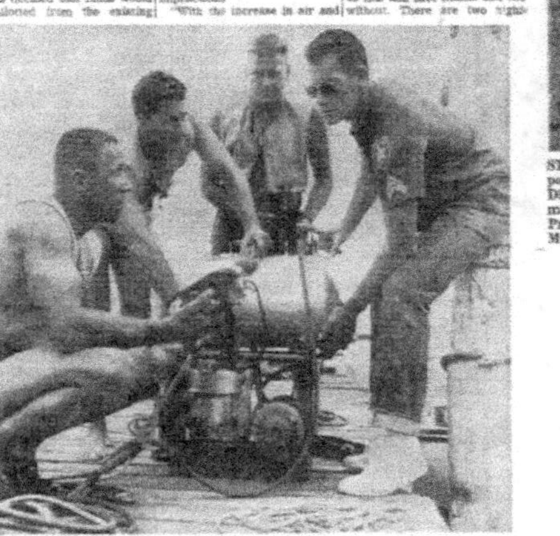

USE OF AIR TANK is demonstrated by Instructor Val Haley, right, to students, left to right, Dave Chasteen, R. T. Baker and R. G. Barton. The training period began April 5 and will wind up Saturday.

John And Dora Miller Meet "Alex" Of "Amaryllis"

AT 2 P.M. WEDNESDAY, Riviera Beach Mayor Jake Bosma took off from the parking lot of Capt. Alex's Restaurant in a helicopter. His destination was the "Amaryllis," and his mission was to deliver two twenty-five pound turkeys complete with all the trimmings to the crew of twenty-nine. The venture was sponsored by the Northern Palm Beach County Chamber of Commerce, the Riviera Beach Industrial and Advertising Committee and Louise Kimmist, owner of Capt. Alex's. The helicopter, owned and donated for the occasion by Spherical Corporation Helicopter Service, was piloted by Norman Reed. He hovered over the ship while Mayor Bosma lowered the turkeys, other goodies and literature on the area, some of which was written in Greek.

John And Dora Miller Meet "Alex" Of "Amaryllis"

By Edith Judge.

Ever since Hurricane Betsy blew the freighter "Amaryllis" onto a coral shelf about fifty feet off Singer Island, it has become the biggest topic of conversation in the area in many a day. Thousands of interested and curious spectators have thronged to the beach since the ship crunched ashore in eight feet of water in Wednesday's pre-dawn hours.

The first people to see the ship, at 5 a.m., were Riviera Beach Police Officers Bob Barton and Gene Armstrong. The men ran across the beach and called to the crew to ascertain if anyone had been injured. They received a negative reply. Sgt. William Copithorne and Lt. Jeff Waites arrived at the scene just as a message came off the ship, asking "Where are we?" A man wrote "Riviera" in the sand. Another message came from the ship (one crew member Alex Romanakis speaks and writes English), "Please contact agents in Baton Rouge."

Behind every story, there is another story and this is not an exception. Late Tuesday evening, Mr. and Mrs. John Miller of 2672 Conroy Dr., Lake Park, stopped by the SUN office and told of their experiences with the "Amaryllis." We are happy to relate this exclusive story.

Friday night the Millers went to see the ship. They were impressed and decided to return Saturday to take pictures. While there, a crew member (Romanakis) asked for a copy of the polaroid picture. Miller swam out to the ship and attached it to a line that Romanakis lowered. He then lowered a picture of himself and a thank you note. This, then was the first of several notes passed between the two in the next two days.

John And Dora Miller Meet "Alex" Of "Amaryllis"

On Sunday, the Millers returned with some Florida souvenirs in a plastic bag, which he again attached to the line and Romanakis pulled aboard. In the evening, the Millers again returned to the beach, swam out to the ship and tied a bottle of liquid refreshment on the line. The crew then proceeded to do a Greek folk dance on the deck, one played an accordion and they all sang "God Bless Jack and Dora Miller." Romanakis then called and asked them to wait for another letter. A copy of the letter follows:

9-12-65

Dear Captain Miller,

I have seen in you a man with a great heart and we are all really much obliged or rather in debt.

But as you are in such a position and we are in this position you see. I ask from you to speak to the Immigration for us, so that they can give us permission to come ashore as we are going to remain here for a few more days.

So if you will be kind enough to talk to some one in charge in the Immigration we might then have the honor to come ashore, and meet you wonderful people, then we will really give you everything we have in our hearts.

Mr. Miller please see about this matter because I want to see you personnally and your dearest wife Mrs. Dora so that I could have the honor to shake your hands and to thank you the way we do in my country. Captain Miller receive all our respects and friendship from all the crew, many thanks for everything you and your wife have done for us, I think you are wonderful people, and I personnally will never in my life forget you.

I hope God will give you and your dear wife Dora all the best of luck and happiness forever

John And Dora Miller Meet "Alex" Of "Amaryllis"

and ever.

Yours faithfully,
Alex

John and Dora Miller were so touched by the letter that they felt that somehow they must try to help their new friends. They walked across the beach and as they approached the street, they saw a Riviera Beach Police car. They showed the letter to the officer and much to their surprise, it was Officer Barton. He said he would do what he could to help and then radioed headquarters. Dispatcher Betty Hallison took it from there and called the Immigration Office.

When John Miller returned to the beach Monday morning to tell his friends that perhaps something could be done, he found that the Immigration officers had just left the ship. By Monday afternoon, the crew was cleared to leave the ship and visit shore at will.

Tuesday evening the Millers went to the beach and the captain, Florias Galatis, invited them aboard for coffee. They swam out to the ship and following coffee, invited Alex Romanakis to visit them at their home. Romanakis, who speaks 8 languages visited this reporter at the SUN office Wednesday afternoon and expressed great appreciation from the crew to the "kind people, who have made us feel so welcome here."

Thus far salvage plans for the "Amaryllis" are still not certain, but whatever happens, 29 Greek seamen will never forget this trip. They surely will never forget John and Dora Miller, who reached out the hand of friendship and helped make it possible to turn what could have been a long, lonely wait on a strange island into a warm enjoyable visit.

APRIL 24, 1965   SCUBA-DECSO RIVIERA BEACH DEPT

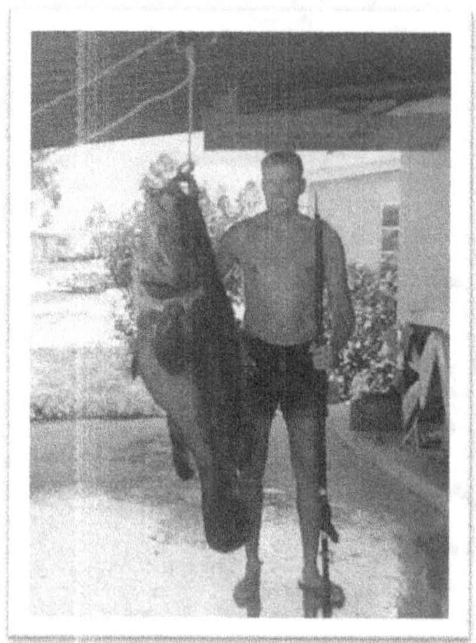

OVER THE HILL GANG

This story occurred in the late 60's, between 67 and 69 as I was yet a slick sleeve deputy and I worked mostly in zone 2. The shift was the 3-11 PM. Now back at this time, the sheriff's department didn't have the benefit of, hot sheets. The sheets had all the pertinent information a deputy going on duty would need about lost or stolen license tags, stolen cars, missing people etc. and as a result of no hot sheets, this information was given by the shift sergeant at what is known as, lineup, and prior to anyone going on the road.

We were advised at this lineup by the sergeant that a 400-unit, vice, that through an informant he had developed information that a gang known as, the Over the Hill Gang, had a safe house in the Westgate area.

Now a safe house is a place where people might go to rest and recuperate and lay low, and in this case don't get involved in any crimes and especially not to draw any attention from any law enforcement agencies. The gang was also wearing body armor and we were instructed that if we made any contact that we were to shoot at the head or at the feet of the contact, and not to try any bodyshots.

The sergeant in giving out this information didn't have any street, house number, vehicle or for that matter any other information that might help, just to say that it was in the Westgate area. Now Westgate is a large area having many streets and houses and also Westgate is in my zone. Well with that we were told to hit the road.

A word about the Over the Hill Gang, the gang had committed a series of armed robberies. I think they were all armored cars as they delivered cash to stores, mostly Food fairs, Publix etc. Their MO, (Method of Operation) was to pull up behind an armored car as it pulled up in front of a store to deliver cash, and when the occupants, guards, opened the rear door of the truck, the gang would jump out of a car from the back seat and trunk and rob the guards by taking the cash bags and in some cases, kill the guards or anyone that offered resistance, get back in their car and make a getaway. Supposedly one member had killed over 20 people. So, you can see that it would be dangerous to run across any one of them.

Well, we all had the information that was available at the time when we went on the road. At this time most, if not all deputies carried a shotgun in a scabbard on the floor of their patrol cars, this was in addition to their side arms and of course, a gas billie. I myself was no different but I also carried a 22-magnum derringer in my pocket.

I headed to zone 2 and you can believe that I put a round in the chamber of my shotgun which I normally don't do. Now zone 2 was only 5 minutes away from road patrol and right away I headed for Westgate, but I didn't have any house address, vehicle description or any information other that what was given us at lineup, but I did drive slow in the area as I was on routine patrol in there waiting for a call.

Needless to say, I'm sure there were a lot of other cars, detective and vice, as they were unmarked, but no contact was made this night or any other night that I was aware of, but you can be sure that a lot of looking was going on. Me being in zone 2, I was always wary of most contacts.

****

I heard several weeks later the gang had a shootout with

the FBI and all the members were killed. Now I can't verify this,
but there is justice.

PERFECTION FARMS SID VIENNE

The shift was 3 till 11. The time, early 1970's and I was one of the departments 5 road sergeants. I was in the south end of the county area where we have all our labor camps. I had just got done talking to a Sid Vienne, a Delray Beach substation detective who wanted a road, uniform, assist on trying to catch 2 Puerto Rican males who were wanted for aggravated assault, and 2 other Puerto Rican males at Trevino's last dance. Trevino's is a large dance hall, bar, and restaurant owned by Oscar Trevino, a Mexican who also had a store near by the dance hall. He held dances every Saturday night for all the Mexican and Puerto Ricans, farm labors, who hated each other anyway and we had 200 to 300 people there for each dance. It was very rare that we didn't get a few felony calls at the dances, mostly aggravated assaults, and an occasional murder.

Anyway, both were victims of Vienne's aggravated assault/assault. The victims had been shot and were still on the critical list at the hospital. Vienne tells me he just got word from a CI, confidential informant, were just seen at Perfection farms, a small labor camp to the west of state road #7 and just north of Boca Raton Road, he had called me originally at road patrol headquarters from the Delray substation. That was the reason I was talking with him. I had been at road patrol headquarters a good 18 to 20 miles north and I'd be a few minutes getting there. We'd meet there and go into the camp together. I called the dispatcher and told her I was 10-51 south, enroute, to assist a 300-unit, detective unit, in reference to a signal 31 BOLO, aggravated assault. Now everyone on the sheriff's department had an I.D. number. The sheriff and his staff were in the 100's, uniform personal was in the 200's, detectives in the 300's, vice in the 400's. We sergeants were in the low 200's so when you heard a call to the dispatcher, you would hear on the radio when the caller ID'd himself. You could hear on the radio as he talked to the dispatcher. I went 10-8, 10-511 on a signal 15. Now a signal 15 is a special detail but she already knew the details as I had called her from the road patrol headquarters by land line, telephone, so I didn't have to repeat just what the detail was on the air, radio.

Well I went west on Southern Blvd. to state road #7 and then south on 7 to Delray Road and met with Vienne. I already knew what the detail was and what the suspects looked like and who they were, and so I tell Vienne to go ahead I'd follow him to the camp. It's about 5 more miles south and about 1/4 mile west of 7. We pulled off at the camp and right away a group of Puerto Ricans 15 or 20 start towards us. At that point I don't know if they were friendlies or not, so when I got out of my car my shot gun came first but I held it low. It's a fine weapon, a 12-gauge Winchester model 97 all chromed and just a wee bit over 18 inches, legal limit, well everyone stopped dead in their tracks and Vienne hollers out *"Bob, that's my informant coming, well how was I to know."* I got up to Vienne just as the Puerto Ricans got to us and the one who was the informant points toward the northwest and says that both the suspects ran that way.

Well, we both, me and Vienne, took off running in the suspects direction. We ran up to a bunch of trees and bushes and we saw them both in a clearing up ahead, probably a good 6 to 7 hundred feet ahead of us. Well, I give my shotgun to Vienne, and he ups and shoots all 4 rounds at them or at least in their direction. They were 00 buck rounds coming out of that shotgun. Now Vienne is a retired navy chief in his younger days, and he stays in shape by bending his elbow frequently in some gin mill and this exercise is supplemented by chain smoking. So, after no more than 2/10th's of a mile he's sounding like he's trying real hard to have a heart attack and doing pretty good at it. By now he can't even talk, just take in big gulps of air. So, he falls down and waves me on to keep running after the suspects. The 4 rounds that Vienne cranked out just made the suspects run all the faster. They passed through a barbed wire fence and got into a pasture that had some cattle grazing in it. Now Florida cattle are all pretty wild as there put out to pasture and have to fend for themselves, so not much contact, so they're not to used to having people around. maybe on horseback, but not on foot. Well, the 2 suspects kept heading in a northwest direction towards Farmers Motel, our biggest labor camp, it has about 300 to 400 migrants there. Now Farmers Motel is on state road #7 and about 2 miles north of where me and Vienne had turned west to get to the Perfection farms camp. I can see the suspects footprints in the mud, and they cross a canal that's about 15 feet wide and it don't look deep, so I go right on in and it's up to about my waist. So, I take my side arm out of the holster. Now, it's in my hand so as not to get it wet. I make it to the other side of the canal and my boots are all filled with water and gook and I'm a mess now and I got to go through another barbed wire fence into another pasture and so I follow their footprints in the mud, and they stay right beside the fence. The trail here isn't open pasture anymore. I got the fence on my right side and a cattle trail about 12 to 15 feet wide with a solid row of bushes and trees on my left side. The trees are hanging over the trail and so it's like a tunnel and I walk/run in a hunched over manor. Now just at the time along came 3 or 4 steers in the opposite direction and I've got no were to go and they don't look to friendly, I move as close to the trees and bushes as I can and the cattle go running by, bawling at me. I've got to tell you that by this time I'm huffing and puffing, sweaty, wet, and dirty. My boots are sloshing with water in them when all of a sudden, I see Farmers Motel, the 2 Puerto Rican suspects are about 1000 feet in front of me. I can plainly see them at the southwest corner of Farmers Motel. Well, I'm not going to give up now, so I make it a very fast walk.

Well, I finally made it to Farmers and see the 2 Puerto Ricans laying on the hood of Herbie Nichols brand new green Ford Torino. He handcuffed them and he wasn't even breathing hard. The 2 Puerto Ricans looked just like me, wet, sweaty, dirty and tired, just like we had been in a war. Now Herbie is also a south county detective and so when Vienne told him what was going down, he just kind of moved that way, to the Farmers Motel, and waited in his air-conditioned car. By now Vienne had recovered and was back at Perfection Farm and got his car and met me and Herbie with our 10-15's, prisoners, at Farmers. Zone 8 showed up and I had him transport the prisoners to the jail for aggravated assault. I drained my boots and tried to wipe off my python, handgun, I had to go home as I was a mess. Home was a good 25 miles away, I had to take a shower, and get a clean uniform. I sprayed my gun with WD-40 and put on a pair of shoes. Later I put my boots in the oven, they dried to fast, and they cracked all over, so I ruined them.

****

As far as I can recall, both victims recovered and both suspects were convicted of aggravated assault. This is before plea bargaining.

PHONE BOOTH SUICIDE

It was the 4 to 12 PM shift and I was working zone 2, my steady zone. That's the West gate area. This is where I used to get several felony calls a night. It was a real red neck area that had several bad bars that were always good for a shooting, CCW (Carrying a Concealed Weapon) or a cutting and always had good fights. Now zone 2 covered a much larger area and it had business and residential types. Zone 2 actually ran from 45th Street north, all the way south to Belvedere Road but there was so much trouble in paradise, I mean West gate, that I usually just stayed close by and only left the area when I had a call to respond to. I hardly ever got the opportunity for just routine patrol.

It was around 7:30 or 8:00 PM and zone 3 and 4 combined because of its small size was out for a 10-40, meal, so that meant any calls for that zone would be handled by zone 2, me, on its north side, and zone 5 on its south side. We didn't have any cover cars to fill in while a car went to eat, if he was busy, or just out of service.

The time was early 1968 and the road sergeant hardly ever took any calls, at least I don't remember him taking any. So, when the dispatcher came on the air with, *"Palm Beach, zone 2, 10-23, wait, for a possible signal 32 attempt,"* suicide. This means that I was supposed to stop and copy the information about a suicide attempt, the case number, time, etc. I acknowledged the dispatcher and instead of stopping to copy all that I told her to just point me in the right direction and I'd get all the particulars later by landline, telephone.

Anyway, she advises that the victim is a white male, and

he is in a phone booth at Harney's Trailer Park, that's on State Road #80, also known as Southern Blvd., a major highway in Palm Beach County just east of the turnpike.

Now while the dispatcher is transmitting this information to me, I put on my blue lights and my federal system, siren so I can work it off the horn, then I start west on West Gate Avenue. Harney's Trailer Park is a small park east of the pike and we've had several signal 38's, domestics, there.

I forgot to mention that I had an A man, Auxiliary deputy, with me. His name was Toby Dawes. Toby had the rank of sergeant in the auxiliary. Toby was a little older fellow in his late 40's. As I write this account 16 years later, 40 doesn't seem so old, He worked for Florida Power & Light and put in a lot of time with the sheriff's department.

The Auxiliary were required to ride with a Deputy at least 12 hours a month but Toby rode at least 80 or more, you can see that he really liked being a deputy, but he couldn't afford to work for such low wages. He especially liked to ride with me in zone 2 because there were lots of calls and all were good ones. He carried a 12-gauge, chromed shotgun that was a real attention getter and on more than one occasion he saved my bacon in the Square Wheel Bar while I was on a fight call or some other call that was violent. He would just stand by with that shotgun cradled in his arms, just watching and covering me and not saying a word while I conducted an investigation.

Anyway, I'm up to about 60 mph in a 25-mph speed zone just turning south on Military Trail, another major highway and its 4 lanes, divided. I'm hitting the siren; horn button and cars are moving out of my way. By now the dispatcher had advised that, *"Palm Beach is on 10-33 traffic for zone 2,"* that's emergency radio traffic ONLY.

The dispatcher came back to me while I was south bound on Military Trail. I'm doing 90 to 95 mph and she advises, *"further signal 14,"* information. She tells me the male is in a phone booth, has a rifle, and is talking to his dad, in Belvedere Homes, and is telling him he's going to shoot himself.

I'm a long way past Cherry Road where his dad lived, the main entrance to Belvedere Homes and the dispatch further advised that the dad had another member of the family go next door to a neighbor and call our department, they were keeping a line open also in addition to the line between father and son. So, all was covered as far as communications.

By now I'm at 4 Points, an intersecting highway and turn right on State Road #80 Southern Blvd. I've got my foot jammed on the gas pedal and my hand on the horn rim for the siren and I just moved the Federal system to yelp so the siren yelps automatically all the time.

Toby is all excited and hollering at the cars to hurry up and get out of my way, he didn't think they pulled out of the way fast enough. The dispatcher came back on the air with, *"Palm Beach to zone 2, the complaint desk just advises that the father just heard a shot over the phone."* I acknowledged and told her I was about 1/2 mile south of the trailer park and just to put me 10-97, arrived, she acknowledged me and verified for all listening units that, *"Palm Beach is still 10-33 traffic,"* as she transmits this info, I'm pulling into the trailer park.

Now a word about Harney's Trailer Park, it's shaped like a circle that has a loose end and that's the way in and out so it's one lane wide. It's a small trailer park so I don't have any trouble finding the phone booth. There is a white male laying on the ground outside the phone booth door and a lever action riffle. I jumped out of my car about 25 feet from the male and I hear him moan so I know he's still alive, from the way he's lying on his back you could see that he had been standing in the booth with his back to the door, he had the phone in his left hand, and the riffle in his right hand. He probably had it pointed up at his throat area or lower jaw as he was talking to his dad and in the microsecond when he pulled the trigger, he had turned his head just enough so that the muzzle of the riffle fell down far enough that the bullet hit his shoulder, but anyway standing over him is a big black dog.

Now the dog looked to be about 85-95 pounds and as I tried to get close to the victim the dog snarled and showed his teeth.

The phone booth is a standard Southern Bell telephone booth with glass walls and it's about 30 some inches square. The light was on the ceiling and the left wall was shattered but still up, this is where the bullet went out. Everything else inside was covered with blood, flesh, and bone. The victim kept moaning as Toby and myself tried to get near him and the dog but weren't having any luck.

By now all the residence of the trailer park were out of their trailers standing by but at a safe distance just watching us. I told Toby to get back to the dispatcher and tell her the victim was still alive and to get a 10-71 code 3, an ambulance lights and siren. As Toby was doing this, I managed to get close to the victim, he became aware of my presence and realized that I was trying to help him, he saw and heard his dog growling at me, so he talked to the dog, and I had no problem getting beside him then. The dog was just scared and wanted to protect his master. I knelt down beside him and just at that time Toby was back from my car telling me that an ambulance was enroute code 3 and he also had the first aid kit. I told Toby to take the dog away and tie it up while I checked the victims wound. There wasn't much left of the left shoulder and not much flesh either. All it had was just a few strands left to hold it on, his shirt sleeve was all tattered and in a mess. I didn't even bother opening the first aid kit cause I knew that it didn't have anything big enough to cover such a massive wound like this one.

We had been trying to convince the captain that all cars should carry Kotex just for emergencies such as this one, it was a good example. Well anyway I didn't have anything to cover the wound, so I hollered at the crowd for someone to get a clean towel, wet it and bring it back in a hurry. Toby went with someone and was back with the towel. I just laid it on what was left of the shoulder. It must have given him some relief as he felt it right away and thanked me.

Now I could hear a yelper, a siren, so I figured the ambulance was almost here. There wasn't anything else I could do for the guy, so I just talked to him and told him the ambulance was almost here and he was going to be okay. Toby was busy clearing people out of the way so that the ambulance could get to us.

Well, it pulled up right beside us and the assistant got out, ran to the back, and opened the doors, unlatched the bed and both he and the driver brought it over to us. I told them that we also needed the back board. They got it and laid it down beside the victim. We hadn't moved the victim yet as they were looking at his arm. It was just barely attached to him. I told the attendants that we better secure his arm before any attempt was made to move him, I'm sure they also thought of that. No one had anything close to what we needed so I took my knife out and cut the belt loops off the victims' pants and put his belt around his left wrist and him and cinched it. so at least it was secure. Then Toby and me and the two ambulance attendants lifted him gently onto the backboard then onto the portable bed. We put it into the ambulance and the driver advised that they were going to

JFK Hospital, (John F. Kennedy) since it was the closest one. I got back to my car and told the dispatcher to clear 10-33 traffic and that the victim was enroute to J.F.K. I ask her if the complaint desk still had the guy's dad on the phone and if so, ask him what type

of blood his son had as he was going to need a lot of it, and if they knew ahead of time, they could be ready when he got there, even running code 3 the ambulance was still 10-15 minutes away from the hospital.

She acknowledged and cleared the radio of 10-33 traffic so it could resume normally and advised me that a 300-unit, Detective Ed Johnson, was responding to J.F.K. to get the information for a report and that Johnson would do the face sheet and a more detailed narrative. My supplement report would just contain what I saw and did. I didn't even have the victim's name and all I could refer to was a white male.

I acknowledged the transmission and told her to mark me 10-8, in service, and enroute back to my zone.

I picked up the riffle and examined it, it was a lever action Winchester 30-30 caliber, and it still had the empty cartridge in the chamber, so I put it on half cock and put it in my trunk. I thanked the crowd for their help, none in particular, just thanks for the assistance. Me and Toby got in the car and left.

The rest of the night was quiet so at road patrol I filled out a property receipt on the Winchester, unloaded it, attached an evidence tag and turned it into the property room the next day.

****

I never saw the victim anymore but about a year later I got to talking to Johnson about another matter when it hit me that he had worked the case with the telephone booth, so I asked him how the victim was. He told me that he had gotten his head together, got over any mental problems, and that they had put a Teflon ball and socket in

to replace his shoulder, that after therapy he would have about 75% use of his shoulder and arm. Johnson went on to say that he, the victim, moved to north Florida and that was the last he heard from him. The victim's father said that his son was doing okay.

The Winchester rifle, used in the phone booth, was returned to the father.

PIG TWO LEGGED

The day shift, 7 AM to 3 PM and I don't like it. It was about 10:00 AM and so far, no details for me to do, and none of the calls were very serious.

The day is dark and dreary, and it looks like it's going to rain, and in a few minutes it does. One of the things that Florida is famous for, besides dope, is its rainstorms, and when the rain comes down, it pours. Now that it's raining so hard, I figured hell, now we'll have a rash of signal 4's, accidents. Well, I hoped the complaint desk can get FHP (Florida Highway Patrol) to work some, or all of them, but usually FHP says that they're busy. You know, FHP only has one man to cover 10 million miles and they're short of people and funds, sorry. By now it had been raining for close to 20 minutes and coming down harder than hell. So far, we only had one accident and the dispatcher advises that she had called FHP and they advises that, guess what, they're busy and couldn't take the call. Now to me all FHP was just an overrated traffic agency. I'm going south on Congress Avenue, a busy 4 lane divided roadway, and I was just crossing the intersection of Lake worth Road, another busy 4 lane divided road, when I see a big black pig just walking along. He had just crossed the street and was going behind a gas station on the southwest corner and he was going into a motel complex there. So, I turned into the gas station and went 10-6, busy. on my digital, at LW Road and Congress Avenue and I didn't give any reason. I put on my hat cover cause it was raining like hell and put my raincoat on. Normally I wouldn't get out of the car when it's raining this hard except on a serious case or some emergency, cause a good cop not supposed to get wet, but this was different. It looked like meat on the table. Well, I got out of my car and got a coil of 3/4 inch rope out of the trunk of my car. I started out through the station property into the motel area, the water was in puddles, and it was raining so hard that the ground couldn't soak it up fast enough. The pig was just standing in the grass and rooting around a tree, I made a noose, put it on the pig, and drew it tight. Not bad for a sometime cowboy and never even thinking that the pig was pretty tame to let me do all that. Hell, this was easy and not like another pig(s) incident I remembered.

Now this pig was about 125 to 150 pounds, but it had been so easy so far and I gently pulled him back towards my car, now remember it's raining on both of us real hard, and he just came along, it was like walking a dog on a leash, only this was a big dog. While walking him back to my car I already had him butchered and wrapped in my mind.

Walking back to the gas station I first tied the pig to the tire rack, and it didn't even squeal or try and get away. I went to the phone and called Steve from Steve's Wrecker Service. He was a close friend and an ex-West Palm Beach patrolman; he was on a disability pension. I told him I had a pig and would bring it right over and hung up. I went back and got the tied-up pig and started for my car. It was still raining hard, but I didn't care, I was as happy as a, excuse the expression, pig in the rain. I unlocked it and opened the rear door. Now up to this point the pig was easy to handle, it was just like a little kid, but it got plain real quick that he wasn't fond of any car ride. It squealed and jumped and even tried to bite me and I damn sure knew that it wasn't no little dog on a leash. I finally got the porker in the car and slammed the door shut.

Now I was all sweaty and dirty and my Stetson hat was floating in the water, my raincoat was open and all dirty and a mess, but at least I was going to bring home the bacon. I figured I could tell any anyone at road patrol at the end of shift that I had an RAWV. (Resisting Arrest with Violence)

I just hoped the dam pig didn't tear up the back seat to bad. I figured I could wipe it up at Steve's as I was only 5 minutes away. I jumped in the car, started it up and pushed the function 3 button on my digital, that's 10-8 or back in service.

When I did this the dispatcher came on the air and said, *"213, you were just in the area of Lake worth Road and Congress Avenue, did you happen to see a black pig anywhere, we just had a call from a female who said she just lost her pet pig and didn't want anything to happen to it."* I paused a few seconds thinking, shit, all that work for

nothing. I came back and told her that I had the pig secured at the gas station and she could pick it up there. At least the porker didn't squeal while I was on the radio even though he was in my car. I went 10-6 again at the same location, opened the rear door and had no trouble getting the porker out of the car. Once out he was easy to lead, just like before.

I tied him up to the same tire rack and told the attendant that the pig was a pet and that a female was coming over to get it.

I went over to Steve's and cleaned myself and the car up and listened to him bitch about no ham and bacon.

****

Now, I buy all my pork and bacon at the store and it's real easy, its wrapped and there's no fuss.

PIGS 2 AND 4 LEGGED

Well, it's the night shift, 12 - 8 AM now I'm working in the north end full time and its lineup for the troops. I only have 4 troops to supervise and it's a snap. I give out zone assignments letting the older troops have first choice and the rookies have what's left over. I pass out hot sheets, go over the business of B&Es (Breaking and Entering) from the previous night and then got them on the road. In comparison to the Central or Baker zones or for that matter the south zones, Charlie and Able zones are like a retirement position. Now true to form I think it was around 3 AM and we had only gotten 1 or 2 calls and they were not of any consequence. Well around 3:20 AM the Able dispatcher sends a call to Able 3 on the digital, now not being an emergency, voice transmission wasn't used and so it was sent by digital.

Now a digital is somewhat like a typewriter/computer combined having a display screen that when filled to capacity would display 10 or 12 lines or roughly 250 words total, now all cars are equipped for a digital except the detectives' cars. The only bad thing was you had to remove it at the end of the shift and put it in the car at the beginning of the shift so it was a real pain in the Ass as if you didn't have enough to carry with reports, flashlight, shotgun or whatever else and if it rained, which Florida gets plenty of you can see that it's a real pain. Now all calls are dispatched on a digital, and are received by all cars that have one, so everyone knew what type, and where a car was dispatched to, so no voice transmission was used.

So, all calls were sent, and the status of every car could be checked, and cars could even talk back and forth and never a word spoken. Now this probably bugged the Hell out of cop freaks who listen in on police monitors all the time. Well Able 3, Ron Seifert, gets a call that's in a housing development and it has 2 pigs running around, squealing, and waking up all the neighborhood and could the department respond and do something about it. Well, I got right on the digital and typed out a message to the dispatcher to contact animal control and that we weren't farmers and tell them that we would assist them and that in the meantime Able 3 and me would try to contain the pigs. Now I'm still enroute to the call and every car has a digital so they get the case number, complaint, complainants name, address, and phone number if they have one, and the dispatch time. Any additional messages can be sent to an individual car involved in the case. Being the sergeant and Supervisor, she tells me there is no answer at animal control and she says that the answering machine states they workday shift hours only. *"Well how sweet it is",* what kind of cooperation is this between county governmental units, this is just typical. So, in my most soothing and authoritative sergeant's voice I break radio silence, the hell with a digital, that up to now has only been 10-4 checks on the hour every hour to see if they are okay and their 10-20, location. *"Call their Captain Larry Wilcox and get him out or have one of his troops on call."* Now the dispatcher could feel the annoyance in my voice and gave a hurried 10-4 to acknowledge my transmission.

Word about Larry Wilcox, he used to be on the sheriff's department and in fact he was my sergeant for a while. He only lasted for 6 months, probationary period, on the road and was sent to communications division. Once there he ran the dispatchers and complaint writers like some tyrannical lord. A hypothesis as to why he was like that was best illustrated by a Herb Roberts, another SO sergeant, who used to draw a caricature of Wilcox by drawing a pair of jump boots with a riot helmet on top and Wilcox was somewhere in between with a little voice coming out so you can get the picture how big he was. Nothing else was visible except the sergeant stripes on each side of the boots, anyway who ever heard of a captain of the dog catchers.

Well by this time Able 3 and myself are 10-97, arrived, at the scene of the call and punched in a function 2 on the digital showing we are there. We start at the complainant's house, knock on the door and it opens by a guy in his skivvies, underwear, and he's trying to get fully awake. Able 3 to the sleepy male, *"good morning, sir."*, it's about 3:30 AM. I imagine the guy would argue that it was a good morning, *"you called about some animals in your yard/area, now just what is it?"* The sleepy male, *"its two big G/D pigs in the back yard somewhere trying to get out."* By the sound of his voice, I guess he didn't think it was a good morning after all. Now Able 3 back to the sleepy male, *"Well we'll see what we can do sir to catch them"*. So, off to the back yard we go. First off, all the homes in the area have back yards that are fenced off, all the fences are different, some are cyclone, some are wood, and some even have a thick hedge which was over 6 feet tall. There are no streetlights and so it's dark as hell. I tell the dispatcher that if we get any calls in the area just to advise the callers that 2 deputies are in the back yards trying to catch some loose pigs.

The dispatcher acknowledges and we start to try and locate the pigs in the beams of our flashlights. Along about the second yard I spot this pig, now I mean a BIG black pig, it's a sow, and she's around 200 pounds just standing in the corner of the yard backed up to the fence. Well, I walk toward her, and she lets me get about 20 feet from her and she grunts and looks like she's going to charge or run at me so I back off. Hell, I figured the pig would be small and that between myself and Able 3 that we could just dive on the pig and tie it up and TOT (Turned Over To) animal control. We found out that there is a second pig and it's the piglet and that piglet is around 125 pounds.

Well, no cop in his right mind would have dove on that sow and so I gave Able 3 the keys to my car and told him to get a coil of 3/4 inch nylon rope out of the trunk. I was going to trap that porker. Well, the sow stayed cornered just as long as I didn't crowd her, so I stayed away from the fence. Back comes Able 3 with the rope and I lay out this great plan. I'd lay the rope out in a big circle between the house and fence, and Able 3 can herd her toward me and that way I'd hurry up and pull the big noose tight and catch at least one of her legs. Then we can secure the rope to the fence post until animal control shows up. Now by the way, where the hell IS animal control? So, I ask the dispatcher by walkie talkie just where is animal control? She advises me that Captain Wilcox had to get a troop out of bed and that he had a dog, and he is on his way, but he's coming all the way from Delray Beach area so it will be some time before he reaches our location. I acknowledged her and put the walkie back in the belt holder thinking SHIT. Delray's 35 miles away. By the time he gets out of bed, dressed and on the road and up to us would take a good 45 minutes to an hour. I tell Able 3 the good news and then it's back to the problem at hand. Well, I laid a big noose down by the fence close to the house making it about 6 feet in diameter and then I tell Able 3, *"I'm ready,"* and to chase the pig my way.

Well, he does and now she is squealing like hell and

running like mad in my direction and as she passes, I give a mighty tug on the rope and shit nothing happens. Now that big pig hit the fence so hard that the gate popped open and now, she's out on the street running east and then back into another yard about 4 houses down and she's squealing and hollering all the way. By now I can see lights coming on in about 5 houses, then I hear the dispatcher call me while I'm running. I stop and acknowledge her, and she advise that a call from a female saying there are two pigs in her yard, I advise the dispatcher to tell the complainant that we're trying our best to catch them.

The dispatcher comes back with, *"She's not complaining about the 4-legged pigs but about the 2-legged ones"*. Well with that I pause and became unglued, but in a calm voice I ask the dispatcher the name or address of the caller, she comes back with, *"The complaint declined that information."* I calmly acknowledged her and thanked her thinking, *"you SOB! "*, I'm all hot and sweaty and dirty and trying my best to catch those pigs and we got to take this shit. Well, me and Able 3 start knocking on every door, the hell with the pigs, let's give it a rest, and see if we can find out who made the last call.

The pigs started squealing again so I figured we'd find out who made the call after we got the pigs. Well, lo and behold up drives the Marines in the form of a black male in a light green, screened pickup truck. Animal control has just arrived, and just like I thought, it took about 45 minutes to respond and sure enough he has a dog in the front seat and it's a German Shepherd. I go out and introduce myself and Able 3 and thank him for coming out and ask him about his dog.

Now while we're standing there, we hear a big racket; its tools and lawn chairs being knocked over. A light comes on in a carport not 3 houses away from us and its baby pig squealing like hell and all caught up in carport junk. Well, the dog sees, hears, and smells all of this and goes bananas to get at the pig. The black male releases him and he's off like a shot in the direction of the pig who's still knocking junk around. The dog makes it to the pig in 3 seconds flat, jumps over a bunch of junk and grabs the pig by the ear. Well with that the musical overture really went into high gear, now the pig was really squealing and scared as hell with the dog attached to his ear growling while holding on. Now the pig wasn't able to drag the dog around and the dog wasn't able to drag the pig around, so it was a standoff by both, just lots of noise. I thought, *"I'll be dammed, I never knew a dog could do something like that."* Well with all the noise ole mama finally made an appearance to take care of her baby and I thought we were really in for trouble now cause the dog was all wrapped up with the baby and didn't even see mama, and I was thinking if she comes any closer it's time for me to make bacon and ham, but she thought the better of it and ran into another yard.

By now the dog was able to control the baby and between myself and Able 3 and the animal control officer we just picked up the pig, this is after the B/M convinced the dog to let go of the ear with a swift kick to the ribs. Well, it's one down and one to go, but ole mama was a different story. Now she was almost twice as big as her baby and twice as mean, and I didn't think the dog could handle her so easy. By this time there must have been lights on in every house in the development and various residence were milling around the animal control truck. I know that they had to be pissed off for being awakened with all that squealing, and all their families awakened. It's around 4:30 AM and it looked like round 2 was about get under way and take even longer. Now that we had a lot more help, unwilling but for the sake of law and order and so that they could get back to bed, a resident hollered I found it, it's down here. Needless to say, we all went running down there and sure enough there's ole mama in the back yard. She had run in through an open gate and was in the far side of the yard, now she's madder than hell, grunting and pacing like she was waiting to get it on. Well, we got the dog and again it was bananasville. The animal control officer let her go and she was on that pig like flies on fecal matter. I slammed the gate closed and saw the dog trying to get her feet on the ground, but ole mama just kept spinning and tossing the dog, but it never let go of the ear.

Well, I could see that the dog was between a rock and a hard place and needed some assistance, so I told Able 3, and the animal control officer that we better help the dog and that if we all three dove on the pig we should be able to handle it. Well surprisingly we got the pig off her feet, cause she was concerned about the dog on her ear, with no trouble. Now one of the neighbors saw we had the pig down and brought over some rope and we, excuse the cliché, HOG TIED HER. I had the animal control officer get his truck and drive it right into the back yard and the 4 of us loaded mad mama in with her young'un. Well by this time I'm all dirty, sweaty and mad but glad it's over. Animal control leaves with the two pigs. It's now 4:55 AM so Able 3 and myself start back tracking on addresses and sure enough, one of the houses where we had run through the yard when we knocked on the door and a female answers, she's in her late 40's to early 50's and she's demanding to know what we want and I knew right away from her attitude that she was the caller about the two legged pigs in her yard. Wellbeing the good deputies we just wanted to advise everyone in the neighborhood that the beasties had been captured and that the neighborhood was safe again. I recognized her from a domestic argument about 2 weeks ago, she was a nurse, also an alcoholic and the last time we had arrested her for DOC (Disorderly Conduct).

Well, I knew it wouldn't do me any good to ask her if she had made the second call, but I knew she did. We thanked her and apologized for any inconvenience and left. While in her yard I got the tag numbers of both parked cars, there colors and distinctive marks. I had the dispatcher run vehicle registration checks on both tags and I wrote them down. Now at line up the next night I gave all this information to the troops, advising them that any infraction/violation would be a great benefit to the Able zones. I didn't think much more about it but three weeks later I hear the Able cover car ask me for a 10-56, meeting, and a location and guess what a small world it is. Our pig caller was drunk behind the wheel of her still running automobile, it was just off the highway on the berm. Now I know a good DWI when see one, yes folks, there is justice!

****

Well, the pigs ended up as honored guests at a barbecue as no one claimed them. Able 3 was Ron Seifort and he finally went to the Vice Squad and after a short tour came out and became a K-9 unit.

POLICE FUNERALS COP KILLERS

I attended another police funeral for a slain police officer in our county. He was from the seaside resort town of Delray Beach and like most towns in south Florida it had a large black population. The time was early Sunday morning right around 1:00 AM. Now the city of Delray has more than its share of black clubs and most on Atlantic Avenue on the west side of town. Being its Saturday night, early Sunday morning, all these clubs are crowded, and the Delray PD was busy as usual with complaints on fights, disturbances etc. A white police officer had just come on shift at 12:00 midnight, and already he had answered several calls as he was working the zone that included Atlantic Avenue and black town. He had finished a call and was sitting in his patrol car in a closed service station on Atlantic Avenue and he was on the west side of the tracks that separate Atlantic Avenue.

Atlantic Avenue has a lot of expensive shops and is palm tree lined, but only up to the railroad tracks. On the west side of the tracks, it looks like any other black town USA.

The police officer was just sitting in his patrol car, his window was down, and he was smoking a cigarette and doing a report on one of his previous calls he had handled so that he could keep up with or try and keep up with his paperwork. The window was down on his side of the car as it was a hot night in Florida, as usual, but the hot and busy night was soon never to be a concern to the officer again, because the next thing to happen was that someone put a 38-caliber weapon in his left ear and pulled the trigger. The cigarette fell out of his mouth and onto the seat where it was found still burning

The sheriff's department Uniform Division very seldom

went into the city of Delray other than to drive through to get to U.S. #1, or to the beaches on A1A, or some other unincorporated area of the south county. We never went to any city or business unless requested. Anyway, the substation of the sheriff's department was in the city of Delray, and that's where county cars, both patrol and detective, went to gas up.

This policy of us going into the city of Delray changed right away when the shooting occurred as the Delray Detectives and the sheriff's detectives didn't have lead one at this time. So, the uniform division was ordered to go into the bars, clubs, stores etc., and see if we could develop any leads and interview all party's we met. Now I got to admit that we were not in any mood to be nice and friendly, and like most blacks when interviewed in a bar or club give you a bad eye and say, *"who me, man I don't know nothing."* Actually, it would make you think that as a group they suffered from a disease known as dumb ass. Well, the investigation went on for several months. The Uniform Division got away from this investigation as they had other duties and activities to take care of or else, they would have spent more time on it if able. It was the detectives from Delray PD and the sheriff's office that stuck with it and finally they developed a suspect, and an arrest was made. The grand jury returned an indictment of murder in 1st first degree on a black male known as Willie Simpson. Now Willie was an 18-year-old badass, and I had gotten involved with him once when I had worked out of the Delray Substation. We also arrested his mother, a Maggie Pugh, for aggravated assault, she had shot her husband when she caught him screwing around. Now this was a real salt of the earth family. Willie got convicted of first-degree murder and was sent to Raiford Prison in north Florida and he was put on death row awaiting to meet ole sparky, now he had a lot of company at the time as Florida had 156 citizens waiting to meet sparky. Now sparky was kind of a lighthearted name for a gruesome oak chair.

The funeral for the fallen Delray police officer was quite an impressive and spectacular tribute to a fallen officer. Police motorcycles from all over the state of Florida's various and numerous police departments to sheriff's departments. These must have numbered in the hundreds, and they were followed by patrol cars from their agencies. Now the entire funeral procession must have been a good 3 to 4 miles long, this excluded the unmarked cars and so it was impressive to see as well as probably aggravating to some along the procession route who didn't much like cops or police officers anyway. Then having to wait so long to cross a street or Blvd, or a highway, anyway at the grave site there is nothing more mournful and sad than to see the lines of different uniformed men, all with different hats giving a hand salute while an honor guard fires a rifle salute in tribute to a fallen officer. Then taps are played, and the last thing done in the ceremony is the folding and presentation of the flag to the widow.

Now this had to be about the 12 Th. funeral I'd been to, and they don't seem to get any easier and to attend one really makes you think. Oh yea, the name of the police officer killed is one synonymous with great wealth and great tragedy, his name was John Kennedy. Now Officer Kennedy left a wife and 5 children plus one on the way that he would never get to see. How ironic as I sit here in Alaska having left the sheriff's department in October 1977, and six thousand miles and a lifetime away from all the police funerals, now just memories left.

In 1980 two police officers in Juneau, Alaska, the state

capital, were shot and killed in the line of duty, one had the name of Kennedy. I didn't go to that funeral, but I did say a prayer.

A little background on Willie Simpson, though he was only 18 years old at the time, he had already made his mark on Florida society by having been arrested numerous times in the early 70's. He and several of his friends were indicted by a grand jury in a robbery and murder of a Boynton Beach retiree and had been sentenced to life in prison. He was awaiting transfer to Raiford State Prison in north Florida when he and two other inmates escaped. Well Willie was in the big time now.

The detectives at first arrested two black males for the police officer's death but they were released after a while. Willie was picked up in the state of Virginia at an uncle's farm and in early 1975 he was indicted for the police officer's death.

I left Alaska to return to Florida and back to the sheriff's department only to find ole Willie in the headlines of the local paper.

Now Willie had gotten a retrial in the death of Officer Kennedy, so after 9 years on Florida's death row he was granted a retrial due to a statement made by the prosecutor, now a Judge, named Harper.

Now in addition to the murder charge, Willie had been serving life plus 35 years for the murder and robbery of the Boynton Beach man, also, for the escape charge. Well, I won't go into the logistics of his new trial as far as locating witnesses of which some had died, even good ole Willie's sister was murdered a week before the trial was to begin and she was to have been an important witness for him. She had been stabbed in a Delray bar by another black female. His mother had by now died of cancer, but her sworn testimony stated that,

"Lord I don't want my baby sold for $5,000," the reward for the arrest and conviction of Officer Kennedy's killer. Anyway, Willie was convicted of second-degree murder at the second trial due to the jury being unable to reach a verdict. In May 1983 he was sentenced to a term of life imprisonment for the death of Officer Kennedy. At his sentencing he was quoted as saying, *"I have an advantage in the prison system, I'm a veteran, I want my book to be educational. I want the kids who idolize me to take a warning from all this."*

Well, it seems that time has a way of softening attitudes dulling the pain of a tragedy. Now I'm sure it never will for Officer Kennedy's wife and 6 kids, and for all the police officers involved, or read, or will read about it. Now ole Willie has been tried three times for two murders and he was convicted each time, but he has beat his appoint with ole sparky. Justice! Shit!

Now there's more to ole Willie Simpson's story and in relation to his second trial on the killing of officer Kennedy from Delray Beach Florida.

Ole Willie was declared indigent, poor, no funds, by the courts, meaning he didn't have any money to afford a lawyer, and in so keeping with due process he was to have been represented by the Public Defender's Office, but lo and behold, the case had received such notoriety that I believe the ACLU, (American Civil Liberties Union), contacted a lawyer of renown fame and had agreed to represent Simpson at his upcoming murder trial. None other than the radical William Kunsler. Now what can I say about a lawyer who defended George Jackson and his band of merry men, aka, the black panthers, a fun-loving black organization. They also had a fun-loving member known as H. Rap Brown. Now what could I possibly say against a man like Kunsler, after all, didn't he act as a mediator between the cons and screws at Attica prison in New York state where a total of 43 people died. I can only speculate that Kunsler had a deep and abiding hatred for all law enforcement officers. This is the kind of man who would defend ole Willie on a murder charge. Now Willie was also represented by another lawyer who didn't have the national acclaim that Kunsler had, but in Palm Beach County it was hard to find a better criminal lawyer than Eddie Starr. A word about the man who defended the iron workers at the Spreen Volkswagen riot where they destroyed 3 to 5 million dollars' worth of buildings, cars, and tried like hell to kill several deputies, me included, namely me. I got hit with a 6-foot piece of rebar 3/4 inch in diameter. Also, what can I say about a man that got busted by one of our vice agents right in the courthouse for passing out methamphetamines, upper or downer I don't now remember, and what can I say about a man who did hard time in a federal slammer for income tax evasion. I'll tell you what I can say about Eddie Starr, he shared a deep and abiding hatred for law enforcement officers along with William Kunsler and these are the two lawyers that would defend Willie Simpson against the State of Florida. The jury couldn't reach a verdict, so they gave him life in prison.

****

This next story also involves a police officer and his killer. This time it's before I had joined the sheriff's department and at this time, I was a member of the Palm Beach Gardens Police Department.

I had originally started in police work in the city of Riviera Beach, Florida in late 1964. and I stayed there until October

1966. when I went to the city of Palm Beach Gardens Police Department.

Now the city of Riviera beach had a black population of at least 50%. Anyway, I got fairly used to dealing with blacks and I had my share of fights, cuttings, shootings, etc. Now these seemed to be the norm for a city like Riviera Beach. I'm not prejudiced or biased, but I wouldn't be surpassed if they didn't bring in black sand from Hawaii for their beaches. Now they even had a black Chief of police, Boone Darden. He was the first black Police Chief in the state of Florida, and that was quite an accomplishment.

Anyway, I had just left the RBPD (Rivera Beach Police Dept.) and joined the Gardens PD, this was a retirement type job, to be honest I don't think that I ever made an arrest while a Gardens Police Officer and at this time Riviera Beach Police Department hired a white male named Meredith Runck, called Skip for short. He was a very good and conscious officer and I had met and talked with Skip several times and had told him of some of my experiences while on Riviera PD.

Well anyway Skip had been dispatched to a signal 38, domestic disturbance, while he was a Riviera Beach Police Officer on the black side of town and at the residence of Monroe Holmes, aka "Turkey" who had just beat up his girlfriend and had broken up some furniture.

This was the second call of a domestic disturbance at Turkey's residence but that was unknown to Skip as the first domestic occurred during the previous shift so Skip didn't have any idea as he received no word(s) of caution at his line up or given any information about any previous domestic at that residence, but he should have at least gotten some warning. Well Skip responded to a domestic and things got out of hand right away. It got to the point where Skip lost his service revolver to Turkey, and he shot Skip in the chest and killed him. Turkey was arrested by Riviera PD.

The Palm Beach Grand Jury returned an indictment against Turkey for the first-degree murder of Skip Runck. There wasn't even a trial against Turkey as he plead guilty and was sentenced to meet ole sparky up in Raiford prison. The funeral for Skip was big and was attended by police officers, deputies and troopers from all over the state of Florida and the funeral procession was as big as the one for officer Kennedy from Delray Beach.

Shortly after this incident I left the Gardens P.D. and joined the sheriff's department in August 1967 and stayed until October 1977. I kind of got burned out on crime and corruption and so I went to Alaska, and when the call of the law took over me again, I quit my job and returned to the state of Florida and back to the sheriff's department who were only too glad to have me back, but now I wasn't the senior sergeant but just a slick sleeve. I wasn't back on the department any more than a month when the newspaper had articles every day about the upcoming new trial of a Willie Simpson and then an article appeared about Monroe Holmes, the Turkey, that after having spent 8 years on death row, the Florida Supreme Court ordered that Holmes be taken off death row and to be retried and resentenced for Ruck's murder because the Public Defender's Office, as stated by the supreme court of Florida, *"they had not adequately defended their client at the sentencing where he had been given the death sentence without a trial."*

Anyway, the Turkey was resentenced and got life without a chance of parole for at least 25 years. Now at his resentencing Holmes said he felt, *"pretty fine, and that Runck had provoked me. As I remember, the officer the office provoked me as I told him I didn't know what was going on. I had my hands up in the air and with that billy stick he hit me two times up the side of my head."*

Now folks I wasn't at the domestic and I wouldn't want to quarterback it, but if you believe that story then I think you got the same affliction as lady justice, a case of dumb ass.

****

The time was April 1967, and I was in my third year as a police officer at the time I was with Palm beach Gardens Police Department. Now it was Friday the 7th to be exact. I had just started to work on the 4-12 PM shift. In the city of West Palm Beach, the county seat for Palm Beach County, is a city having a large police department. It was as large, if not larger, than the sheriff's department and it had two police officers who were about to meet a black male by the name of John C. Cooley.

The WPB officers where Sergeant Fletcher and a motorcycle officer by the name of David Van Curler. Sgt. Fletcher was a 19-year veteran of the police force and he had spent the last 4 years working in the jail, so he was a bit rusty as far as road work. David Van Curler had about three years on the police force, and he was a motorcycle officer. Now Van Curler I knew and spoke to often as I had met him while I was a patrolman in the city of Riviera Beach. Riviera Beach is the north border of the city of West Palm Beach, and police officers often meet just to talk, or relay people, or items that need to continue northward. I also used to see him in the county courthouse, also located in their city. and I would see him every year at the Heitzelman Brothers pageant on Flagler Drive where he directed traffic.

Now Heitzelman Brothers pageant was a nationally acclaimed pageant depicting at Christmas time the birth of Jesus Christ and it was done in large statute form and had lots of trees etc. Their Easter pageant depicted the persecution, death and resurrection of Jesus Christ. It was also done in large statute forms and being nationally acclaimed had a lot of vehicle traffic, so it called for traffic control of some sort. Now motorcycle officer David Van Curler was part of that control, and he was a regular as far as traffic control. I didn't know Fletcher as he worked in the jail, so I had no contact with him, however he was a police officer.

Now I was about to have cause to go to my first police funeral, of course, I didn't know it at the time. At approximately 4:40 PM of April 7th, 1967, a black male walked up to the Fidelity Federal Savings and Loan Association Bank at the corner of 45th and Broadway. Broadway is also known as US1, and he started to bang on the door shouting that, *"I'm John the Baptist".* Now Sergeant Fletcher who was fairly new on the road, and his duties just happened to be in the area, so he saw the commotion, not even being sent, or being dispatched, he pulled up and got out of his car and after a few brief words with the male knew that he would need assistance fast, as the b/m (black male) was completely irrational. Fletcher went back to his patrol car and on his police radio called for assistance and fast. Patrolman Van Curler while on his motorcycle heard the request and had to know the urgency in the voice, headed quickly in Fletcher's direction, besides he was on a motorcycle, and it was rush hour traffic and West Palm Beach at rush hour is like any other city. It's a zoo to drive in, and so Van Curler rushed off to aid the sergeant, and to meet his fate.

Sergeant Fletcher, meanwhile, had put his police radio back in its holder after calling for assistance. He went back to the black male who was still belligerent, and he started to wrestle with the Sergeant Fletcher. Now Fletcher was 52 years old at the time and the black male was 31, so it didn't take long to overpower the fallen officer. When he did, the black male took Officer Fletchers service revolver out and shot Fletcher in the chest. Just at this time Patrolman David Van Curler was pulling up on his motorcycle and he was just going 10-97, arrived.

The black male who was standing over Fletcher saw the motorcycle, he aimed and shot him in the chest, the bullet first passing through the Plexiglas windshield of the motorcycle. Van Curler never got the chance to put the kick stand of his motorcycle down. Now the black male walked over to the downed M/C officer, and emptied Sergeant Fletcher's service revolver into him. While this was going on, Sergeant Fletcher was able to crawl to his patrol car by some superhuman effort, being wounded, and he called for help on his police radio. Now the black male saw the sergeant, so he reached down and took the now dead Van Curler's loaded weapon and returned to Sergeant Fletcher, who was lying by his patrol car. Now that he had a new and loaded weapon, he shot the sergeant and then started to pistol whip him, the sergeant, who was now also dead. He was grabbed by a white male named Tom Gorham, now Gorham was a recently returned Vietnam veteran. He held him at gun point until responding officers arrived. Gorham had grabbed the gun and it still had one live round in it. Gorham held the black male at gun point until responding West Palm Beach police officers arrived. He did so even while getting cries of, *"Shoot him, shoot him,"* from the crowd of people.

It was more than just a brave act by a civilian. Gorham had won a silver star in Vietnam and was a true hero.

Well, I got to be a member of the Palm Beach Gardens Police contingent that attended the funeral(s) and four of us went. Now at this time there were only six police officers total in PBGPD (Palm Beach Gardens Police Department) Patrol cars and police motorcycles from all over the state of Florida attended, this is not even counting unmarked, detective, cars. The procession had to be several miles long. The service was one of the saddest and mournful that I had ever attended at this point. and it had a profound effect on me. Hell, that could have been me.

****

Sergeant Fletcher had three kids, all grown, and he was a grandfather.

Patrolman Van Curler left five children that he would never see again. This is what made me think," *am I in the right line of work"*. I had a three-year-old daughter and one due in 4 or five months.

The black male, John Cooley was indicted and convicted of murder(s) and by reason of insanity was sent to a mental institution in Hollywood Florida where he died after several years.

The black community of Riviera beach started a memorial fund for the Cooley family, they also built a house for them. Patrolman David Van Curler's five children also had a trust fund in their name given by the community.

****

In 1976 I had attended a funeral for a Florida Highway Patrolman and a Canadian Constable who were both killed together. It happened on Interstate I-95 and in Deerfield Beach. Now Deerfield Beach is not even in Palm Beach County. It is a community just south of Palm Beach County limits.

The FHP (Florida Highway Patrolman) whose name was Philip Black had previously gone to Canada with his family on his annual vacation where he met Constable Donald Irwin. Having a lot in common they became fast friends so when Irwin took his vacation he went to Florida and stayed with his friend, Trooper Black. Now black was working so he apparently got permission from his superiors to have Constable Irwin ride with him while on patrol.

Now on the sheriff's department if a deputy wanted a rider while on patrol, he had to get written permission in the form of a release liability so that in case of an accident or injury the department wouldn't be held responsible. I assume that FHP Black's agency had a similar policy.

Well anyway trooper Black had his passenger, Constable Irwin. They were on I-95, an Interstate, and had just pulled off on one of the many rest stops. Now rest stops on Inter states are a place a traveler can pull off, stretch, go to a restroom, or take a nap. The time was early morning, and I was working as the able sergeant and we were to get off shift at 8:00 AM, so this incident probably started around 6:00 AM or close by.

Our department had gotten so big by now that we had

three substations on the east coast, Able, Baker and Charlie.

Able being the north end of the county went to 45th street and is where I was working. Now Able, Baker and Charlie zones all had their own radio channels. The Charlie zones were the south end of the county and it bordered Broward County and Deerfield Beach, just inside that county. Now we all had different radio channels and so we really didn't need to know about something happening 25 to 30 miles south, but we all had digital computers in the patrol cars and the dispatcher would send messages back and forth to the sergeant and to the deputies that they got along with, telling them about interesting calls in other zones and make small talk about a choir practice etc.

Well trooper Black and Constable Irwin pulled into the rest stop on I-95 and for some reason one car stood out of the many that were there as it must have had a suspicious look. So, they pulled up closer to check it out. Trooper Black would have told his dispatcher by radio communication that *"he would be 10-6 and 10-17on a vehicle."*, busy on an investigation. He would have given the tag number, color and occupants if he knew how many. Trooper Black and his friend got out of their patrol car and walked up to the car in question and saw that it contained two white males, a white female and two small children.

Now back in 1976 the Florida Highway Patrol didn't have individual computers in their patrol cars. They only had multi frequency radios and some, or all, had Vascar units, these are radar units used on vehicles. FHP is primarily a traffic enforcement agency, so to run individual names the troopers had to call the names into their dispatcher who wrote the information down, then in turn this information is checked on

NCIC, FCIC and Palms. So, it's a through and complete check. NCIC is the (National Crime Information Center), FCIC is the (Florida Crime Information Center) and Palms is a local check. These are checks for any wants or past criminal histories. Now NCIC and FCIC only carry information on felonies and not on misdemeanors. Palms carried any and all information on an individual.

Well, it came back to trooper Black that one of the males in the car by the name on Rhodes had a felony past and was currently on parole. Rhodes was in the back seat with the two children and the driver was a Jesse Talfaro. His girlfriend was in the front passenger seat, her name was Sonia Jacob's Linder. Now all this information was given to the trooper from his patrol car and most likely the five occupants of the vehicle didn't know that the trooper knew that Rhodes was on parole. Anyway, this information gave the trooper more reason to be suspicious about his original concern, the car, and its occupants. He must have looked more closely into the vehicle taking time to check the dashboard for things like roach clips, marijuana seeds or anything that might indicate some sort of criminal activity. He probably then looked to the floor of the vehicle to see what he could see by the seat when unfortunately, he saw what looked like several gun handles, and now he knew that some criminal activity had, or was to take place, as Rhodes was a convicted felon on parole and there were guns in the car. Under Florida law, a convicted felon cannot be in possession of a firearm as it's a felony offense in itself, and if a P/O (Parole Officer) finds out he can have the parole revoked and send the felon back to prison to serve the remainder of whatever he was sentenced for in the first place.

Now at this point it looked like all the occupants would go

to jail and the children would become wards of the court, just because of Rhodes's past. Now just a split second after trooper Black saw the weapons, Jesse and Sonia each grabbed a 9-millimeter automatic and one-shot Trooper Black, dead, and the other one-shot Constable Irwin, dead.

Now Jesse who was driving took off in a hurry and its unknown to me who reported the shootings. I believe it was one of the other travelers in the rest stop who had seen both officers killed, and just talked into the trooper's car radio as he alerted the dispatcher. Now Deerfield Police Department, Broward Sheriff's Department and our department were immediately alerted and given the description of the car and its occupants.

It was then that I got the message on the digital compute, and I typed back a message that I would have my radio on the Charlie channel if she wanted me to send me a message.

Almost immediately troopers anywhere in the south Florida area of Deerfield Beach began convening on the area. The local police departments and the sheriff's department started for I-95 as it's the interstate and it goes north and south and has so many exits available. By now the entire state of Florida knew that two police officers had been shot and killed in Broward County having been notified by teletype.

Anyway, the suspect car was spotted in the city of Deerfield Beach, and in a place called Century Village, but only after it was reported that two white males, a white female, and two kids had jumped out of a car and stole a Cadillac at gun point, and that they had taken the owner with them.

Now Century Village is a condominium type settlement that really is a city within a city, the population is all retired, and 95% are Jewish. Most come from the state of New York, and most are from New York City. There are about 20,000 people living there.

Well, the description of the stolen Cadillac was put out right away and all unit's listening were advised that there was a hostage also, the vehicle's owner. Now the car was spotted as it sped north into Palm Beach County. By now the troops working in the Charlie area were either there or were approaching the three main highways and roads that are accessible from one county to the next. Now Palm Beach County and Broward County are separated by the Broward Canal and so there aren't that many roadways that a car could escape on. On the east coast is the city of Boca Raton and their Police Department and they would cover US! Also, A1A, which was an Atlantic Coast roadway right at the ocean. I-95, U.S. 442 and Palmetto Road were the only three other roads to cover plus the Florida Sunshine Parkway, turnpike, and roads were well covered.

The chase included marked units from Broward County SO., the Florida Highway Patrol and now members of the Palm Beach Sheriff's Department. A lot of gun fire happened during the chase and a roadblock was set up on Boynton Road after an FHP trooper blew the tire off the suspects' vehicle. Now one of the occupants of the vehicle was wounded in the knee, Talfaro I believe, the hostage was okay. Now of course the car wasn't okay, and it was later towed as evidence.

I had listened to the radio transmissions since they had entered our county as I'm sure most deputies did, though I wasn't at the scene I most remember what one of the deputies said in regards to one of the children in the vehicle, who was about a nine or ten year old girl, that she showed absolutely no fear, remorse, and even had contempt for the two slain officers, and also the ones who apprehended them.

****

Well, I attended another double funeral service. Constable Irwin was returned to his providence in Canada. Rhodes, the parolee turned state's evidence and testified that Jesse and Sonia had both shot and killed the two police officers. Rhodes was sentenced to life in prison after he plead guilty to 2nd degree murder and kidnapping. The two children became wards of the court.

In October 1977 I left the department and returned in 1981, and in that same year the Florida Supreme Court commuted the death sentence of Sonia Jacob's Linder to life in prison because, *"She was the mother of two children, one of whom was fathered by Jesse. Now isn't it a shame that Ma Barker had to die, it would seem that the Florida Supreme Court deems motherhood as an entitlement to an open season on cops."*

In 1982 a female lawyer named Elizabeth Du Fresne appealed Jesse's death sentence to a commutation to life. In a life sentence, and after so many years, an inmate is eligible for parole. In her arguments she stated that, *"Two police officers were killed, there seems to be the impression that someone must pay the ultimate price,"* She also said, *"Tafaro is not the appropriate one to do this."* She mentioned how Rhodes got a deal because he was," *staring a death penalty in the face."* The felony murder rule as applied in Florida, and she went on to say," *I believe this is the kind of case where you must say, "Why is Jesse Tafero on death row? when Rhodes and Linder aren't, why is he under the death sentence."*

Now that's an easy question to answer, I know what me

and 100,000 other cops would answer.
            "BECAUSE THE SOB KILLED TWO COPS."

PORTHOLE BAR

It's the 4-23 AM shift. The weather is nice and none of the troops had any serious calls, just small domestics, maybe an accident and a larceny or two. The shift is about over and best of all, I start my vacation at 00:01 hours, that's 1 minute after midnight, A whole month away from cops and robbers and my troops, who I'll miss. The last thing I want to do is get involved in any crime or any incident.

All year long that's all I do is cover troops on their calls, answer some calls myself and I've even been called *"Mother Barton"* by some troops, but that's okay, that's my job, but vacation, well that's different. No booking someone into jail, filing charges the next day with the County Solicitors Office and I even had contacted them to advise them of my vacation and to reschedule any subpoenas or trials. I didn't want any, *"failure to appears"* against me, they drop the case if you don't appear. So far, it's strictly DGI (Don't Get Involved).

Well, I'm north bound on Military Trail on my way to the gas pump and as I pass the Porthole Bar, I can't help look at it as its only about 30 feet from the curb and highway, Military Trail, so you just can't miss it. The parking lot is on the north and south side of it, and you can park several in front of it, that's on the west side, or highway side, and there are 3 cars visible.

Now the Porthole Bar is a real red neck bar, and it could have been renamed the *"Ass Hole Bar"*. I recall some shootings and several stabbings and there are always fights, it's just that type of bar.

Well, I see this guy standing in front in the open, not even close to any of the parked cars and he's highly visible to any highway traffic, it's only 30 or so feet away. He's just starting to relief himself. Well, I swing into the north end of the parking lot and advise the dispatcher that I'd be 10-6 10-17, busy on an investigation at the Porthole Bar. I came to a stop on the south side of the bar after driving around behind it. I got out of my car and walked around to the front and the guy is still taking a leak.

Now when anyone checks out at a bar it's good police work and he's doing his job as high visibility in bars, so this keeps murder and mayhem to a minimum. A zone man tries to check the bars in his area as often as possible. It's also good for the zone man to swing by the bar, especially if the sergeant is checked out there.

Well, this time it was Paul Sheridan, he was a good buddy of mine who had made Detective just after I had made Road Sergeant Paul had heard me check out at the Porthole Bar and he was close, so he told the dispatcher that he'd be out with me. Now Paul and an ex- deputy named Roger Hunter go a long way back, as the 3 of us used to go around to troubled areas and de-trouble them, and we were known as," *Bendick's Bastards,"* because of our aggressive patrol tactics. Anyway, detectives on the sheriff's department all had new fast cars and what the department did was to pay $150 a month toward the payment and they also got their tires and maintenance at cost, so it was a good deal. Now Paul being a new detective had just gotten a new car and he was sure proud of it.

Well back to, *"El Leak. "Now just before Paul pulled up beside my car I had walked up to the front of the bar and to the guy who's feeling no pain and I say to him in a low and easy voice,* "come on buddy, why don't you finish behind a tree or a car or go behind the bar so that people can't see you from the highway." Well, he gives me this drunk and I'm bad look while he's stall holding his crank says, *"I'll finish pissing when I dam well, please"* so he continued. Well drunk or not, vacation or not, I wasn't going to take this shit, so I reach in my back pocket and took out my slapper. Now this is a long flat leather blackjack and it's weighted with lead, Texan, and I just tap him on the crank. Well, I got his undivided attention with that, and he lets out a big scream just as Paul walks up. Well with this guy screaming, the front door of the bar opens and outcome 12 to 15 patrons and they're all guys. I told El Leak to quit hollering that he was under arrest for DOC (Disorderly Conduct), and I tell him to put his crank away and I'm starting to push him toward my car. I got one hand cuff on him; Paul is helping me guide the guy who's still screaming toward my car. We finally got the guy's hands cuffed behind him, and we put him in my car. While we are doing this our backs are to the crowd when all of a sudden, we hear this loud crash and feel this wet stuff on us. Well, its beer. Someone in the crowd had thrown a bottle of beer at us and it hit Paul's new car on the roof right over the driver's door and when it hit, it smashed and put a big dent in the roof.

Now when Paul saw this, he lost about 26 cards out of his deck cause we had no way of knowing who threw the bottle, so he whips out is gun, turns and fires a round over the crowd's head, I hoped. All the while he's swearing and hollering at them. Well with that the crowd takes off running, either back inside the bar or into cars or trucks, some were in the rear, and leave. I thought Paul was going to cry he was so mad, and shit this is gonna spoil my vacation plans, at least for a couple of days. So anyway, I tell Paul who is still swearing," *let's get the hell outta here,"* I turned back to my car and though its dark I can't see any movement in the back seat. I open the left rear door and shit, my prisoners gone. I called the dispatcher and told her am okay and that I'd be out a while longer. I still didn't tell her what I had or what happened, a privilege a sergeant has or so I thought, anyway she acknowledged me.

Now a sergeant's car isn't equipped like the other patrol cars as it has its rear window and door cranks that are still attached and there's no cage separating the driver from the arrested subject, so it would be easy to get out of. A sergeant's car wasn't meant to transport prisoners. I told Paul to stay by the cars, his and mine, and I went back inside the bar thinking maybe someone slipped my prisoner inside through the back during all the excitement. The bars not that big so when I go in no one says anything. I checked the men's head, restroom, then I knocked on the ladies, no answer, so I went in. I then checked behind the bar and still no suspect. I went back outside with Paul. I'm standing by my car, and I tell Paul, *"Now this is a crock, I got a prisoner, and I don't even know his name and the bastard got my handcuffs on, now he's gone and I gotta put it on the air as a signal 6, prisoner escape, and start a dam man hunt. This is a hell of a way to start a vacation."* Paul was checking his new car and still swearing at the dent, so I was just about to grab my mike when I hear a loud, *"hey deputy, over here."* I looked up and off to the southeast of our cars about 150 feet away a door had opened, and a guy is standing in the light of the doorway. He waves to us to come on over. Well Paul and I lock up our cars, so they don't get vandalized. Now that's a laugh, and so we walked over to his house and the guy lets us in, and hell, there's our prisoner sitting on the couch, his hands still cuffed behind him. Man, I was so relieved, and I was SO glad I didn't have to put that out over the air. Well, the guy told us that the young fellow sitting on the couch was his son who had just run home after opening the car door. Even though he was drunk he told his dad what happened.

Well, the dad also heard the shot and when his son told him about the arrest the dad told his son," You *turn yourself in, I don't want you in any more trouble than you're already in."* We advised the father of the charge(s) against his son, DOC and escape, but being that he turned his boy in we wouldn't charge the escape, just DOC which was a misdemeanor.

Well Paul was so mad about his new car that he just upped and offered to book the guy into jail and to file criminal charges.

****

I left next morning for Cherokee, North Carolina, and vacation, right on schedule.

PUERTO RICAN MALE RECOVERY

Well, it was the 12 to 8 AM shift and it was about half over when the dispatcher came on the air with, *"Palm Beach to zone 2, the complaint desk just received a call from a hysterical female at the Lil General store at 45th and Military Trail. She's so hysterical that they can't determine the problem. It's a 10-17, investigation, for now, 213 you copy?"* I acknowledged with a 10-5, enroute, and hung up my radio. I figured she got raped or something out west of the Florida turnpike and just got dumped. I headed north on Military Trail and punched my car up to about 100 mph, hell at 4:00 AM there's no traffic anyway. I hear zone 2 go 10-97, arrived, with the female, zone 1 is still enroute and now I'm only 2 minutes away. Just before going 10-97, arrived, I tell the dispatcher to just tell the OD (Duty Detective) to be aware of the call.

Now back then the OD was detective sergeant, hell all detectives were titled detective sergeant, so it made for some great feelings for one of equal rank to give another detective an assignment or order. Thank God in police work there's never any personality conflict and one detective would gladly do what was ask or told by another detective

Anyway, the OD, for this night, was a Sergeant Ernie Di Now Big D, as he was called, had come to the sheriff's department from the city of Riviera Beach Police Department. He was just like me in that aspect as far as coming over. He had spent some time on the road and then he made detective in about 1 1/2 to 2 years. Now Dee was a good detective, but he had a tendency to fly off the handle real fast if things didn't go his way. I never had any conflicts with Dee as we just seemed to agree on any procedures at a crime scene, and we just agreed on how things should be done at a crime scene such as signal 5's, murders, etc. Now one of Dee's attributes was that he spoke Spanish, Cuban or Puerto Rican which in south Florida is the current language used in crime and corruption circles.

Well, now at the scene, zone 2 was having some results in calming the female down. It was determined that she was Puerto Rican, and she was also accompanied by a Puerto Rican male. We could smell the booze on both of them and finally got the story with Dee's interviewing the male in Spanish We found out that these two, plus another Puerto Rican male were off to the side of the next road west, Haverhill, along the canal. While they were drinking, and trying to make out, the one Puerto Rican male had stepped into the canal, and he didn't know how to swim. The male and female waited for a while thinking maybe he was just fooling around but after a 1/2 hour he didn't show up and they got scared. The female got hysterical, and the male couldn't speak English so he just stood there, and you could tell he was scared. I advised the dispatcher of a signal 26, drowning, and that we would be 10-12, have civilians in the car, and gave her a starting mileage because one was a female, and that we were 10-51, enroute, to a canal off Haverhill. She acknowledged and we took the two P/R's west on 45th street and at Haverhill Road we headed south about a 1/2 mile. Now we got there in about 3 or 4 minutes from where we had started. The canal was only about 1/2 mile south of 45th street so it wasn't far at all. Zone 2 advised his ending mileage because of a female, and I advised that we would be 10-6, busy, along the dirt road, beside a canal and to try and determine just were the missing P/R male had gone in. She acknowledged and asked if I wanted a diver to respond and I told her to just 10-23, wait.

Now we were out of the cars and walking the canal bank and by now the female had calmed down and was rational enough to help us. She pointed to a spot where their friend went into the canal, but we couldn't find any footprints, or any grass disturbed or any that was uprooted. Now Dee spoke Spanish to both the male and female and confirmed that this was the place their friend went in. I shined my flashlight on the water, and it was clear with just a little surface current as there was a spillway on the west side of Haverhill and we were about 200 feet on the east side. The canal was about 30 to 35 feet wide at this point and had just a few water hyacinths in it. I tell Dee that rather than call out a diver at 4 AM that I'd just run home and get my mask and fins and do it myself, hell I only lived one half mile away and besides trying to get a diver would be a lesson in futility. I believe at this time that I was the only diver on the department, now it isn't that no other deputies could dive, but it was because no one had submitted their names to dive for the department to be called out when a diver was needed, there was just me as I was gung-ho and it didn't bother me to dive in canals, lakes or ocean or whatever. Sometimes I dove by myself, a no, no, and other times I was able to get one of my friends to dive with me, but they never submitted their names for any dive duty as they weren't to chocked up about diving at 4 AM for some P/R. Anyway, I told Dee I'd dive by myself, and he agreed so I jumped in my patrol car and drove home, it only took 3 or 4 minutes.

At home my wife Claire got up and was all worried that something had happened as I had been known to come home at some odd hours with blood all over me or a torn uniform and had to change. Well, I told her to take it easy and explained the case to her while I took my uniform off and put on my cutoffs, Levi's, and put my flip-flops on and got my diving gear bag. Now before leaving home, I called the dispatcher by land line and told her I was home and that I would dive myself rather than try and get someone to go with me. It would have taken a good hour to an hour and a half just trying to get someone to go diving and to finally get to the canal. Well, she acknowledged and wished me good luck. I kissed my wife and ran out to the car. I must have looked great, a guy in cutoffs and flip-flops and no shirt getting into a marked green and white patrol car. I punched in and it didn't take 3 or 4 minutes to get back to the canal bank. I park my patrol car with the head lights shining out over the canal where the P/R was last seen. I got out and sat on the hood and put on my rubber boots and my fins. I strap my diving knife to my leg, jumped off the car, and walked backward about 15 feet to the water and got in. It was warm just like the night air.

Well, I was glad for that. I spit in my mask until it squeaked, rinsed it and put it on. I had a light in one hand, and I pushed off from the bank. I turned the light on under water, it was crystal clear, and visibility was as far as the light beam. Now the canal was only about 10 to 12 feet deep, and it had lots of grass and hyacinth. I saw some garfish and some brem swimming in and out of the light beam. Now I wasn't worried about alligators, but I did have some concern about water moccasins as any waves disturb them and they swim at you with their mouths open. They seem to be always in a nasty mood and will bite at anything and everything. Well, I swam no more than 20 feet when I saw the guy just sitting there on the bottom in about 10 feet of water, it was kind of eerie as he just kind of come into the light beam as I swam. He was in a sitting position with his legs spread out, his head hung down on his chest and both his arms where just straight out with the hands just hanging limp. His arms looked like they were suspended in mid- water. I could see some brem swim close by, they had lost their fear of this intruder as he hadn't made any moves in a while. I thought to myself, *"you poor bastard, just for a few drinks, a good time with you friends and maybe even get laid and now look at you."*

Well, I jack knifed down and grabbed him by the hair and started back up. A body has a neutral bouncy in the water and so he was no problem weight wise. When I got to the surface, I was no more than 15 feet from the bank where Dee, zones 1 and 2 stood by. I spit my snorkel out and had turned out my light and hollered to Dee that I had him and when the P/R female saw her friend dead and laying on the canal bank she went bananas again. Dee took her to his car and tried to comfort her. I told zone 2 that all he had to do was a supplemental report and that the detective would do the death report or face sheet. He gave me a big smile and an okay Sarge. He was glad to have been busy and not have to do much paperwork. I told him to go 10-8 just as soon as the OD was done with any need of assistance, namely just to standby for a funeral director to take the body to St. Mary's Hospital to be officially pronounced dead and then to be released back to the funeral director. I told zone 1 to go 10-8, got into my car and went home. I showered and put on my uniform and called the dispatcher for all my times for my log, she came back with everything I needed, and it only took 11 minutes from the time I called from home to advise her that I was going to do the diving until I got back to the canal and found the P/R male. Now I thought that was pretty good time.

****

Now the end of the shift and it's around 8 AM and I get a call at road patrol for me to 10-23, wait, for 200, captain. I saw him around 8:30 AM and he chewed me out first for diving by myself and second because I was the shift sergeant and night shift supervisor and should have called out a diver, we didn't have anybody anyway. I tried to explain that it only took 11 minutes from start to finish but all he could say in his rough voice, *"what if you had been needed by one of your troops during that time." "Shit, I could never please the man."*

RECOVERY 7-YEAR-OLD

The 3 to 11 PM shift and I was already in the squad room of the road patrol waiting for lineup. I had just started working in the south end of the county where all the migrant labor camps were. I was broken in by a deputy named Bob Bressimer, a big deputy who, during the regular season carried a 38-caliber revolver, but when the labor camps opened, he carried a 45-caliber long Colt.

I had come in early so that I could get some information on an aggravated assault I had worked 2 days prior from a Delray substation detective that had been following up on the case. Now the monitor was on in the squad room when I heard the dispatcher say, *"Palm Beach will be on 10-33 traffic,"* emergency. Then she immediately called, *"Palm Beach to Harbor Patrol, Palm Beach to Harbor Patrol, 10-21 call in reference to a signal 26,"* drowning.

The 10-33 meant there was to be no voice transmission unless it was of an emergency nature because an emergency call was about to be dispatched to the Harbor Patrol Unit, as he was out somewhere on the water and being that his radio wasn't strong enough to transmit so all he could do is monitor the dispatcher, so what he had to do was dock his boat somewhere and call the complaint desk by landline (phone(for the call.

The deputy on the Harbor Patrol was a fellow by the name of Larry Jobes and his job on the department consisted of traffic control on the waterways within Palm Beach County and which had many miles of inland waterways such as the inter coastal waterways, lakes ponds and lots of canals and even the counties part of the Atlantic Ocean. Now Jobes was the departments diver used in accidents involving drowning or any water related incidents like stolen property etc. Now even if the property or victim was within a city limit of the 30 some law enforcement agencies within the county, they would still call the Sheriff's department for driver assistance.

Now back in 1968 the radio system of the sheriff's department wasn't equipped with boosters throughout the county and so as a result the distance was so great from car to car that no one could listen to what one car had to say except the dispatcher, as the radios in the cars weren't strong enough to transmit. So, any information from one car to another was a 10-55, relayed through the dispatcher. However, even the dispatcher was unable to hear the Harbor Patrol unit when he was out on the water, so when the dispatcher went 10-33, and gave a signal 26 to the Harbor Patrol Unit, the only way she knew that the Harbor Patrol Unit got the message was if he broke the squelch on his radio although he didn't know at the time what the call was about. The only thing that he knew was that the message, or call, was for him, and that he had to dock his boat and call by a telephone to the complaint desk for his call.

Well, the dispatcher cleared 10-33 traffic and resumed normal radio traffic once again. The complaint desk at this time called road patrol by landline and informed the captain of the nature of the call that the Harbor Patrol Unit was getting, as this was the procedure in 1968. The captain had to be aware of the nature of any 10-33 calls, along with this everyone at road patrol would also know the nature of the emergency call and affirmative action could be started immediately, especially if it was a shooting or a robbery or any call involving violence. However, on a signal 26, drowning, that was dispatched to the

Harbor Patrol, so all the complaint desk had to relay to the captain was the location of the drowning.

I was still sitting in the squad room talking with a detective named Herbie Nichols who was from the Delray Beach Substation when the day shift sergeant came in and said, *"Barton, just the man I'm looking for. Jobes got a signal 26 up in North Palm Beach and he's going to need assistance to dive for a 7-year-old boy somewhere in the Erman River."* I said, *"but I'm ready to go on the road."* I had my uniform on and had just gotten information from Nichols on a probable labor camp to look for my suspect in the aggravated assault. I ask the sergeant, *"what about Murray and Chasteen, their divers."* He replied, *"Barton, they're Detectives and they ain't gonna do no diving, they're prima donnas and anyway the captain says for you to assist."*

Back at this time I was a new man on the department, and I never signed up to be a diver, but they all knew that I had gone through their dive school, I was on a different police department at the time. Besides I would never think of saying no to the captain, that would be like committing career suicide. Ok, but I thought those goddamn detectives dove one time up in Juno on a body recovery. Secretly I thought they were chicken and now, I was sure. They had gone through dive school and were divers.

Hell, with me gone our shift would be short a man for however long the diving detail took. My personal car was out in the parking lot, so I went out and got my SCUBA gear and came back to the squad

room. Now I always carried my own gear with me, the sheriff's department had diving gear, but I think Sergeants' Bishop and Haley had taken all the good tanks and regulators, masks, and fins, and all I could see was just junk, and I wouldn't trust using it one dam bit let alone in the ocean or canal or at any depth.

I knew that Jobes, from the Harbor Patrol, was on his way to road patrol to pick up some gear and me. I put my uniform on a hanger and locked up my gun and gun belt along with my shotgun in the trunk of my car. Put on my ole cut offs and an old skivvy shirt, rubber boots, put the rest of my gear in the doorway and was ready to go so we could leave right away. The guys from my shift started coming in, Bressimer, Goldstein, Randy Lee, and Sergeant Lennie Wilson. They saw that I was dressed for diving, so they knew that someone had to cover my zone 8 until I got back. (My zone was from Delray Road south to Broward County Line and just driving around the outer perimeter was a god 35 or 40 miles)

Anyway, the Harbor Patrol unit pulls up with Jobes. I get my diving gear and put it in his trunk, He's telling me its North Palm Beach and their police department has 7-year-old boy that's been under water now about 25 minutes, and that they have a patrolman 10-23, standing by, at the docks at the Camelot Motel which is right on U.S.#1.

Now I never dove with Jobes, so I don't know what kind of a diving partner he was or for that matter I didn't know anybody who had dove with him. Anyway, this would be the first body recovery since I had joined the sheriff's department. The only other time I dove with anyone from the sheriff's department was when we were in dive school, and I was still on the Police Department of Riviera Beach. A prominent attorney and his wife had gone down in their airplane off Juno Beach in a storm and I had assisted in the recovery of the airplane that went into the Atlantic Ocean. The only 2 divers from the sheriff's department were Murray and Chasteen.

Anyway, Jobes had all his diving gear in the car and all he had to get was a rig fitted to drag on the bottom in case for some reason we couldn't dive and had to drag for the body from a boat. Now it consisted of a piece of angle iron about 6 feet long attached in five spaced holes and hanging down was about 18 inches of chain, each chain had a large tine of hooks on it, but no barbs, it was a grapple. Now this was meant to be dragged behind a boat on the bottom. This is how they drag rivers, lakes, and the ocean for bodies.

It wasn't for me to question what we needed or didn't need. Not knowing Jobes I figured he knew what he was doing and had probably done it a lot of time. Anyway, I had my gear and I trusted it, so I wasn't concerned. Well, we started on Military Trail and headed north after calling the dispatcher by phone and advising her we were 10-51, enroute, to the signal 26. Now she would go to the intercity channel and advise North Palm Beach dispatcher that the sheriff's department divers were on the way, and she in turn would advise her troop that was standing by at the scene.

Now North Palm Beach is a good 15 miles from road patrol, and it was that time of day wherein traffic was heavy. Even speeding it still took a good 30 minutes to go 10-97 to arrive in the North Palm Beach area and advising our dispatcher at this same time that we were switching our radio over to intercity channel so that we could get directions from the North Palm Beach dispatcher just were to go.

Anyway, Jobes switches the radio over and we were advised to go north on US 1 to the Camelot Motel turn right and go down to the dock area, that a patrol car was standing by. We had no trouble finding it and besides Jobes knew where we should go. So, we went 10-97 & 10-6, arrived & busy. We were right on the east side of the North Palm Beach bridge called the Parker Bridge it's over the Ermine River which runs into the inter coastal waterway, which was about 200 yards away. Now from where we stood on the dock, the bridge was around 100 to 150 feet west.

The North Palm Beach patrolman told us that the boy and his mother were in the area between the dock and the bridge when the boy went swimming. He had just swum out about 25 to 30 feet, dove down and never came back up. No one else was in the immediate area at this time except an ambulance, dispatched by the North Palm Beach dispatcher and a few people standing on the dock. They were curious about a patrolman, an ambulance and 2 deputy sheriff's with SCUBA gear. Now none of these people seemed to be aware of the drowning that just took place. The victim's mother had already been removed from the scene by the North Palm Beach detective. The tide was still coming in and we were about 2 or 3 miles from Palm Beach Inlet. The water never gets crystal clear this far from the Inlet, just looking at it looked like the visibility was about 7 or so feet. That's not too bad, and in addition the current on the Ermine River wasn't swift, just easy going. The North Palm Beach officer said that as of now the boy had been underwater 1 1/2 hours. I ask Jobes if he wanted us to tie a line to both of us so that we were no more than 6 feet apart from each other, also if he had a search pattern he wanted to use, I guess my newness must have been obvious with all my questions and I suppose Jobes was wondering about my diving ability, anyway he said,*" no we'll just go in and look, if you find the boy just tap on your tank, I'll surface, and you do the same."* Well, that was okay with me, and I started putting my gear on.

Now the water was warm, so I didn't wear a wet suit, just my SCUBA tank with the regulator attached. I put it up over my head and on to my skivvy shirt. I used a skivvy shirt so that the webbing didn't rub me raw, then the weight belt, 2 pounds, and walked to the water's edge, put my fins on and secured my knife sheath to my leg, I spit in my mask and rubbed it and then rinsed it so it wouldn't fog up. Stood up and put on my gloves. I always wore a pair of cotton gloves that had rubber dots on them so as not to get cut on barnacles, coral or burned on any fire coral etc. Jobes was almost ready to dive at the same time. He came over to me, mouthpiece in hand and said, *"you swim east toward the mouth of the river where it empties into the inter coastal, and I'll swim west toward the Parker Bridge."* Now that sounded okay to me, so I put my mouthpiece in, checked my air, and started walking out into deeper water. When it was about 4 1/2 feet or so deep, I took a last look toward Jobes, but he was already underwater, and I could see his bubble trail on the surface.

I turned east, submerged, and headed in a northeast direction so as to get into deeper water and find a channel. The visibility was about 7 or so feet so it wasn't bad at all. I had been moving slowly and I guessed I was about 30 feet from shore when the bottom dropped off sharply and I was going down in the channel, so I just turned east and swam along the channel edge. I'll bet I didn't swim any more than 20 feet when I saw the boy, he was dressed in a white tee-shirt and dark swim trunks and looked as if he was reaching for the surface as both his arms were stretched up over his head. Now swimming up to him I had sunk below the edge of the channel so I could see the bottom and also ahead of me, also to my right side, or the shallow side.

In saltwater like the Ermine River where the visibility is somewhat limited, I wanted to be able to see any fish or whatever. I always got a lump in my throat when something went flashing by and it was as long as I was. As long as I could see it didn't bother me.

Now as I got up right next to the boy, I could see that he on tennis shoes and his right foot was stuck in the Y part of a submerged branch that had long been stuck in the sand and muck of the channel edge. *"Poor kid, I thought as I released his foot, a hell of a way to end your young life, if only you had known to sink down and move your foot it would have been so easy to release yourself."* I could just see him now at peace with the rays of the sun shining down on him with his outstretched arms and being able to see the surface just a few feet away. I could well imagine the terror he must have felt when he knew it was just a futile attempt to reach the surface and air. He probably thought something had grabbed him and he didn't have a mask, so he didn't look down and saw that it was just a branch, so he fought for the surface His outstretched hands where no more than 3 feet under the water.

I released his foot and held him in my left arm and with my right hand reached for my knife, reached behind me, and tapped on my SCUBA tank several times. I replaced the knife and started to swim shore ward with the boy. Now under water a body as no weight, neutral buoyancy, so there's no problem swimming. Almost immediately I was in water shallow enough to stand up in. When I did, I saw Jobes about 70 or 80 feet west of me standing also. He had heard my tapping on my tank. One thing about underwater noises or sounds, water is about 900 times as dense as the atmosphere so it's an ideal conductor for sound. Sound travels about 4500 feet per second so Jobes heard me right away. Anyway, he took off his tank, dropped his fins and hurried east to me. Now, I stayed in water about 3 feet deep and threw my mask and fins on shore. I picked up the boy in my arms and started out of the water. The boy didn't weigh any more than 50 or 60 pounds at most but Jobes got to me and took the boys legs, so I just held him under the arms, and we walked to shore where the ambulance crew had a stokes, a portable gurney, all ready at the parking lot edge.

I could see the North Palm Beach patrolman sitting in his patrol car and transmitting. He was telling his dispatcher that the boy's body had just been recovered and probably asking if he should go to the hospital for the body to formally be pronounced dead by a doctor or should he go directly to a funeral home. Now at this time when any death occurred, they were investigated by the sheriff's department only, regardless where in Palm Beach County they may have occurred. So, the body went to St. Mary's Hospital to be pronounced dead and to be investigated by our department's detective. The ambulance crew covered the boy up and put him in their rig and left. The North Palm Beach officer came over and thanked us for the assist and recovery and he left.

Finally took off my tank and gathered up all my diving gear and loaded it into the Harbor Patrol car. Jobes came over to me and said, *"that was a good recovery Barton, bet it didn't take 10 minutes underwater time."* I took a last look around for any gear left but there was none, then took a last look at the water, it was calm and peaceful as it was before, and no one would know that it just took, and gave up, a little 7-year-old boy.

Well back at road patrol we washed our diving gear off with fresh water and the captain says, *"ain't you working today,*

Barton," now not a word about a good job or about the recover. There was just an inference that I should hurry up, get dressed and into my zone. I found out several years later that he cared a lot about the diving details I did and just how dangerous they were, especially the body recoveries, but that was just his way.

"Yes Sir, just as soon as I put my gear away and my uniform on." Nothing was said about the boy's recovery except a small piece in the paper stating the drowning and recovery of a young boy in North Palm Beach.

Several days later my mailbox had a card in it, it was a thank you card from the mother and father of Joseph Sweat, thanking me for assisting in the time of need.

****

I still have their card.

RECOVERY LAKE OKEECHOBEE

The time was January 1969. I had been deputy sheriff for just over 2 years, and I was the only diver on the department. Now I knew other deputies that dove with scuba gear as well as free diving, but they did it for sport only and never volunteered for work dives for the department, such as for a body, evidence etc.

So as a result, I often got called at home when someone drown, or a diver was needed for some sort of recovery.

This time it was no different except it was the Belle Glade Substation a branch of the sheriff's department making the request. Now the BG substation is a part of the department that handles all of the sheriff's department functions but from 20 Mile Bend to the western border of Palm Beach County. This is all farming and cattle country plus a lot of sugar cane fields and the earth is black it's so rich, so it's good growing whatever.

The only time deputies from the east coast, Atlantic Ocean to 20 Mile Bend, go to BG is for riots, which BG had plenty of in the late 60's and early 70's, they were with migrant workers at different farms and packing houses. At this point I believe I'd been to BG 8 different times, 7 being on riot calls and the 8th was to meet a deputy at 20 Mile Bend to pick up a case of corn, BG had the best corn in the world.

Belle Glade requested a diver as on the previous night a young white male, 17 years old, had stolen a small plane from the BG airport and after flying around a while attempted to land at the BG airport, but now the circumstances were a little bit different than when he first took it. First off, it was dark when he tried to land, and the pilot/suspect by now had been ID, identified, and he had had only a few flying lessons, and besides, he never had made a nightlanding.

Now Belle Glade airport is nothing but a flat grassy field with dome lights, but it's got to be a little trickier than a regular airfield that has several landing strips and a lot more lighting.

Well anyway the lad and the plane never made it to the field as on his approach to the airport, and being out over Lake Okeechobee, he angled the plane too steep, and instead of landing on the field, he crashed into the lake. I don't know all the technical aspects of the flight, or what the kid did wrong other than to steal the plane and kill himself.

The complaint desk advised me by landline that the BG Harbor Patrol unit had located the downed aircraft from the seepage of oil and gas from the aircraft, but that the BG unit wasn't a diver and so the request. Well, it was about 0700, 7:00 AM, Sunday morning so I told our complaint desk that I'd be at road patrol in about 20-25 minutes, so I grabbed my wet suit and all my diving gear and headed to road patrol to meet with Sergeant Marks of our Harbor Patrol. Now Marks was our Harbor Patrol unit on the east coast but he also didn't dive because he had a busted ear drum. Marks was retired from the Army airborne, and he was a little bit older and had no desire to go on the road as a regular deputy. So, he hired on the department as a Harbor patrol deputy.

He was good with boats and people and that was a must. Palm Beach County had so much water within its boundaries that a full-time harbor patrol was more than justified. When you stopped power boats and yachts that might cost several million dollars for a wake or any traffic violation or just a warning, you better be diplomatic, and he was.

When I got to road patrol Sergeant Marks was also just

pulling into the parking lot and he had 2 civilians that I didn't know with him, and he tells me he contacted them when he heard about the diving detail. That both of them were certified divers and that they offered to dive along with me. Well, I was glad to hear that I wouldn't have to dive alone in Lake Okeechobee.

We got some extra scuba tanks that belonged to the department and also a converted streetlight that was now a sealed beam light with cables for surface supplied power. We all jumped into Mark's Harbor Patrol car and took off for Belle Glade.

Now it took approximately 3/4 to an hour to drive to Canal Point to meet with a BG deputy who was to direct us after we had switched to the BG channel, they were on a different radio channel. Well, the harbor BG harbor patrol deputy met us at the dock in Canal Point with about a 15-foot open hull boat belonging to the department. He told us that he had already been to the crash site on the lake and had left just to pick us up. The lake at the dock was flat calm and looked like sand colored mud, so that meant no visibility. The HP unit told us the site was about 1/2 hour away and that another boat was anchored to the plane. During the trip out to the plane we put on our wet suits, put regulators on tanks and tested them.

Like the man said, 1/2 hour out and there we were. We tied off to the boat already anchored to the plane and started putting on our scuba tanks. I told the 2 civilian divers that they would dive together in the buddy system, and I would go down myself but with the big underwater light. I would go down one side of the boat, port side, and they would go down the other side, starboard. The plane wasn't any problem to find because of the oil seepage and we could just follow the anchor line down.

Well after masks and fins were put on, I went over the port side, left side, and came right upholding on to the boat and adjusting my tank and weight belt and then took the big underwater light from Marks who had hooked it up to a 12-volt battery. The 2 civilian divers went over the starboard side of the boat and we three all met at the anchor line. I signaled and we all went under water. I turned the light downwards and turned it on and it almost blinded me. The sand-colored water reflected the light right back to me instead of penetrating the depth, so I turned it off and took it back to the boat, it was useless.

I started down again since the sun was out, I could see maybe 2 feet, now that's laying on the surface. Around 7 feet down the visibility was around 1 foot and then I saw some jagged metal, it was the plane. I don't know anything about planes but this one had thin aluminum skin and not canvas.

I swam on down to my left till I touched bottom, and I was only about 12 or 15 feet in depth. The plane was upside down, so I felt around real easy as on the bottom there was no visibility, and I didn't want to get cut like I did on another downed plane. I found the cockpit but couldn't find any handle for a door, it must be on the other side where the 2 civilians were. I found the anchor line and went up to the surface to see if the civilians had come up yet.

While I was there, they both surfaced, and they had the body with them. I swam around the boat and the 3 of us pushing, and Marks and the BG unit pulling, we got the body into the boat. We all climbed back onto the boat and took off our masks, fins, and tanks. That's when I got a good look at the body, hell, he was just a kid, and he was lying on his back on the bottom of the boat. He had his eyes open and his face, or what was left of it, was all tore up from his hitting the controls, he died with the look of. *"I'M ABOUT TO DIE".*

His eyes had the wide-eyed terror look of someone who was going to die and that's the way he died. I covered his face with a rag and told the 2 civilian divers that they did a good job.

The bottom of our small boat was all red from the water we brought in, from the 3 divers and the clothes on the victim plus his blood.

Now blood is not supposed to seep out of a dead body, but none of us living were cut. By the time we got back to the dock, everything on the deck was covered in red.

The Belle Glade Harbor Patrol Unit had advised his dispatcher of the recovery and so another deputy was standing by at the dock with a detective and a funeral home hearse, along with a news reporter.

Well, we docked and lifted the body out of the boat and put it on the dock. I was on the head end and the 2 civilians were on the feet end. We were all done as the B.G. units took charge, so we packed up all our bloody gear and headed east to the coast after thank you's from the BG, deputies and their dispatcher. I didn't think any more about it until the following Sunday when I bought the paper. There on the front page was a colored photograph of my big Ass in a wet suit. I was bending over putting the kid's body on the dock. The body was visible but not the face.

****

My one big moment of fame and they take a picture of the wrong end.

RIVERA BEACH RAPE

Well, it's the 4 to 12 shifts, I was working in the Able zones only. The department had grown and had 3 substations on the east coast, north was Able, central was Baker and south was Charlie. This night the north zones weren't particularly busy, well at least not in the Able zones. I couldn't say for the Baker and Charlie zones as they were on another radio channel, I didn't monitor their calls anymore and was sure enjoying not being as busy as when I had worked central, now I could kind of relax. Well around 10:00 PM the Able unit gets a call of a signal 35 a rape, and the victim is at Rivera Police Department. All this information comes out of the digital monitors in each and every car, and as it had already occurred, the victim was in no danger, and was now at the police department.

All calls of a routine nature are dispatched over digital computer and only calls of violence or a serious nature in progress are dispatched over the radio. I immediately tell the dispatcher via computer that I was 10-51, enroute to the Able units' call, and changed my status from 10-8 to 10-51. Now all this is done by computer, so no voice transmission takes place. I also tell their dispatcher via computer to call the north substation and to advise the duty detective of the nature of the call. She acknowledges me and while I'm still enroute she sends me a message that its 10-39, message delivered, and that detective Jerry King is the detective working and that he will monitor the call.

A few words about Rivera PD. It's were I first started in law enforcement back in 1964. It's a busy PD that at least had

50 to 60 percent black voting population. A typical shift was 3 white officers and 2 blacks for the west side of the railroad tracks, this was all black.

In addition, we also had a road sergeant. Now the present Chief of Police was black. He was the first black Chief of Police in the state of Florida and possibly on the eastern seaboard of the United States, so there was no question of any favoritism going on toward any black officer. But anyway, that's not my concern now. Even though Rivera PD has all good detectives they still turn over all felony calls to the sheriff's department, such as robberies, rapes, murders, and death investigations. From my years on the sheriff's department, I kind of got the impression that all departments were just lazy and mickey mouse for turning over these cases to another department. I always felt that most cops were proud and concerned about what happened in their city and wanted it handled in their city. Now all they had to do was get permission from the states attorney's office to conduct any felony investigations, but at this time in Florida they didn't.

Well, I arrived at the PD along with the Able unit at about the same time, punching in a 10-97, arrived, and a function 2 on the computer which put me in a busy status at the PD. Now we went inside. A black dispatcher advised us that the victim was in the back being interviewed by a patrolman. We walk to the back-interview room and there sits a black patrolman taking a report from a black victim. She is a very young female and she's giving the patrolman a report. She is quietly sobbing as she does this. The female has blood on both of her shoulders and her head is completely encased in a swami type bandage. The patrolman was very young and diligent and caring, so I figured I'd wait and not interfere even though the case was now the sheriff's departments.

Now in walks the Rivera PD shift Lt. and it's a Howard Conway, hell when I was a patrolman on Rivera PD, he was just an auxiliary officer who drove a bottled gas truck and now look at him, anyway I ask him what happened and why the sheriff's department wasn't notified sooner. He tells me that St. Mary's Hospital ER had called, and that the victim had told the ER. personnel that she had been raped in Rivera Beach, so they had called that city and the patrolman responded. He had brought the victim back to the PD. as they were finished with her. By that time the black patrolman was finished with his report so I told the Able unit to start getting his information for his report, at the same time telling him that it appeared that it would be handed over to a detective. I called one and knew that it would be King. I spoke briefly with the victim, a very scared female who related that she went to this man's house to clean, and he started attacking her and he raped her. She had tried to get away, so he smacked her with the flat side of an ax. He then hit her with a rake.

At this time, she got all hysterical and crying again so I had to calm her down so she could continue. She then advised that she finally made it to the front door and as she got it open, he hit her again on the head with a gun. She ended up getting 15 stitches in her scalp. I ask her if she knew the name and location of the black male who raped and assaulted her and she said, *"yeh,"* to both questions. We got the name and approximate age by checking Rivera's files and came up with an address that the girl gave us and found that our suspect had a history of violent assaults, and had an extensive rap sheet, criminal history. I then asked Conway if he could have one of his men just drive by the address. He called his sergeant and zone car to check it out. All I wanted was just an exact location and if any activity was going on like lights, people etc.

Now I didn't expect them to make any contact with the suspect, just to drive by. At this point the Able unit was wrapping up his report information so I called our dispatcher by land line and told her to have our shift Lt. meet us at the outskirts of Rivera Beach, and also have the Able detective meet us at the same 10-20, location, in about 15 minutes. She acknowledged and I hung up. I then told Conway my plans and ask him if he wanted to join me and my Lt. He affirmed and we all headed west of town for a 10-56, meeting, as we had stopped at a mini warehouse parking lot.

Now Rivera Beach is where the crime happened and was where the address was given but it was in the unincorporated area of the city, so it was in the county and not in the city of Rivera Beach itself. We were stopped no more than 5 minutes when up pulls Lt. Mathias, Jerry King, and Dave Mulberry. The last two being detectives, but Mulberry being a central detective. I introduced them to Lt. Conway and filled them in on the case so far. I also ask Mulberry what he was doing here as it was an Able case? He told me that nothing good had been happening in the central zones, so he was having coffee with the Lt., and when he heard the call, decided to come along. At this point Conway's sergeant pulls up. He came over and told us the house had only one light on and that he could hear music from the inside. The house was halfway down the block and no streetlights in the immediate vicinity and that we could drive fairly close to the residence without any lights on. Lt. Mathias ask what I wanted to do so I told him that we had a good rape case on a juvenile victim, an aggravated assault, and a weapons charge, and that we were going to arrest the black male suspect. He agreed so I ask Conway if he and his sergeant could cover the back of the house while we entered the front. He affirmed and so the Able unit, myself and Lt. Mathias, King and Mulberry from the SO. and Conway and his sergeant for a total of 6 men piled into 2 detective cars, securing all the others, and advising the dispatcher on computer where we were and what we were doing.

Now for armament the Able unit and the two detectives had shotguns and I carried a mini-14, 223-caliber, with a 30-round clip plus one of my ever-present federal CS gas grenades. I called them my Hallmark grenades, when you care enough to throw the very best. Beside all this we still had our side arms. We then drove with our lights out, stopping by stepping on the emergency brakes so as no break lights came on. We got to about 3 houses from the target house and all got out without a word or a noise. The two officers from Rivera Beach went right to the back of the house, Mulberry and Lt. Mathias got behind a tree in the yard, King got down and duck walked from the edge of the property to the front door. Now the front door opened into a Florida room. This is a room with lots of windows, the Florida room had 3 rows of jalousie windows that went from the ceiling down to about waist high. I just snuck up to the Florida room and was close to King. He tried the doorknob very slowly, but it was locked. King twisted and twisted and when nothing happened, sat down, and put his foot against the doorknob and pushed it sideways till it bent and broke.

Well, that didn't work to good, so I slung my mini 14 and found a foundation block in the yard and brought it over by the windows. Now this was an 8-inch cinder block weighing around 45 to 50 pounds. I stood and listened for a couple of minutes, and we could still hear the music coming from the inside and apparently the noise of the knob breaking didn't cause any alarm, so I picked up the block over my head and brought it down onto the windows breaking a whole row of them. I hurriedly unslung my mini and jumped into the house and opened the busted door from the inside but I don't wait for King to enter and so I ran into what was a kitchen and I saw a closed door; music was coming from the other side. I gave it a kick and it flew open, and I jumped aside hollering, *"the first thing out of that door better be two empty hands held high"*, well almost right away I hear, *"yes sir"*. Outcome two hands held high, and fingers spread. The hands are attached to two skinny arms that go with a scared black male who was almost ready to do something in his shorts. King comes in at this point and we handcuff the b/m, hands in the back and there's no need to frisk him for any weapons as has in his skivvies. Now the Lt., the Able unit, and Mulberry advise the prisoner of his Miranda rights. We found the ax and the rake standing in the corner of the Florida room by the door. In the bedroom on the bed, we find it all covered with the victim's blood, and on the dresser, we find a pellet gun that looks like a .45 caliber automatic. There's even still blood and hair on the barrel from where he pistols whipped her. The arrestee advised that he only wanted to have his house cleaned but he got a case of the hots and when she got scared, he became violent.

****

This incident happened in 1975/1976. I left the sheriff's department in October 1977 for a 3-year period returning in January 1982. Returning to the S, I had to start as a slick sleeve all over again. The department had grown and changed dramatically. Gerald King had since left the department I think to join a sheriff's department in Montana. Dave Mulberry also had left the department to successfully start a security business and also to become the Chief of Police in the city of Royal Palm Beach. Lt. Mathias retired and was now a patrolman/fireman in the seaside community known as Manalapan, a small Atlantic community where most of the residence probably were on the Forbes 400 list. He already had a retirement from the city of West Palm Beach as a police officer. He also had a retirement from the sheriff's department, and I guess working to become a triple dipper. Well, he deserved it. A finer man and law enforcement officer would be hard to find.

As far as my old alma mater Rivera Beach PD and the black police chief, Boone Dardin, who had the dubious honor of being the first black Police Chief in the state of Florida he also had the dubious honor of being the first Black Police chief to be indicted by a federal grand jury. The feds had set up a sting operation in the city of Rivera Beach and got some nice 8 x 10 glosses of him accepting about 4 grand in bribes.

The new chief of police in Rivera beach was a Ron Lentini who had been a patrolman with me back in 1964. Another Lt. from Rivera Beach was a Brunell Bruton who also had been a patrolman with me back in 1964, he was a big black guy, and he was sure good to have on your side in a fight. Well, it seems that now Lt. Bruton had run around for several years in a stolen car, he also was caught in a sting operation in the big city of Rivera by our department. The Police Chief, Boone Darden, suspended Bruton immediately but Bruton didn't go on trial for close to, or just over a year so the black Rivera Beach City Manager says that Bruton was a good man and needed a job so back in uniform goes Lt. Bruton to resume police duties. Well very shortly he went on trial, and it took the jury about as long as it took to secure the jury room chambers to convict Lt. Bruton of auto theft and the last I saw of Lt. Bruton he was a resident of our new jail complex.

Well, such is crime and corruption in the county. P.S. forgot to mention that's several years prior Burton had bought and gave a gun to his girlfriend and by some accidental quirk of fate, his wife died of a gunshot wound, now if that don't sound accidental then Castro ain't Cuban.

SANDALFOOT COVE B&E

This is another story about Sandalfoot Cove, I won't give another description as I had given one in another story. I will say it had lots of trailers and was out of the way, it bordered Broward County and they, likewise, had several trailer parks in the vicinity. Now, we had an individual who had B&E, (Breaking & Entering) trailers in both counties as they were out of the way and response time was very slow for both sheriff's departments, that's ours and Broward County so he knew he had more than ample time to commit his crime and escape. He was responsible for close to 300 B&Es. He had also vowed to never be taken alive. He carried a 45-caliber automatic.

Now Sandalfoot Cove is located on U.S. 441, or the Range Line. It's a 2-lane highway that runs north and south, and around the Cove. No other roads were present, at least not in PB County. At this time there was a Delray substation of the sheriff's department, and they handled all cases in the south county area. Now the Delray substation didn't have any uniform personal but it did have detectives and they were all good ones.

One of the detectives developed a stinger, a snitch, rat, informant, in regards to all the B&Es at Sandalfoot Cove, and the guy responsible was to hit a certain trailer on a certain date, so the detective called me as I was the sergeant and supervisor of all the uniform personal on this shift.

The detective asks me if I could assist him and some south end detectives on a signal 15, detail, and I agreed as long as we weren't busy, at the time he said that 2 troops would be enough. Well, I called the dispatcher and told her that myself and zone 8 would be assisting the 300 units, detectives, in the south end of the county later on in the evening and to try and give the calls to someone else if possible.

Well as I remember the shift was quiet and so myself and zone 8 went 10-6, signal 15, busy on a detail, and we met the detectives at a southern location, of course it was dark with no cars or people around. He outlined just what the detail was and ask if we could keep the uniform cars out of the immediate area but available when needed. He advised that all the detectives would be in the area of the trailer that was to be B&E as all their cars were different makes and colors and they looked just like *Joe Civilian*, cars except that they all had sheriff's department radios.

Myself and zone 8, a deputy named Allen Branich waited with our marked cars well away from Sandalfoot Cove and just off the Range Line highway. The detectives staked out the targeted trailer and we waited, how long I don't remember but lo and behold, here comes the suspect. As it was night, and dark and I wasn't right at the scene but I'm sure the suspect parked his car at, or close to, the trailer he was going to hit, B&E knowing that no one was home. I don't know if the detectives let him break in, anyway the suspect knew he was had so the chase to catch him was on. Apparently, the detectives weren't to close as the suspect made it to his car and after some wild and reckless driving made it out of Sandalfoot Cove and he chose to go north on the Range Line highway at a high speed with the detectives right behind him.

Now zone 8 and myself could hear all this as we had switched our radios to the detective channel so both me and zone 8 started south on the Range Line highway. The suspect and detectives were all north bound and speeding when a detective named Alvin Fuller pulled up beside the suspect while both are speeding and Fuller in his excitement and haste, raised a sawed-off 30-06 rifle that he carried and fired at the suspect's car, unfortunately Fuller didn't raise the rifle high enough and shot a hole right through his door, that's from the inside out, needless to say the door was nothing but scrap and he had a new car like all detectives.

The suspect was forced off the road at what's called, *"The Country Store,"* and as it was late the store was closed and none around. The suspect pulled up, jumped out of his car and started to run. We also were right behind him and after a short fight with us he was handcuffed by the detectives but with his hands in front. Now looking at the cuffed subject he had a small abrasion on his nose, and it was bleeding so after all was quieted down, the detective in charge asks me if I would take the subject to the nearest hospital as the jail wouldn't take any bleeding prisoners, so I agreed.

The subject was placed in my car. He was cuffed but my car had no screen or cage. The detectives were taking care or all the reports such as towing the subject's car, and all the paperwork such as the trailer and its owner.

Now I had the cuffed subject sit on the right side of the back seat and put a seat belt on him and I told him, *"I'm taking you to Bethesda ER, in Boynton Beach, the closest hospital."* Well at the hospital I took the subject out of my car in the parking lot of the ER and also took my shotgun, and told *"If they can't fix you here, nobody can,"* and with that I chambered a round into the chamber. Now the subject knew what I meant, and he said in a meek voice, *"What you want me to do Sarge."*

Well, I took him inside and the very first thing the ER doctor says is, *"take the cuffs off him so I can treat him,"* and I told the doctor, *"No way, we just had a high-speed chase and a fight with him and I'm not taking any cuffs off, and if he gets unruly, just get out of the way."* Now the Doc saw me sitting away from him and the prisoner and holding a shotgun, so he treated the prisoner and didn't say anything else. He treated the wound on his nose and the Doc didn't say anything at all to me.

Needless to say, I didn't have any problems with the prisoner, he had been treated and released from the ER. I booked him into the county jail for the detectives as I was just the transporting officer. When I went back outside to my car, I switched back to the uniform radio channel and found nothing pressing.

The next day Sheriff Harris received a phone call from the doctor who advised that he worked at Bethesda Hospital Emergency Room and that one of his deputies had brought a prisoner in, in handcuffs for treatment and he carried a shotgun and wouldn't take the cuffs off the prisoner and that he didn't appreciate the way the deputy handled the situation.

I don't know the outcome of that phone call, but I was never chastised or brought on the carpet either from the Sheriff or from my Captain.

****

All involved in that stake out and chase so long ago got a letter of commendation from the Sandalfoot Cove Association. I believe there were 7 involved in the apprehension.

Years later Detective Fuller left the department and went

to Martin County Sheriff's Department.

SANDALFOOT COVE SIGNAL 20

This is a story about Sandalfoot Cove and a little old lady who lived there, and no it's not about a lady who lived in a shoe, but a trailer and all alone. Now Sandalfoot Cove is a large trailer park in southern Palm Beach County. The trailer park is very large, and it has a section for people with young children, and another section for retirees and also a part for people who are older and don't want to have children in the area. Now the sheriff's department went to Sandalfoot Cove only on specific calls as it was out of the way. It was just north of the Broward County line and so far out of the way that there wasn't what you would call routine patrol in the park. So, if any calls came in for zone 8, which Sandalfoot Cove was in, that he would have to drive fast and far to get there in a decent response time.

The department did get calls with reference to domestics, fights, etc. and a car would respond. Now in the section that had seniors and older folks lived a nice old lady by herself that always had aliens or the FBI bombarding her with X-rays or else someone was on the roof of her trailer. So, she would call the department and a deputy would respond, usually zone 8, and he would satisfy her by checking the roof or clearing up any needless X-rays and knowing that she was a lonely, harmless old lady went through all the motions knowing she was signal 20, mentally unstable. Now she was never any problem to anyone, just wasn't completely right in the head. I myself had been to her house several times and I guess I was a regular respondent. I would check the roof for any one there, get rid of any brain waves or X-rays I found, she was just like a grandma, so I didn't mind the call. Now as I said I had been there several times and it was always the same type call except this one time

I responded to her residence. Well, I knocked on her door, like I always do, and announced myself as a deputy sheriff and the door finally opened. There stood grandma with a gun in her hand pointed at me. Well, I always figured I'd get shot on a call but never from a nice ole lady. I tried not to act to excited and just moved out of the way of the muzzle of the gun, knowing that it didn't take much pressure on the trigger to make it go *"Boom."*

Well after talking nice to her and getting out of the way of the gun, I took it off of her and ask, *"where did you get the gun?"* She replied sweetly, *"I got it today down in Deerfield Beach at a gun shop."* Now I had the gun and I told grandma I was taking it with me, she didn't protest or ask why so I wrote her a property receipt for her gun and told her that she could pick it up from our property room as it was going to be turned in. Hopefully the property room attendant could see that giving her a gun, even though she had a receipt, was not the proper thing to do and it would take a court order to get it released. I casually ask her who she had bought it from, and she gave me a business card that had all the information I needed. Well, I left the residence after checking the roof, glad that grandma didn't put a hole in me. Well, I turned in the gun the next day after explaining the case to the property clerk about the old lady and not to be conned as she was a nice old lady. I then called the gun shop in Deerfield Beach and was told that the gun was sold by a certain individual. So, I ask to speak to him. After waiting for several minutes, I got to talk to the clerk that sold her the gun and I find out he's a police officer from Deerfield Police Department and he just moonlights at the gun shop to make extra money. I couldn't believe him when he told me this. I ask him in talking to her, couldn't you see that she was a signal 20, so why did you sell her a gun? and he answered, *"She was a nice old woman and said she needed protection.”*

****

Now I was glad that grandma didn't put a hole in me and I could understand how she felt, but I couldn't get over the fact that a police officer sold her the gun to begin with.

SARI B.

This incident happened in 1960 when I was just a rookie cop in Riviera Beach. The shift was 3-11 PM and I had just received a call of a drowning. The victim was just a little girl, the call, a signal 26,drowning, had taken place in what is known as Palm Beach Isles. This is a series of homes that are all estates, they border on the inter coastal waterway and all have boat docks and the majority of people that live there have big boats, or yachts that they cruise the inter coastal or even go into the ocean with as the inlet is only a 1/4 mile away. Every home in the isle had a swimming pool. This is common in Florida.

Now Palm Beach Isles is also known as Singer Island to anyone familiar with Riviera Beach, Singer Island also contained a causeway which was a recreational area used by boaters and swimmers. It also had the town of Palm Beach Shores, and all this borders on Palm Beach Inlet on the south side, and the eastern border is the Atlantic Ocean. The whole of Palm Beach Isles is no more than 250 feet at most from the Atlantic. The call I received was of a child who had drowned in the family swimming pool. Of course, I acknowledged it advising that I was enroute. On arrival at the correct address, 10-97, I found a big spacious home and when I knocked on the door and was let in, I entered a big courtyard by a beautiful Asian woman who was sobbing uncontrollably. The courtyard had all kinds of tropical plants and just off this courtyard was an area that had what I believe was a kidney shaped swimming pool. Lying next to the pool was a wet lifeless little girl and a young boy frantically trying to resuscitate her, but from what I could see his efforts were futile, as the little girl didn't respond by coughing or breathing and didn't show any signs of life. When the boy saw me, he immediately moved out of the way as I hurriedly knelt down and started CPR. That's 5&2, five chest compression's and two breaths, sealing her nose off.

I continued CPR for God knows how long but to no avail, I got no response at all from the girl, she was dead. I told the woman who was standing by as I performed CPR that I needed to call my dispatcher and I went with her and the young lad into the house. I called our dispatcher and told that we did in fact have a signal 7 due to drowning. She in turn notified the sheriff's department as at that time all cities were not allowed to investigate deaths within their city or bailiwick, and they were handled strictly by the SO (Sheriff's Office).

At this time doctors still made house calls as one showed up and he was identified as the family doctor, and someone had called him while I was busy. Well with a doctor in attendance and a sheriff's detective just arriving I secured and TOT, (Turned Over To) to him and the Doctor after getting the victim's name, and the names of all involved in this tragedy.

The poor little girls name was Sari Kasin Benoit, and she was only 2 years old, she had been pulled from the bottom of the pool by her 14-year-old brother who tried in vain to resuscitate her. The beautiful hysterical woman was Sari's mother, who was Hawaiian. Her husband, who was not present at the time was the president of the Permatex Co.

****

Years later the state of Florida passed a law that was called, "ATTRACTIVE NUISANCE", law making it a criminal offense to have a swimming pool or anything else that was attractive to kids where they might get hurt or killed, meaning the attraction had to be fenced in or secured in some manor so that kids couldn't just get in. I still see little Sari lying beside the swimming pool and wonder if my CPR attempt was good enough. Every man who has ever worked on his car to replace a water pump or timing chain knows just what Permatex is, it's a putty like substance used to make gaskets.

I never me Sari's dad but my heart went out to him as I had a daughter, just a bit younger than Sari and I can't imagine how I'd feel to lose her in such a senseless accident. I taught my daughter Heidi, to swim right away.

SECOND CHANCE THE VEST

The time was back in the early 70's, and police body armor wasn't that well known about or at least thought of by most police officers, or for that matter, deputy sheriff's. I think at the time very few law enforcement officers had a vest, and if they did, chances are they bought it themselves because the departments weren't furnishing them.

I think it was a company called, Second Chance Body Armor, that at the time, advertised a vest, what type of bullet(s) it would stop and from how many feet away, also what type of gun and barrel length was used.

They put out a very impressive brochure in color, it had pictures of police officers who had been shot while wearing one of their vests, and it showed in graphic detail the large ugly black and blue marks where a slug had hit them. Instead of killing them or wounding them it left what they termed as, Traumatic Shock, and it looked like the cure was far worse than the cause, but also proof positive was that the police officer, though hit with a bullet, was able to return fire and neutralize, kill, his assailant and in some cases, assailants.

Now as a reward for being shot while wearing one of their vests in the line of duty, the Second Chance Vest Company awarded the officer with a brand-new model 29, that's a Smith & Wesson, 44 magnum revolver, in his choice of barrel lengths.

The 44 magnum was just like the one that inspector Harry Calahan of Dirty Harry fame, or infamy used, as he was the rage at the time, me, I'm for fame.

Besides that, they also had various awards that depended on the degree of, neutralization, of three assailants.

You know, like the assailant was made a basket case, you might get 2 boxes of your favorite ammunition, or possibly some leather gear or something related to your job as a police officer.

Well, it wasn't too long after that, the ACLU, (American Civil Liberties Union) had the prize distribution of the Second Chance Armor Company declared unconstitutional for awarding a prize of a model 29 for, total neutralization. So, they just dropped the model 29 but continued with the other prize that they offered.

Now I really liked the model 29 as the ultimate crime crusher because inspector Calahan already proved that it worked and besides I liked the vest. It was made up of 16 layers of Kevlar.

Kevlar was a nylon type of material and the vest fit over your head. It had a strap resting on each shoulder and it protected your vital organs, front and back from any lethal shots and it came down to your waist. Now it came in 2 sizes, small, which was 12 by 14 inch, and large, which was 12 by 16 inch. It left your sides exposed, at least mine did, 3 or 4 inches, but hell you figured if you were going to get shot it would either be from the front or the rear. It came with two elastic straps, each about 2 inches wide and had Velcro to secure it around your body. These straps fit through loops on the panels so that the elastic would stay in place. Another feature was that it was supposed to withstand a knife attack, but I don't think it would withstand an ice pick. I would never let anyone with an ice pick get that close.

Well, it sure looked good to me, and I wanted one, but like always, and like most young cops I never had the money at one time to be able to get one until good old uncle Sam refunded me some of my hard-earned kopecks that I had overpaid on my income tax return.

I finally convinced my spouse, Claire, of all the good points of the vest and how it would stop a bullet and how I would almost be invincible and to hear me you might think that I would be able to leap tall buildings in a single bound, in the not-too-distant future. Anyway, Claire saw that it was a good investment for me and besides we had all the money at one time. She relented so I ordered a 12 by 16-inch size vest. Now it took about 6 weeks to get, but oh boy, I was just like a kid with a new toy when it finally came.

I hurriedly took it out of the padded envelope, and it came with another brochure of its merits and prizes offered, they still offered the model 29 at this time. I hurriedly put the two elastic bands in place and put it excitedly over my head and secured the Velcro straps and proudly modeled it for her.

Now you talk about invincible, hell in my mind I was already thinking, *"do I want a 4- or 6-inch barrel, or a blue or chrome model 29,"* I punched myself in the ribs and boy, the vest felt solid as a rock. The vest weighed 4 pounds and I read the brochure all over again. Now I wanted to show Claire just what a good investment we made with our $80 and besides it was tax deductible as a work-related item. I called her into the living room and told her to hit me in the gut as hard as she could and she laughed and said, *"you're silly."* Now my wife is not one for physical contact, and she don't like violence. So, I plead with her, and she can see that I'm sincere as I want to prove a point about the vest, and she says okay. She hauls off and hits me as hard as she can in the gut before I expected it or could brace myself for the blow and down, I go to my knees, wheezing like a pole axed steer. It hurt so bad I couldn't even breath.

Now she laughed so hard as she thought I was joking but hell, it hurt and now she sees that it's no act on my part, so she gets down on her knees and is concerned now. I finally tell her that I'm okay, that's cause I can breathe now, and the only thing that hurt was my pride. I'm sure glad my troops didn't see ole 213, my ID number, on his knees. Well, I wore the vest one time and then took it off and put it in the closet cause 4 pounds was to uncomfortable to wear for 8 hours, as it was so hot and heavy. As the years went by, better vests appeared offering better protection and a lot of police officers wear them religiously. Some departments even furnish them to their troops.

****

As for the model 29, I bought one 6 months later for $195, police price from, Jones Supply, in Fort Lauderdale. This is before Jones declared that the model 29's are not a police weapon and stopped selling them to police officers at their special price.

I had the vest all these years packed away, the only thing it stopped was my wife's punch.

SEMINOLE MANOR

I had been on the sheriff's department about two years and at the time I was the only deputy that did any diving for the department. Now it's not that no one knew how to dive, it's just that no one wanted to volunteer for it as you didn't get paid extra for it, nor got any compensatory time off and really, not even an atta- boy. Something that's kind of recognition for a job well done. Anyway, I liked to dive and so I volunteered when the need for a diver arose. In the two years I had been on the department I had already recovered several bodies, cars, plus numerous pieces of evidence. Anyway, we had a series of armed robberies in the county and the detective(s) working the case(s) developed a lead, I guess, through a CI (Confidential Informant) that a 12-gauge shotgun and a 45 automatic, used in these particular robberies had been thrown into a pond bordering a sewer plant in a development known as Seminole Manor, a housing development, in Lantana Florida. The detective in charge of the investigation was a Richard Sheets, a detective sergeant, and he needed to recover those weapons. He didn't have a diver. Now detectives don't dive for the department but depend on the road deputies or uniform personnel to do the job for them, it's still only on a volunteer basis. Well Sergeant Sheets ask the road supervisor, uniform Sergeant Bendick if he had a diver available, and if he could spare him? I just happened to be on Bendick's shift at the time. Well Bendick came to me and tells me what Sheets has, what he wants, and what he needs, and if I would dive for him? Well now I'm not a big fan of Richard Sheets and I tell Bendick how I feel and also knowing that Bendick don't like Sheets also, but that it might be important to Bendick, so I tell him OKAY, I'll dive but only because you ask me. Well it was dark when I got to Seminole Manor, and I already had my wet suit and scuba gear. At that time the sheriff's department had hand-me-down scuba gear and to tell you the truth, I didn't trust their gear and so I carried my own scuba gear, carrying it daily in my personal car to whatever patrol car I was assigned to.

Well anyway the pond is connected to the sewage plant and as best that I can recall it's about an acre square. Well, all I got to go on is that the guns are in there some were and with no location to go on, *"they're just in the pond"*. Well I put on my booties and fins, my tank and mask and just start to walk into the pond. Now the sewage has been treated one time and so it didn't stink much. I believe it was a settling pond. I didn't go under the surface and just kind of walked out and found the depth of the water about 5 feet deep in average and so I walked back to shore and took off my tank and removed my fins and went back into the water and walked the whole area as best I could for about 2 hours trying to feel with my feet for the two guns. I could feel lots of slimy stuff that my booties just slide over and off, also lots of hard objects that I tried to pick up with my feet, I really tried to keep my head and mouth above water, but I wasn't able several times and so when I did go under water, I just kept talking to my self-saying that *"I wasn't there but some were different than were I was and in different kind of water"*. Well after about two hours and no guns I wadded into shore, you might think that all I found was crap.

Well the dive was called off and I secured. Now the county nurse knew that I dove for the department and also the kind of water that I had to dive in sometimes and so she gave me a quart bottle of Physohex liquid soap, now banned. Well I got home and right into the shower, wet suit and all my gear, that's mask, fins and booties and tank with regulator still on it. I spent close to three hours scrubbing myself with special attention to body cavities and all of my gear. Surprising I didn't catch anything, this time anyway, but I did say to myself while in the shower, *"canals, ocean, rivers, lakes, okay, but never again no crap creeks or ponds."* Well about three days later I get another request to dive for the same guns in a canal that runs parallel to the Florida Parkway or Sunshine State Parkway on its west side. Detective Sergeant Sheets had his CI confidential informant working again. Now this time I had a guy named Murphy who agreed to go and dive with me. Murphy just joined the sheriff's department and had come over from West Palm Beach P.D. He had about seven years' experience at the time. Well it was mid-afternoon, bright and sunny so Sheets goes along with us. It was really hot and so I was anxious to get started as I had a wet suit on and wanted to get into the water. Well we get to the Florida turnpike and the canal is on the west side on the pike and would be on your right as you head toward Miami.

Now where Sheets stopped us, the canal is about 25 to 35 feet wide, and all covered over with hyacinths. The canal is completely covered over with plant life, bank to bank. I took one look and could just picture water moccasins all over the place and it even looked good for an alligator. Well even though it was hot as hell, we had our wet suits on because of creatures, snakes, and things in the water. We put on our tanks and gear and went into the water and lo, it was crystal clear water and about four feet deep, bank to bank. We spent over an hour swimming back and forth but no guns, snakes, or gaiters, just a couple of gar fish. The dive was called off and we secured.

****

I never did recover the guns, but two days later Sheets' CI finally gave him the right location. They were right were we had dove on the turnpike but were dug up under the mile post marker on the median strip between north and south bound traffic and not in any water at all, that's another dive I did with no atta-boy. Here's to CI's and the games they play.

SHOOT THE TOILET

I had been on the sheriff's department just a few months and the time was in later 1967, I was on the 3-11 PM shift. Dick Hall was my sergeant, and after giving out the BOLOs (Be on the Lookout) and the zone assignments, I got zone 2, West gate area. I was the rookie, so I always got Zone 2. Hall advised that vice was going to have a raid after our shift was over and they needed some uniform volunteers to go along and so I told him that I'd go, this was the first raid I was ever on, several troops also volunteered, so it was all set at least uniform wise anyway.

Well, strangely enough, Zone 2 was kind of quiet and I was able to keep up with my reports as I got the calls, usually I would just go from call to call and then have to stay at road patrol until 3 or 4 in the morning, but I was new, a rookie, and gung-ho, and I didn't mind because it went with the territory. That's why I always got Zone 2 cause no one else wanted it and I WAS the rookie.

Well, the shift got in after gassing the patrol cars and I turned in all my paperwork, several citations, several no nothing reports, my trip sheets and I'm done. Now we just sat around and shot the breeze with the night shift sergeant who happened to be Bendick, when it comes Grady Lisk, he's the senior vice agent, then comes in Ed Mann, another vice agent and he's known as pretty boy.

Now Grady goes to the blackboard and draws a schematic of the target of the raid, it's in Riviera Beach, where I first started in law enforcement, it's in a black section of town, west side of town, and it's on First Street about halfway up the block. It's a single story, four-unit apartment complex. The target apartment they wanted to hit was apartment number 2. Lisk made sure that everyone knew that it was the second apartment from the east end and that the second apartment from after west end was apartment number three.

Now there was a total of seven men going on the raid. Three vice units and four uniform. List also advises that all the agents would be going in the front door, and they would take two uniform deputies with them through the front door for a total of five in the front door. Now there wasn't any back door, but he wanted two deputies in back stating, *"that the bathroom was in back and when he kicked in the front door, a deputy was to break the bathroom window and shoot the toilet bowl with a slug, this was so no evidence got flushed down the toilet drain."*

Wellbeing that I was a rookie on the department and raid, I was given the detail in back. Agent Lisk was taking the senior deputies in the front with him. Everyone knew their positions and the game plan, so we all go outside and pile into two patrol cars and two vice cars. The agents already knew that three arrests would be made if all went according to the stinger, source, so that was another reason for the two patrol cars, so that they could transport prisoners.

Well by now its 1:00 AM and we head north from the south side of Palm Beach Airport towards Riviera Beach. We had about seven or so miles to go, we went to 45th street and then east to Old Dixie Highway and north again. Riviera beach was only a mile or so north on Old Dixie Highway. We had past St. Mary's Hospital on a hill to our left and the FEC, railroad tracks, on our right. Riviera city limits where just ahead and the first street was First Street. The street was all quiet and had no lights on in any residence at this time in the morning. We parked at the beginning of the block and started to walk softly west towards the apartment. Now there were no houses on the south side and all residences and apartments where on the north side. The south side was all a field with some scattered trees and sand, as it was still land belonging to St. Mary's Hospital.

The fourth unit was visible even though it was dark, I had my flashlight in my back pocket, my side arm, and I carried a 12-gauge Ithaca riot shotgun, and it was loaded with four deer slugs. The only portable radio we had for the whole group was a walkie talkie and the Senior Vice Agent Grady Lisk carried it. It was already determined that we in back would hear them kick in the front door and that's when I was supposed to bust the bathroom window and shoot the toilet. Anyway, back in 1967 walkie talkies, or portable radios, were not in abundance on the sheriff's department.

Well, I went to the rear of the apartment along with another deputy and Vice Agent Mann, now Mann had visions of himself as Adonis, a Greek God, and I won't say anymore. He came to the rear with us and pointed out the window. I was supposed to break and then shoot. Now it was a frosted window and up about seven feet or so, so I got a garbage can to stand on. When I got into position, agent Mann left us to go to the front. Well, there I stood, on a metal garbage can holding a 12-gauge shotgun right up close to the window and hoping I didn't fall off when the raid started, with the other deputy standing there in a semi-crouched position. I had already jacked a round into the chamber and had my finger on the safety and easy to release it while I was breaking the window.

Well, I hear a big commotion in the front, and I start to stand up straight and am ready to punch the barrel of the shotgun through the window when I hear a shout, *"Barton don't!"*

so I stop and look. The agents are inside, and a light is on, but they're in the next apartment to my east and it's defiantly NOT the apartment, I'm scooped out on. Now I stay on the garbage can and Mann comes running back to me and saying, *" shit, I put you on the wrong window, that's apartment number three's bathroom where you are, and we hit apartment number two."*

Well, I got down and thinking, *" Mann you dumb shit,"* anyway we all walk to the front door with the agents and the deputies inside, and just then the door to apartment number three opens and this little old black lady comes out and wants to know what all the commotion is about. Agent Mann tells her it's the sheriff's department, that all is okay and to go back into her apartment. Now the agents, Herron, were busy inventorying narcotics that was seized as evidence, and they also had three 10-15's. prisoners. Well, at least they got that right.

****

I thought to myself, that would just have been great for me and the sheriff's department if I'd have broken that ladies window and shot her toilet to pieces. Well, it all ended okay anyway.

SIGNAL 4 ACCIDENT, GAS TRUCK

The shift was a 12-8 AM tour. I was the sergeant and nothing much had happened so far; all was quiet, and we still had about 3 to 31/2 hours left till shift change. I happened to be in the south end of the county as that's where most of the labor camps were and I always liked working with migrants and labor camps. It was early in the morning and was still dark. Not much had happened so far this night.

The dispatcher would do hourly checks on the troops to check on their wellbeing. A D/S Mahay was working zone 8, the southernmost zone, when the dispatcher came on the air with, *"Palm Beach will be on 10-33 traffic,"* emergency traffic only. She then calls zone 8, signal 4, accident, on State Road 7, south of Boca Road, that's Boca Raton Road, unknown injuries. Now State Road 7, or U.S. 441 is a major 2 lane highway that runs north and south through the county. It's all rural country and being that it is a major highway it is well kept, or maintained, but it is far out in the western part of the county, so it's used very little, especially at this time of the morning. So, traffic is very light or hardly any at all. I know it runs the entire length of the county, but I don't know how far south it goes. Only that it goes into Broward County. Well zone 8 responds that he is enroute code 3, that's blue lights & siren. I also advise that I'm enroute with blue lights and siren.

On our arrival at the scene the first thing we do is park in a safe manor out of the way of any traffic that might come along, and we do leave our blue lights on. Now what we have is a tractor-trailer, in this case it was a gasoline tractor-trailer, and we found out that he had just gassed his tractor at Port

Everglades in Broward County with 7,400 gallons of gasoline. He was north bound on State Road 7, State Road 7is a rural highway and no traffic at this time in the morning. He had to be doing 70 MPH and the impact was so great that there was no sign that he even attempted to brake his truck when he saw, and soon hit, a 4-bedroom house just sitting in the middle of the highway. The driver, nor anyone else, could ever imagine a house, big house, just sitting in the middle of the road, but this morning there was one and he paid dearly for it.

Well about the house. Now there was a company that's specialty was moving large objects. In this case it was a large house, from point A to point B. What they would do is to jack up whatever the object was to be moved off of its foundation, block it up securely with heavy wooden timbers, and of course the timbers were all mounted on heavy duty tires. After securing all the necessary permits to move such an object through towns, counties, and roads, they would wrap what is called *"Christmas tree lights"* around the object they were moving. Now Christmas tree lights were just bare light bulbs around the object and were plainly visible on the 4-bedroom house, as they were on at impact.

These objects that were moved travel very slowly and never over 3 or 4 miles per hour if even that. It was required by law that when such objects were moved that they had to have a motorcycle escort, so the company doing the moving hired off duty m/c police officers, and their job was to go ahead of the object moving and warn oncoming traffic, block intersections etc. Now the house, all jacked up and lit up, was just sitting still on State Road 7 as the moving crew had stopped to take a break, and besides there was no traffic at all. The house had also come up from Broward County and was north bound, the same as the gas truck, he also was north bound as having just filled up at Port Everglades. Well, the truck hit the 4-bedroom house so hard that he blew out 64 of the 66 heavy duty tires that supported it. The impact was so hard and violent that the big diesel engine of the truck went through the 2 front windshields and the driver never had a chance, he was dead. The tractor ended up at an odd angle, and all that gas stayed in the tanks and not a drop leaked out as far as we could determine. It was a mess, a big mess, but fortunately there was no traffic to contend with. There were no injuries as the only one injured was dead and to tell you the truth there wasn't much left of him so we didn't even need an ambulance

Well, the next thing that I had zone 8 do was to put flares out but well away from the crash site. Now the wreck was south of Boca Raton Road and north of a place called Sandalfoot Cove, so we had to block off State Road 7 at Boca Road for south bound traffic to turn east on that road. I had the dispatcher call Boca Raton Police Department, the Highway Patrol, FHP and Broward sheriff's department that we were blocking off State Road 7. That we just had a bad accident, and the road would be closed for some time. I also told her that a gas truck was involved and that any responding fire departments bring plenty of foam because if that gas truck blew up, we would really have a fiery mess and we would really need lots of foam and not water. I told her that we didn't need any ambulance and it would take some time to get what was left of the driver out of the rig, especially if it blew up. We were fortunate that the accident occurred on State Road #7 and in a rural area that had very few homes and none in the immediate area. There was a store, but it was in no danger. The house hit, was a 4-bedroom, one story CBS block covered with stucco and was all cracked up and almost all of the heavy-duty tires were blown out on impact. I then helped zone 8 get all his witness statements from the moving crew for his accident report and also helped with measurements etc.

Our night shift was coming to an end by this time, so I told the dispatcher to advise the oncoming day shift of the bad accident, and they came and relieved me and zone 8 at the scene. By some miracle the gas truck never blew up. I was advised the next day that due to the mess of the house, all the flat tires, the gas truck and trailer, and a dead driver, the road was closed down for 18 hours before normal traffic could resume.

****

Several years later, Mahay and myself appeared in federal court in Miami to testify in a civil suit about the accident. Neither of us stayed in Miami to find out the result but you can bet it was a big, big, civil suit.

Dennis Mahay made detective and he later left our department to become Chief of Police in the village of Royal Palm Beach, he also had a successful security company.

SIGNAL 20, UNSTABLE PERSON LAWRENCE ROAD

I was working the 12 to 8 AM shift and the time was early 70's. I was the shift sergeant and Begley was the shift Lt. I just had gotten the troops on the road and me and Begley were just finishing up our nightly pie and coffee at the Ranch House Restaurant when Begley's walkie talkie speaks up, Palm Beach to zone 7, report of a signal 20 a mentally disturbed person in the canal behind the orange grove store and packing house on Lawrence Road, *"do you read 204 and 213?"* Now she says all this in one breath knowing where me and Begley were and making sure we know the nature of the call. Zone 7 acknowledged her with a 10-4, 10-51. I knew the call and was enroute. Now Begley advises by walkie talkie that both he and I are also enroute. Zone 8 and the cover car are also responding. Well, me and Begley have separate cars, his not having any light bar on the roof, so he gets behind my car and I put on the blue lights and away we go south bound and, in a hurry, as we got 7 or 8 miles to go. I advised zone 7 to just 10-23, wait for me and the Lt. before he took any action or got involved. At 90-100 MPH it don't take long to get from point A to point B especially since this time of the early morning there's no traffic. So, me and Begley go 10-97, we arrived and right behind is zone 8 and the cover car. Zone 7 has been 10-97, it had arrived just a few minutes before. Now Lawrence Road is a 2-lane road and is a secondary road and has no traffic at this time and it's kind of in the boondocks or woods as it just has orange groves and a packing house and somewhat of a tourist store. Now naturally the store was closed at this time, and no one was around the store or parking lot. At first it looked like a prank call as there was nothing going on when all of a sudden, we hear this commotion going on from the direction of the canal about 50 or 60 feet to the north of the store and our location.

We stopped to listen and again, all was quiet, and then we hear this God-awful whoosh noise coming from the canal area. At first it sounded like a manatee breathing. Well, we all walk over to the canal and walk east along the bank, and we find a leather belt and a sleeping bag just lying under a tree. Now the canal is only about 10 or 12 feet wide and its completely covered with water hyacinth so that you can hardly see the water. The night is not really dark so you can see fairly well. At first all looked quiet and serene when all of a sudden up from the canal, and all covered with hyacinth, jumps this guy and he gives a big whoosh, takes a big breath and goes back underwater and starts swimming. Boy what a squirrel we got; it scared the hell outta all of us as we stood on the bank. Hell, he was just like the creature from the *Black Lagoon*, but this was no movie. Well, the guy came up for air again and we ask him to come out of the water, but he just took a breath and went right back under. He was easy to follow cause you could see the hyacinth and algae moving. Now this kept up for a good 15 to 20 minutes so we figured we would just wait him out and that he would get tired and just come out on his own. It looked like he wasn't tiring as we thought and that he was going to make a night of it and I wasn't about to stand around all night and watch this squirrel swim. Now it just so happened that there was a big pile of green coconuts stacked close by. I guess the tourist stand was letting them ripen before they shucked them and sold them to the tourists.

Well Begley got the idea just as I did and so we both picked one up. Now coconuts you buy in a store are small and full of milk and maybe weigh 2 pounds at the most. Green coconuts in the shell got to weigh 15-18 pounds. We never had any intention of hitting or even hurting this guy, we just wanted him to stop so we could find out his problem. Well, we started bombing the canal in front and back as he swam, and after a bomb run of 5 or 6 coconuts he comes up for air and shouts, *"you dirty m/fer's, you make me go to Vietnam and kill for you and now you do this to me."* He then breaths and goes back underwater. I can't understand how he can keep this up for so long without getting tired, his endurance was tremendous or else he had to be really high on something. I tell Bendick that I'm going in after him, because I'm not standing all night on the canal bank with a crazy, and besides we got at least 5 troops tied up on this call and I wasn't going to ask anyone of them to go in the canal, he said OKAY. I take off my hat and put it on the hood of the nearest patrol car along with my gun belt and my keepers, also my wallet and the last item was my boots. All this time Neptune is still making it in the canal, and he still showed no signs of slowing down.

Well I get right on the edge of the canal bank and wait for aqua man to surface close to the bank, Begley throws another coconut and up he comes with another, *"you motherf'rs,"* now this time he is close to the bank on my side and so in I go trying to land right on top of him but I miss and land right beside him, almost at the same time the smallest deputy Don Cusack jumped right after I did, and now I grab at the guy and get my left hand on his adams apple and at the same time grab the back of his neck with my right hand and start dragging him toward the canal bank. Now Cusack is on the other side and has him by the arm. We drag him up on the bank telling him he was sure trying to kill himself. Now he was about my size, 6 foot and about 210 pounds, and around 20 years old.

So, I figured I would have had a hell of a fight if he hadn't been so tired from all of his activity. Anyway, big Jon Akins and Brad Mecham, both good sized, pick him up and drag him to the nearest patrol car, cuffing him also with his hands in back and also searching his pockets for any weapons or any ID. He didn't have anything. We checked out the sleeping bag that we saw earlier and found a plastic baggie with cotton in it which was saturated with transmission go, an additive for car transmissions, and it gives a real cheap high but constant use deteriorates the brain cells, anyway I had the cover car take the guy to mental health clinic.

I heard Begley advise the dispatcher that we had a 10-15, prisoner, and a wet sergeant. Hell, I give credit to Don Cusac when he saw me jump in; he got excited and jumped in too, the only trouble was he still had on his gun belt, wallet and boots.

The signal 20 got dried out but he was a chronic sniffer and was already well on his way to idiots ville. He was 21 years old and had the mentality of a 7-year-old as he was just burning up his brain. The closest he ever came to Vietnam was watching about it on TV.

****

About 4 or 5 months later we got another call on the same guy off on another trip, he lived in a trailer park, Whispering Pines, just south of the canal where we had first contact with him but this time, we didn't have any trouble with him. He got dried out again and the last I heard his family took him back to New York state.

****

Little Don Cusa stayed on the department first making detective and then going to the Warrants section, all the while he kept up with his schooling and he finally got a master's degree, so he left the department under not to friendly circumstances. Big Jon Atkins made it to the vice squad for several years and got out to be a detective sergeant, still with the department. Brad Mecham is a road sergeant, Begley made Major in charge of all uniform units. Me, I faded away in 1977 to go to Alaska for 4 years. When I returned to the department now as a slick sleeve. Hell, everyone that I had supervised was now promoted up. I guess I learned to just regress. I still have the belt the guy had.

SKIVVIES (SHORTS)

Well, the time was the late 1960's and I was just a slick sleeve and I worked on the 3 to 11 PM shift in zone 2, an area from 45th street north, to Belvedere Road to the south, and it had been raining hard just about the entire shift. I had a couple of signal 4's, accidents, and a couple of signal 38's, domestic disturbances, but nothing heavy enough to write home about. I got all my reports done and turned in, but my uniform was soaking wet from all the rain, so were my boots and gun. I go home and the first thing I do is hang my uniform up on a hanger to let it dry on the shower curtain rod in a bathroom. Right then all I had was my skivvies on, under shorts. My wife and 2 girls were long in bed cause it's about 12:30 AM. So, I empty my gun, wheel gun, get a cup of coffee and was about to spray my gun with WD-40 as it had been wet most of the night.

I was thinking someone once told me, *"A good cop don't get wet,"* and I think to myself, that was a bunch of shit, it's the lazy cop that don't get wet. When all of a sudden, I hear this God-awful noise just outside the kitchen window. The window faces to street, and it sounded like a car being dragged down the street but on its side. Well now my kids are up and crying, my wife gets up and so I turn more lights so I can see what's going on outside. What I see is a station wagon, and it was going really slow. Couldn't have been going 4 or 5 miles an hour. The driver must have been drunk out of gourd (head) cause what he did was to run over my neighbor's metal garbage can as tomorrow was pickup time. Now the can was stuck underneath the station wagon, going slow and dumping its contents all over the street. Well, I had my empty gun in my hand and just my skivvies on. I don't see any other lights on in the neighborhood, so I run out the door and through the grass and up the street to the intersection. Where I lived was on a horseshoe curve at the end intersection where the vehicle was now stopped. I got to the driver's door and yanked it open. Now I had my gun in my hand but didn't point it at the driver but just held it close so the driver could see it. I was right, it was a white male, and he was drunk out of his gourd, my gun didn't even phase him in the least. He wasn't even concerned about me being a deputy sheriff. Well while all this is going on zone 2, area patrol car, was dispatched to my home and he arrived about 5 minutes later. He laughed at me being out of uniform, skivvies only, and I helped him put the drunk in the back of his patrol car and hurried home. I still didn't see any lights on in the neighborhood so I figured no one saw me.

****

Just before I left for work the next day my wife says to me, *"O yea, Pat up the street called and wanted to know if I knew anything about the car and noise late last night and the guy running around in his under wear."* I don't think my wife ever told her that it was me running around, but I'm sure Pat knew.

SNOOKS BAR SIGNAL 20

This incident occurred in 1965 and when I was just a rookie cop working in the city of Riviera Beach. I was in the long process of becoming a police officer with some sort of understanding that there are truly bad people in this world and there are truly people in this world that need help. I found that there was a possibility that I could get hurt from either group.

As a rookie police officer, I attended all the law enforcement classes that I could. At the time there was no police academy in Palm Beach County. In the county, classes were conducted by certified state instructors. As I recall, all the ones that I had been taught by were the city of West Palm Beach Police Department and it wasn't until 1967 that Florida adopted what is called, POLICE STANDARDS. These are standards for police officers nationwide.

By police standards I grandfathered in by virtue of being an active police officer at the time. What police standards meant was that to be a police officer in the state of Florida, or anywhere nationally, you had to attend various law enforcement classes until you reached a certain number of hours toward being certified. The hour requirement increased yearly. Those police officers that completed the required certification from the state of Florida received a certificate from police standards attesting to the fact that the required number of hours were completed. The certificate that you received was recognized nationally and it had a blue seal on it. Those who already had been police officers and grandfathered in also received a Police Standards certificate, but it had a gold seal, mine was gold.

Enough background information, the shift was 7-11 AM

and it was just early, around midnight. The city of Riviera Beach is a busy city and it's located right on US 1, a major highway, it also has a large black population. The dividing line in the city was alternate A1A, any calls east of this were handled by white police officers and everything west of this road was handled by black police officers since this was where the black population lived.

Now the sergeant was a man named Howard Wyatt. A man and I named Howard Friess worked on the east side this night and we also had two black officers on the west side, this made up the night shift. The dispatcher just put out a call of a signal 20, a mentally disturbed male at Snooks Bar and that he had just broken a beer bottle and then just left the bar. Now Snooks Bar is on the black side of town and would have been handled by the black officers, but they happened to both be on a call at the time, so they were 10-6, busy. The bartender gave a description to the dispatcher on the male and the kind, and color of clothes he had on. Once the call went out, and the two officers were busy, Sergeant Wyatt called me and Friess and told us to meet him as we were going to look for this black male and he gave us a clothing description, he also told us what the male had done.

It only took a few minutes for the three of us to assemble and go off and search for the black male as he was just walking. Now the three of us were driving slowly west on the road and we spot this male walking. Sure enough he's wearing the same clothes as described. We all stopped and Sergeant Wyatt, being the man in charge, walked up to him and after a brief conversation with him placed him under arrest, myself and Friess put him in the back of a patrol car. He was no problem, just wild eyed and ranting about his sister.

Being that Riviera is not a large city, we went 10-19, the station, in no time so we took our prisoner in to the booking area, that's where you frisk a prisoner for any weapons and all articles they have in their pockets, that's wallet, change etc. That's where you inventory it.

Now Sergeant Wyatt and Friess left the booking area and told me to stay with the prisoner, so we were alone. Friess and the sergeant went to get cuffs, leg, and hand, that are made out of leather and padded to be used on people who might have questionable sanity, so they don't hurt themselves. Now the booking area is enclosed in glass so you can see what's going on so all can see me and Mensa man.

Now Friess and the sergeant had been gone several minutes to get these restraints in a room that was used to put people in who had a mental disorder. It had a bunk bed, and it was attached to the wall and a commode and sink combined, nothing else.

The regular jail cells were off in a different section also just of the booking area. While I'm in the booking area alone with this black male who has been passive and no trouble so far, we had just made small talk and I had him empty his pockets and turn them inside out, when all of a sudden, he gets wild eyed again and says, *"look at my hands, they got blood on them, I killed my sister."* Well not thinking, and about to learn a very important lesson, I grabbed his wrist, held up his hand and said, *"There ain't no blood on your hand."* Well that definitely was the wrong thing to say cause he up and punched me and knocked me down. A good thing that all three of us had secured our guns in a gun locker before all this took place as I could have been shot right then, this male is about 5'11" and 195 pounds or so and he's now wild and crazy. I jumped up and was wrestling with this nut when Friess and Wyatt saw all this and they rushed in and after a violent tussle, we managed to get the leather restraints on him. We walked him over to the quiet room, put him on the cot and secured his legs with leather restraints then we left and locked the room.

I didn't have anything else to do with him nor did I see him again. I'm sure Sergeant Wyatt had the man taken to a mental health facility for an evaluation as to his mental ability.

****

Officer Friess left the department to go to Palm Beach Gardens police department. He and another police officer, a John Davis, eventually talk me into joining the Gardens PD Sergeant Wyatt also left the department later to join the sheriff's department where he remanded a slick sleeve deputy.

Also, what I learned from this incident is that I had to agree with whatever signal 29 said to pacify him.

SUICIDE ATTEMPT JUPITER INLET

The 4 to 12 shift. I had 12 cars on the road, that's 8 zone cars and 4 cover cars. So coverage was good and that's not even counting detective cars which was probably another 3 cars. Now that's 15 people on the 4 to12 shift. It was around 9:00 PM and it was dark already. We had been real busy up to now as I hadn't even gotten a 10-49, meal break, yet. Now fortunately all the calls so far where just minor in nature, just constant, like fights, domestics and this was the time for a lot of signal 30's and signal 65's, both are larcenies.

One thing about working on the 4 to 2 shift, traffic stops are at a minimum because there's just not enough time when your busy as it's one call after another. Anyway by this time most of the zone cars had already gone 10-40 as I had the cover cars take the calls so the zone man could eat, and like I said it was about 9:00 PM and it was a warm light breezy night, it was scary, and the moon was almost full, so it was easy to see without lights. The radio transmissions had ceased for a couple of minutes from its customary flow of voice traffic. The dispatcher broke the silence with, *"Palm Beach will be on 10-33 traffic,"* that's emergency traffic only, and she sounds the familiar signal 3 times with the emergency tone and the emergency call was about to be dispatched, and that routine traffic was to stay off the air until it was given out and 10-33 was cleared. The dispatcher came right back with, *"Palm Beach to zone 1, signal 32 attempt at Jupiter Inlet,"* suicide. Now normally the case number and all the information relating to the case was given to the zone involved along with his dispatch time. This was so he can keep an accurate record on his time sheet that he had to turn in daily and also for his report. However, on 10-

33 calls all this is a relatively minor detail when time is critical, and a life or lives may depend on a quick response and besides the dispatcher had a written log with all the particulars on it in reference to the call. All the zone man has to do is to call the complaint desk when the emergency is over, and all the information is available to him.

Anyway zone 1 acknowledges the call with a *"10-4, 10-51,"* received and enroute. Now I happened to be in the 4 Points area and just coming 10-8, back in service, as I had just assisted zone 3 and 4 on a domestic call and we had a 10-15, prisoner. On hearing the call I advised the dispatcher that I was 10-51, enroute, to assist the zone. She acknowledged and advised me that Jupiter Police Department is 10-23, standing by. at the inlet. Now J.P.D. is a small-town department and even though Jupiter Inlet is not in their jurisdiction, and they are always willing to stand by the sheriff's departments calls, now we in turn assist them, I always felt that they were glad to do it as it gave them something to do and also, they didn't have to write a report, just go 10-6, busy, with the dispatcher, our dispatcher, advising her that they were assisting the sheriff's department. I was a good 20 miles south of the inlet, so I put my blue lights on, put the Federal system on manual control so it worked off the horn rim. I always ran code 3 in this manner, blue lights flashing, as if you have the siren on automatic or constant yelp, the noise gets inside your head in the car and just stays with you. You can't pass the sound and if you have far to go the sound just stays with you and you end up with a headache.

Now in addition to the blue lights and Federal system I flipped another switch and it activated 2 aircraft landing lights mounted in the grill and they both pulsated. These two lights certainly provided a lot more light and offered a lot more visibility to all traffic. Now as I headed north on Military Trail, I was almost doing a 100 MPH. We remained in a 10-33 status; it would be my responsibility to clear it so that normal radio traffic could resume. Now as I ran out of road I turned east on Palm Beach Gardens Blvd., I got to thinking that I'd use the northern most cover car for the call and that way zone 1 can be ready and available in his zone and besides I felt that we would probably be tied up for a while, so I advise, *"213 to Palm Beach, 10-22, disregard, zone 1 and send the cover car."* Now she didn't even have to call him, the cover car just acknowledged my transmission with a 10-4, 10-51, he understood and was enroute. Then I got to thinking that the suicide attempt was right at the inlet, and we might possibly need a boat. So I advised the dispatcher to call the Coast Guard and see it they can standby off the inlet with a boat if we might need one? She acknowledged my message and it didn't take 3 minutes and she was back with a, 10-39, message delivered, and the CG is 10-51. I then told her to advise the OD, not that I wanted him to respond, but just so he was aware of the nature of the call as it was his responsibility to keep an accurate log in the detective bureau. Now this log was read by the Detective Captain, Chief Deputy and the Sheriff, and this call seemed to have the potential to be on the log. Anyway, the dispatcher comes back with, *"The OD is 10-51, enroute, 213."* So it meant he was monitoring the radio and was responding.

Now the OD was a senior detective by the name of Ralph Wiles, he was a good troop and he had been a grunt with me. He and I were among the first 4 deputies to attend Dade County PSD (Public Safety Department) in 1968, a 13-week ball buster of a police course, complete with uniforms, spit shined shoes and short haircuts etc.

Well I turn north on U.S.1, a 4-lane highway divided, and traffic is very light, so I punch it up to about 115 to 120 MPH and from here it's only about 5 miles and I'm there in 3 minutes. Now we're still 10-33 traffic on the radio, so the radio is real quiet, the OD gets on the horn, radio, and says directly to me and by passes the dispatcher, *"213 what's your 20, location?"* I tell him I'm just turning off U.S.1. into the Jupiter Inlet Park. Wiles back. *"I'm just in North Palm Beach on US 1,"* so I was around 8 miles north of Wiles. He had a new car and like all detectives all he had was a tear drop blue light with a magnetic base that he put on his dashboard. When these lights are on all they do is rotate and blind the driver because they reflect off the windshield as they rotate. He didn't have a federal system either, so he wasn't able to truck as fast as a patrol car and keep up with us. Now while I had been north bound on US 1, I was able to catch up with the cover car that I had assigned the call too. He wasn't moving as fast as I was and so when I passed him, he fell in behind me.

We were now east bound on Jupiter Inlet Park which consisted mostly of a large parking lot, almost empty at this time of night and it also had several restrooms. At the northeast end of the lot was a single lane road that went through a wooded area and came out with the ocean about 200 feet to the right or east. The road looped along the south jetty wall of the inlet and then looped back south to the parking lot. We stopped along the jetty wall and advised the dispatcher we were 10-97, arrived. Where we were parked was about south of the jetty wall. The distance between us and the wall was about 50 feet, and it was all soft sand that separated us. The jetty wall from where we looked at it was about 20 inches high on the land side and was about 3 or 4 feet wide and made out of concert. Now on the inlet side it probably dropped down a good 6 to 8 feet and it was reinforced with large granite boulders as the tide really ran through it. Now this wall ran east and west and was about 400 feet long. From where me and the cover deputy stood the wall extended another 80 to 100 feet into the ocean, or east. It was well past the beach. The Jupiter police officer was there and glad to see us. Like I said it was dark already, but the moon put out lots of light and there was just a slight breeze, it was just a typical night in Florida, the kind snowbirds just dream about.

Well in the moon light I look east on the jetty, and I see a male standing all alone, quiet and watching us. We were still on the hard surface next to the patrol cars. Now this male don't have a fishing rod or a cast net and he's just standing on the edge of the jetty wall. Now while we were at our patrol cars the OD, (Officer of the Day) goes 10-97, arrived. Wiles gets out and walks over to me and I fill him in on the subject on the jetty wall. *"What you going to do Bob?"*. Me, *"will try and talk to the individual but I bet I end up getting wet."* I just had a funny feeling that I'd end up in the ocean so while we talked, I took off my gun belt, keepers, shoes and wallet and put them in my car as we had moved on the blind side of the patrol cars so the guy wouldn't see what we were doing. I took my radio out of the Convertacom and told Ralph I was going to clear 10-33 traffic and that units with me would be on 10-91, detective channel. This way the main channel would stay clear, and that the dispatcher could advise me if I was needed anywhere, and she could keep me posted of anything else of a serious nature that I should know about.

Ralph and I switched channels and started walking northeast toward the lone figure on the wall, we walked slow, and I told Ralph that we would try and talk to the guy and if that failed, I would whisper, *"go,"* and with that we both would run and jump on the jetty wall and grab the guy. So far, we hadn't seen any weapons or advised that he had any. Ralph agreed and we continued walking slowly and when we were about 30 feet from the guy he hollered, *"stop,"* and stop we did, from here I could see that he was a white male and looked about 30 years in age, and about 6 foot 1, about 180 pounds. I looked east beyond the guy, and I saw a Coast Guard boat laying offshore just beyond a sand bar about 6 to 7 hundred feet out in the ocean. Just then the dispatch called to advise that the CG was on the scene. Well I started talking with the guy and he was crying and in an emotional state, but he talked easily to me, and Wiles and he told us his name, where he lived and worked and the fact that when he came home today from work that he found a note from his wife saying that she was leaving for good and also taking their 4 kids with her. He cried some more and then he took a cigarette and not being able to find a match he asks me for one, I told him I didn't have one, but I would find him one. Now Wiles didn't smoke and so I walked back to where the Jupiter officer was and got a pack of matches and then I walked back toward the guy on the wall, now with the matches. I figured I could get close enough to him that I could grab him. Well he was one step ahead of me and let me get within 15 feet of him and he hollered, *"stop, and just throw them,"* and that's what I did.

Also, at this time Wiles moved up and stood by behind me, and there we stood, a uniform sergeant and a detective, both holding walkie talkies, and a guy who wants to kill himself. Now he must have guessed that something was going on cause aren't cops supposed to do something and try and stop a thing like this, and now he says, *"don't do anything funny cause I'll jump."* Now the guy seemed sober and not high on anything, and I wondered if he could swim, all he had to do was to jump out a little to miss the granite boulders and he'd be in the water. Well I told him, *"No way, I got a radio worth over a $1000 and I'm not about to lose my job cause my radio fell into Jupiter Inlet."* He accepted that and started to light another cigarette so I ask him if I could have one and he said, *"okay,"* so I took a few steps closer to him and again he hollered, *"stop!"* and so I did and he just threw me one, he lit up and threw me the matches, now I'm only 8 to 10 feet from him and I lit up. Now this is the first cigarette in my mouth in over a year, I used to dearly love these coffin nails and smoked 2 or 3 packs a day, but I was to the point where I'd wake up at 2 or 3 or even 4 in the morning coughing like crazy and it got the to the point that it was effecting my diving, so I decided to quit and it was no problem cause I enjoyed my diving, so here I was tempting myself. Well I started puffing and thought, O boy how easy it would be to just start inhaling and that I would probably be hooked again, but I figured shit, it wouldn't be worth it, so I just puffed away and talking with the guy as he started to cry again.

Now at this time the dispatcher comes on with a *"213, that's me, are you 10-4?"* Now she hadn't heard from me in a while and so it was just a check on me and us, and I acknowledged her, and she gave the times as a dispatcher normally does, but it also made me realize that we had been out with this guy close to an hour and a half, and I couldn't see any end in sight soon. So as I was talking with the dispatcher and the guy I slipped in a *"GO Ralph,"* I never looked back and just dropped my radio in the sand and tried to leap forward but all I did for a split second was to further sink in the soft sand. The guy knew he was had, and he hollered as he jumped into the water, *"you SOB."* Now I'm committed and so I make it to the wall in two strides and jump up on it with one big leap, I hope, toward the inlet. Now I'm hoping that I clear the dam boulders cause if I don't, I'm gonna break something real bad and even if I pass the boulders below, I hope I'm far enough out to clear the ones submerged that you can't see cause they would be covered with barnacles. Anyway, I got my eyes closed and I'm falling and yea, it's all water, I cleared all of it.

Now Jupiter Inlet was made mostly to relieve pressure from the in-coastal waterway, but it did have boat traffic and it's a very dangerous inlet. There is a sand bar that shifts with every tide and there's two tides in and two tides out every day. The water moves through it around 10 to 12 knots, which is pretty fast, and I just happen to hit an outgoing tide. When I jumped in, I sank about 6 or 7 feet and by the time I came to the surface I looked and shit, I was already 2 or 3 hundred feet out in the ocean and moving like hell. I looked for their guy and he was just east of me in the ocean and was real close as we were only a second or so apart when he jumped. Well he heard me break water and started in my direction shouting, *"you lying SOB, I'm gonna drown you,"* I figured, *"what's a nice guy like me doing in a place like this."* Well I let him get about 5 to 7 feet from me and now we're almost 6 or 7 hundred feet from the shore. I dove down and let him go over top of me and when he did, I grabbed his legs and jerked him down and locked my left arm around his throat real tight. Well he had swallowed some water when I had jerked him down, so he was gasping and was no trouble. There was no way he was getting me now.

The CG boat was following us and pulled up alongside. There were three troops in a utility boat and two of them pulled the subject in with no problem. He was exhausted and had no fight left in him. Then they helped me aboard and I asked the troop running the boat if he could put into shore just south of the inlet at Jupiter Park Public Beach. It was no problem, and we went right up onto the beach as the ocean was calm.

The cover car and the Jupiter Police Officer met us and handcuffed the guy. I told the cover unit to take the guy right up to the mental health faculty under the *"Baker Act,"* I was soaking wet, so I walked the short distance to my car. I was just taking my shirt off to wring it out when up walks Wiles laughing and says, *"you crazy SOB. you looked so G/D funny going through the air into the water."* That's me folks. a laugh a minute.

****

I learned about 4 months later that he had gotten back with his wife and kids and that he and the family moved out of Palm Beach County. Wiles who was a rookie with me on the department back in 1967 stayed just a short while as a detective, took a job as an investigator with the County Solicitors Office, that name was changed to the States Attorney's Office and now Wiles became Chief Investigator and had a staff of 12 to 15 investigators under him.

I remember his family back when he and I went to Dade Police Academy in 1968. He had a little boy and a little girl. I left the department in 1977 only to return in 1982 as a patrolman/deputy and I had the opportunity to work with a patrolman named Craig Wiles, Ralph's son.

SUICIDE MILLER ROAD

The 4 to 12 PM shift, I'm in the middle of line up for the troops. At this time on the department, lineup was 30 minutes long, so I have to come in 30 minutes earlier, prior to the troops going on the road. First off, I give out the zone assignments, that's 8 zones plus any cover cars I might have and myself, and that's the shift.

I was still reading the BOLOs, (Be on the Lookout) the department had not yet started putting out what was called a hot sheet that had all the necessary information a deputy might need, like stolen cars, missing people etc.

The day shift Lt. came into my lineup and says, *"Sergeant, the dispatcher is on the phone for you, and they have a signal 33 and 32 on Miller Road,"* shooting & suicide. *"Yes sir,"* and I go into the sergeant's office, pick up the phone and it's the dispatcher who advises, *"Sergeant Barton, there's just been a signal 32 on Miller Road. It's just off 2nd Avenue, and just west of Congress Avenue, north of Lake Worth Road. The day shift units are already at road patrol for shift change, what do you advise?"* also signal 14, information. Deputy Sheriff Hallen from the night shift was at the residence about 0500 AM on a signal 33. At the residence was a white male who had shot two dogs, but further advised that the dogs he shot were his.

Okay first take it easy, the female dispatchers all excited. Deputy Sheriff Farkas is zone 6, the area of the shooting, so he's enroute, so I'll go with him. Now I'm back in the lineup room and tell the troops to hit the road, I tell Farkas about the signal 32, the location and I also give him the information about the dogs.

Fortunately, I already had my gun belt on as I normally just sling it over my shoulder or leave it in my desk, but not today. I grab my hat, car keys, run outside and see Farkas is all ready to roll. I start up and call the dispatcher with, *" 213, I'm 10-8, 10-51 with zone 6 and we're code 3."* That's my ID number, I'm in service, and we're on our way with blue lights and sirens. We already knew where we were going and why.

We were still on airport property, and I put my landing lights on also. These are pulsating, high intensity lights mounded in the grill. I put the federal system, the siren, on yelp, and on manual to work off the horn button, not automatic, otherwise the noise would drive you crazy. As I pull up to Belvedere Road, zone 6 pulls in behind me, he also is running code 3. We got a good 5 miles to go to get to zone 6's north boundary and it's all through traffic to get to the scene. It's all rush hour traffic at this time and cars are everywhere and they do pull over for us. We're pretty lucky on the Airport Access Road and make it to Southern Blvd., a 4-lane divided highway. We're doing close to 70 mph which is dam good for the traffic. We're south bound on Congress Avenue and it's also a 4-lane divided highway. Now we're coming up on the north boundary of zone 6 so I ask the dispatcher to again give me the street name and number, she came back right away with the information, and I see we're only a couple of blocks away, so I advise the dispatcher to put us 10-97 arrived, and 10-33 traffic, emergency.

At this time in the department, only the Lt. had a walk talkie, so once away from the car there was no communication until you returned to your car or else called the dispatcher by landline. I normally don't have one as the Lt. always took it,

RHIP, (Rank Has Its Privilege) but today I had one, as we had no Lt. We're now on the scene and I see an elderly white female crying and waving frantically at us. Both myself and the zone man park our cars, kill the blue lights and run over to the lady whose hysterical and shouts, *"oh my God, he's in the back yard,"* I told zone 6 to stay with the lady as she looked like she was going to have a heart attack and I wanted someone with her at this time. No other neighbors are out, and we don't have any time to canvas the area for any information.

I ran between two houses, and I find a 4-foot cyclone fence, the damn gates on the other side of the house. I see in the back yard a white male lying on his back about 30 feet from the house right in the middle of the yard. I jumped over the fence and as I got close, I saw what was left of the male and a lever action riffle by his left side, his head was missing from where his left ear was, to up around his right eye. About 6 feet away was what was blown away, and the damn Florida weather, the goddamn flies where already over both of what was left of him and also the part blown away. Ah shit, I shooed them away, but they came right back. I ran to the fence and yelled for Farkas to bring an emergency blanket. It's a yellow, disposable blanket, made of paper and covered with plastic. He was just handing it to me over the fence when an elderly female cried out, *"Oh God,"* and here comes his victim's mother. Crap, that's all I need, I can't let her see her son like that, she'd die beside him.

I jumped back over the fence and ran out to the front of the house just in time, the mother already knew that something was awfully wrong and frantically cries, *"Officer, let me see my boy,"* she came at me in a frantic, scared, and tearful state and had her arms open as if I could make things right. I put my arms around her and held her and after a several seconds said, "*Ma'am, there's been a bad accident and I'm sorry, I can't let you see your boy just now.*" Fortunately, the neighbors from across the street saw me with the woman. They were an elderly couple, and they came right over to us and offered to take the mother over to their house if that was okay with me. You bet it was okay with me, I asked the fellow if I could see him first and he came over to me and I told him, *"Sir whatever you do don't let her come home or go to the back yard for any reason. I'll have a detective here shortly and he can come over to your house."* He nodded and left with the woman, mother.

I then realized that we were still on emergency traffic, so I called her on the walk talkie and told her that the signal 32 was also a signal 7, dead, and to send a crime scene unit along with a detective, and to lift 10-33 traffic. She acknowledged me and advised Palm Beach was back on regular radio traffic.

As I walked back to Farkas I thought what a shit job this is. Well the victim was covered up and part of the disposable blanket was torn off to cover the blown off part so the flies didn't get on it, we covered the blanket ends with rocks we found in the yard so the wind wouldn't blow them away or off. While looking for the rocks I found two fresh mounds of dirt but I didn't pay much attention to them at the time.

I told zone 6 to start a supplemental report as the responding detective would do the face sheet and most of the report. I bent down to look at the riffle but didn't touch it as it was evidence and wasn't to be moved until the crime scene unit had taken pictures and any measurements in relation to where found, and how far from the victim. It was a Winchester 30-30 and was lever action. I thought, boy, it did a hell of a job. I stayed with zone 6 and we talked about the suicide while I waited for the crime scene unit and detective. They respond in about 15 minutes. The crime scene unit had his ID case and camera and got to work after hearing about the case. I told the detective that the boy's mother, was across the street at a neighbors and how she almost ran in back and saw her boy. I sent zone 6 back on the road as calls were backing up in his zone and they didn't need me anymore so I went 10-8, back in service.

I spent a busy night but nothing major, just so busy that I didn't even get to eat chow. I got back to road patrol around 11:15 PM, ate some candy and had a coke, filled the night sergeant in on our calls, particularly on the signal 32 and 7. I saw a deputy named Ed Hallen, he was a night shift deputy, and he was around 6'4" to 6'5", then I remembered of the dispatcher advising me that Hallen had been at the residence where we just had the suicide. He had been there on a signal 33, shooting, last night. So I stopped him and told him to come into the sergeant's office as I wanted to talk to him.

"Sure Sarge," and he followed me into the office. I sat down at my desk, looked at him and said, *" tell me about your signal 33 last night on Miller Road." "It was nothing Sarge, some young guy was pissed off and he shot his dogs." "Why in the hell didn't you arrest him for cruelty to animals." "Ah Sarge, they were his dogs." "Then why didn't you Baker Act him into mental health and take his guns?"* Florida has what is known as the Baker Act, it's a tool for law enforcement officers. What it does is to give an officer or deputy the power to take an individual into custody and take him/her to the county mental health faculty for evaluation, and though it's not an arrest it's a sort of protective custody situation where the officer or deputy answering a call sees it's apparent that the individual involved has a mental disorder and is likely to injure someone or himself. The only

requirement is that the erratic behavior be witnessed by the officer or deputy. Under the provisions of this Act, the officer or deputy is protected from a false arrest charge.

The bad part about the whole matter is the long drive to the mental health faculty located on 45th street. All calls for this zone are TOT (Turned Over To) a cover car if you're lucky to have one, if not they go to an adjacent zone or a cover car if the shift had one. So a troop Baker Acts an individual only if it's really necessary. Now the Baker Act has solved a lot of potential problems that could have ended with serious consequences just like this one did. I told Hallen, *"If you had Baker Acted that young guy and took his guns, he probably wouldn't be dead now."* Deputy Hallen didn't know about the suicide and this last statement kind of floored him.

A word about the taking of guns, back at this time a deputy, responding to a domestic or any type crime involving guns, could legally take the guns in the residence, leave a property receipt for them, and in a few days the owner could come to the property room and claim them after for whatever reason things calmed down. *"Ed, you're lucky I'm not your sergeant, you handled that call all wrong, you'd better get into your lineup."* He left, and I went and checked my troops paperwork, made a log entry, reference the suicide and went home. I thought to myself going home, *"what the hell was his sergeant doing when all this was going on, he should have been there at the scene."*

I didn't think about any more until the next day when I came to work, I found out that Captain Sanchez had suspended Hallen for three days because of his poor judgment and also the way he handled the call.

****

I stayed with the department until October 1977, leaving for a four-year period. On returning, Deputy Sheriff Farkas, who was zone 6 on the day shift was now in charge of the motorcycle unit as a sergeant.

Deputy Sheriff Ed Hallen made road sergeant just as I returned to the department. Looks like past sin(s) are forgiven.

SWAT THE TAC SQUAD

Back in the mid 70's the sheriff's department saw a need for a really well trained, disciplined group, or team of men to respond to unusual situations such as hostages, barricaded subjects etc. The type of calls not normally handled on a daily basis. Now not that the zone deputies couldn't handle any of these calls along with their sergeants or with a cover car as had been done in the past, but by now the department had grown in size and population to where it was more professional to handle calls of this nature by a specialized team trained to cope with these situations.

One good reason was to free the zone deputy from a situation that could take many hours to resolve and like it or not, crime and corruption don't wait to be resolved. Beside at this time the team concept was beginning to gain more acceptance and recognition throughout the country. Even though this concept had already been instituted by many large departments the SWAT TEAM was about to be born in Palm Beach County Sheriff's Department. Well after the Swat Team was approved of by the Sheriff and his staff it only remained to have it formed. Now it was decided that a total of 10 personal would form 2 teams, 5 on each, and it was decided that a Lt. would be the OC or (Officer in Charge) of the entire unit, and he would be a team leader. It was also established that a sergeant would be the leader of the 2nd squad, or team. Now in order for a deputy to become a member, or even be considered for a position on any team, Major Hinns, who was in charge of the entire uniform division, had a memorandum posted on all bulletin boards and in effect stated, *"that if you're interested in joining the newly formed Tactical Squad, they changed the name from SWAT to Tactical Squad, to submit a name with your qualifications and it would be considered".* I was always gung-ho and so was Begley We had talked about it and figured that he had the best chance of any Lt. for the OC slot and when he got it, I would be made the sergeant by Major Hinns. Now Lt.'s didn't have to submit any memos. It took about a week to decide who they wanted on the tactical squad, and it was announced that O'Bannon would be the Lt. in charge and not Begley for whatever reason, but anyway I was picked as the sergeant even though I hadn't submitted any memo.

So I was quite surprised, but I still wished that Begley was there too. Now some background on O'Bannon, he had come to the sheriff's department from some department in New Jersey and had only been on our department just a short time. The thing that irked me, no, pissed me off and everyone else, was that he came to the department and went right to our vice squad and his career was no less than astronomical as far as promotions go. Didn't stop at Lt. but that's 6 or 7 months down the road, boy I'm sure glad that politics never influenced the Sheriff.

Well a meeting was held with all prospective applicants at the road patrol squad room with Major Hinns outlining the function(s), training schedules and the deployment of the TAC squads. He advised that each squad would get the opportunity to attend SWAT school at Quantico Virginia at the FBI academy. Now this was a 2-week course on swat operations that the FBI conducted for law enforcement agencies throughout the country. Personally I always thought that the FBI had plagiarized LAPD (Los Angeles Police Department) when it was Daryl Gates who was the chief, of course I could be wrong. Now being that they had the faculty and the funds they just expanded on it.

Well it really sounded okay to me, and I was getting into the spirit of the movement up until the Major brought up the fact that the members would have to come in 2 hours earlier every day and we would work on physical training, running and at least once a month we would have to go to our rifle/pistol range and run an obstacle course, also for weapons training. Now I was already thinking what I could tell my wife about the additional time that I would be tied up with the departmental activities. What with me coming in early every day to make up line ups, get hot sheets or see the captain about whatever, and all the other things a road sergeant has to have ready for lineups. Besides all this I still got to go to court once in a while. Hell, my wife Claire must think that I married the sheriff's department, and she was just my mistress. Well I figured I'd smooth it out somehow when the Major's next statement brings me back to reality when he says, *"I'm sorry we can't pay you or compensate you but you'll have to bear with it for now."* I figured there would be a big star in the east and three wise men before I'd donate any time, and with that the meeting concluded.

Now the sheriff's department had a policy known as the Chain of Command that was a big issue if not adhered to and basically what it means is that your keister is in dire jeopardy if you don't do it, or send a memorandum to your immediate supervisor, and just go and see or address his supervisor. First, it's grunt to sergeant, sergeant to Lt. etc. and this goes all the way to the Sheriff if it's necessary and then all the way back down, thus the chain of command. Well like I say, *"no way*

José," am I donating any time. No more free time from me and since O'Bannon is the Lt. in charge of the Tac Squad I just wrote and addressed my memo to him to pass on to the Major and not wanting to stay on the Tac Squad and not donate any more free time I'd just stay a road sergeant. Hell, I get more than enough excitement.

So what follows is verbatim from the memo that I wrote to Lt. O'Bannon to pass on to the Major Hinns. The meeting that I attended on Friday the 15th of November 1974 at 2:30 PM in relation to new policies and procedures applied to the tactical unit under your command and answerable to Major Hinns.

It is my understanding that to remain a member of the unit, which I never submitted a memo for as a number of deputies had, also in addition to this that of days off, a certain amount of time would be required toward a physical fitness program. Again, it was made clear that this time would be donated, but mandatory, in order to stay in the unit. I have been with the department just under 8 years, 5 of them as a road patrol sergeant. I feel that I have done my job to the best of my abilities. But there comes a time in every man's life when he can no longer shit a pile this high and of a certain color and I have reached that point, so I'll go back on the road and as you stated for the Major, No Animosity.

Well I figured that when the Major read that gem, I'd be a slick sleeve or a civilian. I gave it to O'Bannon, and he read it and didn't say anything. I had written the memo on November 16, 1974. and the Major wanted to talk to me on November 18, 1974, that's a Monday.

The only reason it took so long was that I wrote it on a Saturday and Majors don't work Saturdays or Sundays. Well I walked into the Majors office expecting the fecal matter to come in contact with the retorting blade, but to my complete surprise he was real nice and explained that they can't pay us, but there are other benefits that were possible, and I'll be dammed if he didn't talk me into staying on as a team leader. He then brought out his copy of my memo and says, *"we can forget about this okay!"*

Well needless to say I stayed on the tactical squad.

****

Lt. O'Bannon and his team got to go to Quantico's SWAT school. Now somehow mine never did, and somehow, I still managed to give the department 2 extra hours each day plus 4 hours at our range once a month on my days off. As to where those BENEFITS are, well I think I learned a lesson in psychology.

Lt. O'Bannon's career continued to skyrocket, and he made Captain on the Vice Squad and on the campaign for Sheriff he backed, and campaigned for candidate X, and "X" made O'Bannon a Major. Me, well I stayed a sergeant.

THE ARMADILLO

This is a story about and Armadillo, but first I have to give some background information about the animal. You say what's an Armadillo got to do with law enforcement? Well I'll explain it all later and I'm glad you ask.

Now the Armadillo is a nice quiet nocturnal armored plated animal that seems inoffensive, and I know just how an animal like that can assist a Deputy Sheriff in crushing crime and help attain justice. Well now that you ask, I've got to go back in time before I even entered law enforcement to around 1962 when I worked at a place called Pratt & Whitney Aircraft. It was located on what is known as the Bee-Line Highway, in rural West Palm Beach Florida. It's set out in the middle of nowhere in swampy country. Now P & W made experimental rockets and jet engines and then they tested them. So in this process they made a lot of noise and that's the reason for being so far from civilization. Now I hope the FBI don't view this as espionage or treason, Anyway I worked at a place called Rough Stores. This department handled only rough metal such as bar, sheet stock, rough castings etc., and all was in rough form. Now a lot of this stock was stored outside as any elements had little effect on them.

I worked on the evening shift, that's 4-12 PM, so one evening I'm out in the compound and an Armadillo came walking across the lawn, under the fence, and into our enclosed area. Now this is the first time that I had ever seen an Armadillo in the wild as I had just come from the Pittsburgh area and Armadillos aren't common there. Anyway, this guy named Kelly said that Armadillos are harmless as they have a real small mouth with tiny teeth that looked like a zipper, and they just don't bite.

Now I told Kelly that I was going to catch him. What an Armadillo does is to dig in the ground like a mole and he is equipped with some very long and sharp claws, of course I didn't know it at the time. Besides claws, he also has an armor plate body, and the only soft part is his underside.

This Armadillo was on a hard surface in our compound, so I figured, "I gotcha now." Now you got to remember this was around 1962 and I was a lot younger and though I was never known for any brilliant bursts of speed I was able to run the Armadillo down, dive on him and knock him over, well I jumped up figuring now I gotcha and when I looked at him the SOB was on his back okay, but he had all 4 feet just flaying away. Now at the end of all 4 feet were some of the longest claws this Polish boy ever saw. All of a sudden, I wasn't so keen on catching him, so I ran away in one direction while the Armadillo exited stage opposite me and got out of the compound.

That goddamn Kelly! I owed him one as he got me good. So, I learned about Armadillos. Well enough about armored plated critters, I did find out that they made ladies pocketbooks out of them and that they were good eaten, and so it's back to the present.

I eventually went into law enforcement and later joined the sheriff's department where I made sergeant after two years, the time was 1969. Now being a sergeant I had approximately 10-13 deputies working for me. One of my troops was a guy named Joel Frye, he was a good deputy and he had prior experience in law enforcement. He came from Washington D.C. Police Department. He had been with me when I caught Daniel Yencho for murder, so Joel kept his cool and didn't let stress get the best of him.

My shift had been working the 3-11 PM and Frye was working zone 2, my old zone. Zone 2 has the Westgate area and has a fine crop of rednecks and assholes. Now Frye came on the radio and in a calm voice advised that he was chasing a white Studebaker Lark and that the driver appeared to be drunk. Wellbeing the road sergeant I immediately headed to Westgate and assist Frye and found him with his drunk. After some name calling and a tussle, we got him cuffed and stuffed into Frye's patrol car for DWI (Driving Under the Influence).

To make a long story short, when Frye finally went to court on him, he beat the rap on a technicality. Now I told Joel, *"Don't worry, he may have beat the rap of DWI, but he didn't beat the ride to jail, have his car towed and also attorney fees."* I was there as I was a witness.

The case would have been, you win some you lose some but, the asshole made some unkind remarks to Joel in the hallway of the courthouse after he was exonerated of the charge. Now this really pissed Joel off, and so was I, but I figured we'd get him again on some other charge as he was always in trouble. With that in mind the background is laid.

It was night shift and was quiet so far. I, like the zone deputies, checked business for breaking and entering, people, and any suspicious cars or anything out of the ordinary. I had just pulled into the Lounge Bar, a redneck, good ole boy bar that at the time had a couple of bouncers who liked to break bones every time a customer said an unkind word. Anyway, in the parking lot I see this white 4 door Lark and it looked familiar. So I run a 10-28, registration check, and sure enough, it belonged to the guy that Frye had for DWI some time ago and beat the rap, charge. Well I stayed close by the lot to see if I could catch him or anyone for DWI or something. I finally left and went over to Westgate as that's where he lived, and I started to check some businesses in the area. I started on some mini warehouses by driving up with my lights off, shut the car off and walking real quiet through the area, shaking doors as I went. As I approached the end of an L shaped complex, I heard a funny noise, it was kind of scratchy in sound, like someone getting ready to break into the building. Well it's dark as hell, I peek around the corner and what do I see, an Armadillo, shuffling slowly along and it was his claws that I heard, and he was coming in my direction.

Back then the order was, *"you get out of the car, you carry that night stick with you."* Now this comes from God in his earthly form and known as, Captain Henry Sanchez, also known as, hollering Hank, of course not to his face. Now Captain Sanchez was in charge of uniform division of the department.

Well the Armadillo gets almost even with the building and me when I nailed him with the night stick right on the head and over, he goes stunned but not out cold, so I got time to grab him by his tail.

Now an Armadillo has a long tail so there's no way he could climb up and get to me. Besides, he wasn't feisty at this point, but he was moving those legs. I hurried back to my car, the window was down so I could hear my radio,

Back then the troops and the sergeants didn't have portable radios so you had to listen to your car radio, all seemed quiet, so I carefully opened the door, sat down and carefully transferred the tail of the Armadillo so I could close the door and I held it in my left hand outside the car. I drove slowly 4 streets to where the asshole lived, his car wasn't there so I drove over to the Lounge Bar parking lot and sure enough, guess whose car is still there, sure glad that no one saw this particular sheriff's car driving down the road. Well at the Lounge parking lot no one was around, and the Lark was still in there and parked in the same place. I got out of my car real careful and switched hands and opened the door. I was right behind the Lark. The passenger door was unlocked, and the windows were all up, so I just put deputy Armadillo on the passenger seat and slammed the door shut. I got back in my car and drove away. Just another deputy on routine patrol at a known problem bar parking lot.

I didn't find out until the next day when I came in and checked the complaint log for any B&Es and their locations, that's when I saw that the owner of the Lark had filed a vandalism report. I got the log copy of just what caused the front and back seats to be all shredded up, but both were beyond repair. To this day I never figured out how deputy Armadillo got out the car, but it was mentioned in the report that a sharp object was used to vandalize the seats. I guess deputy Armadillo just wandered away in the night, pissed at his surroundings and had a headache.

****

I left the department and when I returned as a slick sleeve, Joel Frye was just getting off the vice squad after working there for several years he made road sergeant. I then told him about the Armadillo and the Lounge Bar. It was 2 years later that I left the sheriff's department, the last I heard was that Joel Frye had died on the operating table during some heart surgery.

THE BABY

This is a story about a baby, it was maybe 15 months old and would never live to be any older. The date was sometime in the 70's, the shift was 12-8 AM and I believe the time was around 5 in the morning. It was still dark. I had been on the sheriff's department about 4 years. The shift, as I recall was slow and no meaningful calls up to this point.

The quiet of the morning was broken with the dispatcher coming on the air with, *"Palm Beach to zone 1, a signal 7,"* dead person, and she gave a Riviera Beach address and a number. Now even though it's a Riviera Beach address it's still outside the city limits so it's in the unincorporated area and that means the sheriff's department handles all calls in the unincorporated area.

Zone 1 acknowledges the call and advises he's enroute. Myself, as the shift sergeant also acknowledge it, and I'm enroute also. Now there's 2 of us on our way to Riviera Beach but at almost normal speed, there's no need for us to hurry as someone's dead and there in no hurry for anyone. Both zone 1 and myself drove a little faster as there's hardly any traffic at that time of the morning, besides we both had a long way to go to get there. I had a good 8-10 miles to go from mid-county, and zone 1 had to come all the way from the Jupiter area, he also had about 8-10 miles to go. We both met on what is known as State Road 710, the Beeline Highway, and Military Trail and started east bound into Riviera. We found the address and it happened to be projects, or a housing development, that's where all the buildings looked the same and each had a number of apartments within it. They were just like projects in any other big city, but these happened to be all black residents and all black projects.

By now we had found the right building, there was no traffic, and all the cars were parked as at this time everyone was asleep so we both went 10-97, arrived. We went inside the building and checked the mailboxes and found the right apartment number of the calling party. Well after a short elevator ride to the upper floor we stood in front of the right apartment and knocked on the door. Soon a voice responded and meekly ask, *"who's there."* We ID'd, identified ourselves that the sheriff's department was here and a young black female in a robe, wearing night clothes under it opened the door. She was sobbing and you could see that she was distract, she saw that there were two deputies standing at the door, so she opened it up all the way and had us come into the apartment. The apartment was small, and she showed us into the kitchen area, and there stood a black male, also in night clothes, I found out that he was her husband. Now with the both of them in the small kitchen you could smell booze coming from both of them, and they both were crying and sobbing.

I asked in a very gentle voice that someone had called about someone being deceased in the apartment. Well with that statement the female started sobbing all the harder so that she couldn't even answer my questions. The husband looks at me with his blood shot/crying eyes and says, *"yes our baby's dead."*

I ask him if I could see the baby and he had me follow him into the bedroom and there lay a little black kid, no older than 15 months at the most, the covers were off him and he lay at an odd angle. I went over to touch him, and he was stiff, meaning he had to have been in that position for some time.

A word about people who pass away, the first thing that happens to a deceased person is what's known as lividly. That's were all the blood in a body sinks to the lowest portion of the body. So if someone passes away while seated, all the blood would sink to the feet and legs. The next step is called rigor mortis. This is where a body stiffens up, meaning if was found to be at an odd angle, it might require that something would have to be broken. I'll leave that to your imagination. There is one more stage a person goes through, but I wouldn't go into that. Well, I could feel that the baby had been dead for a while, so I asked the dad just what happened. He told me that he and his wife had been drinking heavily and when they finally went to bed, they had taken the baby from its crib and put it between them in their bed and they then went to sleep. It was plain to see that in their drunken state, one of them just rolled over onto the baby and smothered it. They had to have laid on him for some time as rigor mortis had set in. On hearing this I wanted to arrest them right away for negligent homicide, but I didn't as I knew that a detective had to be called on a signal 7, and after his investigation the baby would be transported to the nearest hospital, probably St. Mary's to have the baby formally declared dead as the ER doctor would have to do it.

Well I called the dispatcher by landline, telephone, and told her to send me a detective as it was a confirmed signal 7. Myself and zone 1 took both parents into the living room and tried to comfort them in their grief while we waited for the detective to show up. Both parents were extremely sad and by now sober, but you could still smell the booze. The detective came and as it was a death investigation, all zone 1 had to do was a follow-up as all the paperwork was done by the detective. When he arrived, I filled him in about the negligence of both mother and dad and their drinking.

****

I don't know the follow-up on the detective's case, or if he filled homicide charges, or if he even filled any charges with the county solicitor's office, but parents or no, these two people needed to go to JAIL.

THE BADASS LOUNGE BAR

The time was in the late 60's or early 70's, I know because I was still an old slick sleeve, just a plain old deputy, and I was on Bendick's shift. Now Bendick was a shift sergeant who just made Lieutenant, and Lennie Wilson was the shift sergeant.

The best way to describe Sergeant Lennie Wilson is to picture a pair of jump/riot boots with a riot helmet on top of them and somewhere in between or under them was Sergeant Wilson. You can guess that he was kind of small.

Now myself, a guy named Paul Sherdian, and Roger Hunter were what Bendick affectionally called, *"The Rat Pack,"* and the whole shift was known as Bendick's Bastards. Sounds like a radical group, well by 1980 standards, we were, but you've got to remember that back in 68/69, law enforcement had a lot more leeway.

I guess the ACLU, (American Civil Liberties Union) never heard of the Rat Pack other than, *"Frank Sinatra and friends"* and vice versa, and we didn't hear much about the ACLU.

Well Bendick formed the rat pack and it consisted of the three of us, when the shift had enough troops to cover all the zones, we three would ride as a three-car unit. The object was, *"Selective Saturation Patrol,"*

Now what that really meant was that if there was a problem in the county that required action, such as a bar fight, or a hippie gathering, Florida had lots of these, etc. Then the three of us would respond rather than the zone car and when we did, someone or more, most always went to jail.

I was the senior of the three, so I was more or less in

charge. Now I got along good with Bendick our shift leader, and he had gotten me on his shift as he liked my aggressive attitude toward law enforcement. I had just been involved in a shooting incident with the president of the Outlaws, Motorcycle Club, a fun-loving group of asshole, Deke Tanner, the president, had gone screaming that some crazy deputy had tried to kill him, a lie, but that's another story.

Well it was the 3 to 11 PM shift and I was the senior man among us three, so since the shift was one man short, Hunter had to work a zone, that left me and Paul as cover cars.

The shift had been quiet so far; myself and Sheridan just covered cars and domestics, signal 38, or other calls as we were needed. We then drove to the Lake Worth Pier to see all the dopers.

Back then Lake Worth Pier was a hangout for junkies and dealers and probably still is, but now it's under the jurisdiction of the Lake Worth Police Department.

Well Sheridan is called by our dispatcher and advised to 10-45, call by land line. He calls and the complaint desk tells him to check the Lounge Bar, a stinger, confidential informant, had just called and said that a white male had just gone in, and we had a capias, warrant, on him for a felony and that he was a real badass. She also gave a physical and clothing description on him.

Sheridan told her that I was 10-12, in company, and that we'd both go and check it out and he hung up. Well Paul gives me the information and we take off for the Lounge Bar.

Now this sounds good, first off, it's a capias arrest, so it's a free arrest meaning no paperwork involved, just booking an individual into jail and no written reports. Only log it in on the daily trip sheet as a felony arrest, and it looks good on our monthly log sheets which every deputy had to keep.

Hell, it sounds like this guy we were going to check on was an unbeliever as far as law enforcement goes. From what communications told Paul, this guy is a badass or what modern day penologists might term as a revisits, repeat offender, in other words he was a con.

The Lounge Bar was a likely place for a con. It was a badass bar and in my years on the sheriff's department we spent a lot of time there and not socially either.

We checked out at the Lounge bar, 10-6, 10-49, busy on a warrant. We both had the physical and clothing description of the subject we were looking for.

Now the Lounge Bar had a square bar inside, so I tell Paul to go right, and I'll go left. It just so happened that I saw the guy on my side and as I walked up to him Paul came up from the other side, so we had him flanked. I just told him to come with us outside, he never said a word or offered any resistance and just came with us passively. Once we got him outside, we tell him he's under arrest on a warrant and cuff him in front, shake him down for any weapons and put him in the back seat of Paul's car, no problems. We loaded up and I tell the dispatcher that we're, 10-15, 1019, that's a prisoner and going to the jail. Now Paul takes off with his prisoner and I'm following him. We hadn't gone a quarter mile and for no reason, Paul pulls off to the side of the road and so do I. Now he jumps out of his car, gun in hand running back to me. I wonder what the hell happened that I missed.

Paul tells me that since we left the bar the guy, prisoner, was hollering at Paul that we needed 2 deputies to arrest him and that if he wasn't cuffed, he'd beat Paul's ass.

Now that's kind of a wrong thing to say to ole Paul

Sheridan as he has a fuse about as long as what you might need a roach clip for, and when he gets that way, he wants to go to fist city.

I have always been able, at least most of the times, to talk to Paul and calm him down, this was one of those times. I had him put his gun away and just cool down and stand by my car and listen for the radio. I was about 20 feet behind his car and told him I'd go up and talk to the guy and get his attitude straightened out.

Paul agrees and stands by my car while I walk up to his rear door. I tell the guy to old up his hands and I take the cuffs off and I don't say a word. He has a bewildered look on his face, and I say in calm, professional voice, *"Okay asshole, out of the f'n car and let's see how bad you are."*

Now this guy is about 6 feet tall and 190 pounds and none of it looks like fat. Well he didn't get out of the car and I'm sure he heard me, so I tell him again a second time, but he still sits there so I reach in, grab his legs and drag him out. He falls to the ground and just stays there. I told him to get up and show me how bad he was. Now I don't like anyone telling a deputy sheriff that he was going to kick his ass. He might kick mine, but he better bring a sack lunch cause hell be a while. All the guy does is lay there with his hands free and his shirt open, so I reach down and grab a hand full of chest hair and as I pulled him up a lot of it came out in my hand. He never uttered a word and I didn't even recuff him, he just got back into the rear seat of Paul's car. Paul was still standing by my car and saw the whole incident, I said to him, *"the guys okay and wants to go to jail now,"* and so he did.

****

As the years passed Paul went into the vice squad and then into the Detective Bureau having his share of ups and downs. He got demoted back to the uniform division where he worked for me as I was a shift sergeant now. Paul made detective a second time.

I won't say why he got busted other than to say it involved, choir practice, and filthy pictures stressing togetherness. He finally got busted out of the sheriff's department along with his CO, his boss, in a bar mooning incident. Today he is a detective in a small town in Palm Beach County, Paul is a story all by himself, he's a mustang.

THE CHASE

I had been out of uniform for some time and in charge of one of the departments TAC squads, another name for SWAT team and with Lt. O'Brien being in charge of the other team. My team happened to be working that night.

Each team consisted of four men, with me in charge, for a total of four men, as long as nothing heavy was going down and the detective bureau hadn't made any special requests, such as assists or special surveillance or possibly any apprehensions. My team would stake out various convenience stores and also various and numerous liquor stores in the county. I would assign one of my troops to go to the north end of the county, one to the south end, the last troop and myself would take the central area.

We all wore civilian clothes at the time and also drove unmarked cars, FORDS, that would have a hard time doing 100 mph even if they were dropped out of a HERC or C- 130 at 10,000 feet. The only thing fast about them was the radio. We all worked 10-hour shifts at the time starting at 1800 (6:00) P.M. to 0400 (4:00) AM. which wasn't a bad shift at all cause it was only a four-day work week. The uniform sergeant in the central area was a guy named Jim Brennan, one hell of a good cop and who also came from my hometown of Pittsburgh PA, and besides that, his whole family was on the Pittsburgh PD (Police Department).

Well it was a nice warm evening, as usual, and all was quiet for me and my troop in the central area and we were just cruising the central area of the county and its convenience stores.

The time was around 7:30 PM when Gary Hill, a

detective who had worked for me for a while in uniform, comes on the air with a 10-50, a traffic stop, giving the vehicle tag number, state and a 10-20, location of stop. The dispatcher acknowledged and all was 10-4, okay, no wants on the vehicle and all sounded fine, just like any other traffic stop. But being a detective made the stop and hadn't asked the deputy working the zone to make the stop for him, the deputy had a marked car with lights and siren, were as detectives only had civilian cars and of their choice. I decided to keep an ear open for the detective on his traffic stop. What could have been 3 to 4 minutes go by and the detective comes on the air all excited and breathing real heavy and talking fast advising 10-33 traffic, meaning only cars in a real emergency were to use the radio, no more routine radio traffic until he clears it.

The detective comes back on the radio that he just been assaulted and that shots had been fired and that the suspect had fled the scene of the stop. The detective advised the type and color of the vehicle and that it was south bound on Kirk Road from State Road 80 or Southern Boulevard, also the driver was a Mason Kimmel, a white male who was about 6 feet tall and about 225 pounds, an ex-marine who had a black belt in karate and who worked as a bouncer in one of the local gin mills bar, so the detective knew the suspect.

Now Mace was the kind of bouncer that liked to hurt people, he was a friend of Mark Herman, a 7th degree black belt and who owned a dojo, school, and who later was convicted of a shot gun murder of an oil company executive, another story, in Palm Beach County. Well the dispatcher calls out a 10-28, vehicle description. owner and address. well the address comes back to a Narcissus Street in Lake Worth. Now that's off of Kirk Road and about 2 to 3 miles south from where the incident started. From what the detective had given as the direction of travel of the suspect vehicle, it looked like Kimmel was headed that way, south which was his home.

I got on the air and advised Bendick, shift Lt. and also Brennan the shift uniform sergeant that me and my troop were close by and would check on Kimmel's residence as we had unmarked cars. By now the sun was setting it was still light, but it would be dark in a while. With me in front and my troop right behind me we passed 10th avenue still on Kirk Road and with Narcissus just a few more streets south and to the left or east bound. Both me and my troop turned on Narcissus and halfway down the block on the north side we saw the vehicle in the driveway and at the same time its driver saw us. He backed out squealing his tires and headed east, the same direction we were headed but still 1,000 feet or more separating us.

Well it was darker now, not black but you could get a ticket for not having your lights on. Anyway, the chase was on, and I advised all units responding, patrol cars and any detective cars, that the suspect car had made it to 10th avenue and was west bound with his lights out. Me and my troop were only maintaining the same distance and never able to gain on the Chevy, ID NOW, with our sick Fords. At this time, I carried a Smith & Wesson Model 29. That's a 44 mag. Mine had a 4" barrel. I had it out of my shoulder holster and in my left hand so I should be able to get a round or two off if I got the chance.

Somehow my troop got in front of my car as his was the same make and model but just a wee bit faster and he even seemed to be gaining on the Chevy which had turned north on Kirk Road. The same road he came south on when all this started. I heard on the radio that Brennan, the road sergeant and two other deputies had set up a roadblock on Kirk Road just south of Forest Hill Boulevard, the next major intersection to the north. By now all cars, except roadblock, were driving around 100 mph with Kimmel still driving without lights. We crossed the intersection on a green light, lucky, and approached the roadblock, I heard several shots from handguns and then a loud boom from a 12-gauge shotgun but nobody stops Kimmel or disables his car and he makes it through the road block and continued north bound. Me and my troop are still behind him not gaining, just maintaining distance, and we pass the next intersection, Summit & Kirk Roads. He, Chevy, busted a red light and so did we, lucky again.

Now all other units, cars involved, are moving into the area of the chase when all of a sudden, the Chevy disappears. I can't believe we lost it in the vicinity of Kirk Road and Gun Club roads, less than one block from where it all started. Now all this time we had remained on 10-33 traffic when Bendick, the shift Lt., clears 10-33 traffic and resumes regular radio traffic. We spent the rest of the 4 to 12 shift trying to find Kimmel and his Chevy. But no luck, the detective who started it all was interviewed, he had stopped Kimmel, whom he knew, just to talk to him when Kimmel knocked him down with a punch to the face. The detective hurriedly took out his shotgun from the trunk, a 12-gauge, it was sawed off enough to make an ATF agent frown and wince. He pulled the trigger and both barrels went off. The recoil of the blast brought the shotgun back with such force that it tore the webbing between the detective's thumb and index finger and later it took 6 stitches to close. The uniform sergeant, Brennan, advised that he had put a 357 round through the back window of the Chevy as it past the roadblock. One of the other deputies at the roadblock hit the lower left fender as it past him, it was in front of the driver with his 12-

gauge shotgun. My troop was also able to get a round, 357, into the trunk of Kimmel's vehicle. Somehow Kimmel got away clean but the next day he called the sheriff's department wanting to give himself up and said that he was in a motel called Camelot in North Palm Beach, a small town in Palm Beach County. He was picked up with no problem.

Needless to say, his car had numerous bullet holes in it. He was convicted of all charges against him. He turned around and sued the sheriff's department for all the damage done to his car, needless to say, he lost the case. When asked. *"Why he ran in the first place",* his answer," *I had a promise of a piece of ass and didn't want to miss it".* After he ran the roadblock, he traveled north and then put his lights on and drove into Gun Club Estates, pulled into a driveway, killed his lights, and just sat and waited for the units, cars, to leave.

****

In January of 1982 I had returned to the sheriff's department, this time as a slick sleeve and not as a senior sergeant. I had several assist calls involving Mason Kimmel for various crimes he was involved in, but he was no trouble to handle. Now he was an alcoholic and weighs 275 to 300 pounds and bald. I guess his martial arts fell along the way with his booze. He can't even hold a job as a bouncer anymore.

THE DANCE SIGNAL 20

It was the early 70's, the shift was the 4 to 12 PM one and I'm at line up with the troops when a troop from the day shift came into the squad room in a hurry saying there's a phone call for me and it's commo, communications. Well I go into the sergeant's room and it's the complaint desk and a woman says, *"213, my ID number, we got a signal 20, mentally deranged person, he's real wild and tearing a house apart."*

She gave me a location and I guess it's about 1 1/4 miles from road patrol, my location. I told her, *"Okay I'm on my way and I'll take 3 troops with me."*

The Road Patrol is on the north side of Palm Beach International Airport as we had just moved from the south side because the department was growing and needed more room.

Well, like all cities of any size, the traffic was heavy and rush hour was just starting. I told the troops in the line up to saddle up and get going into the zone. I told the zone 3/4 deputy that we had a real bad signal 20 and also the north and south adjacent zones, 2 & 5. Plus a cover car and that we would all respond code 3, blue lights & sirens.

The zones had already been assigned so we just hurried from the airport complex and headed west on Belvedere Road. It's 4 lane and straight until Congress Avenue, then it goes to 2 lane and snaky until Military Trail cause it goes around Palm Beach International Airport.

Now all 4 cars had blue lights and sirens on and were in a caravan. The traffic was heavy on the 2-lane part but unless you were already dead, you couldn't mistake the noise from 4 patrol cars in convoy. People east and west bound pulled off the road to let us pass and even some pulled onto the median strip on the 4-lane part. I told the dispatcher, signal 14, information, for the troops responding with me. That at that time there was no talking car to car and all transmissions had to come through the dispatcher, *"leave your guns in the trunk of your cars and just take your night sticks with you, that I'd be the only one with a gun inside the residence."* I didn't want to go inside and get into a big fight and have the subject grab a deputy's gun and start shooting.

Back then all the sheriff's department used was a Border Patrol holster and all it had was just one strap over the hammer of the weapon. It was really easy for a weapon to fall out in a fight or, worse yet, the intentional grabbing of a weapon by a subject.

We all went 10-97, arrived, at the residence, and the dispatcher immediately goes, *"Palm Beach is 10-33 traffic.",* emergency. Only myself, or a unit at the scene can advise it to be cleared. Now back then we didn't have any walk talkies or portable radios and all radios stayed in the cars.

Once out of the cars we could hear all the screaming, hollering and racket coming from the house, so we all ran up to the back door.

It turned out to be the kitchen door and we just went in, holy hell, there isn't anything left standing or unbroken in the kitchen anymore. All the cabinets were pulled off the walls, and all the dishes and glasses were on the floor and broken, the refrigerator was pulled over and all the silverware and pots and pans were on the floor. By the door going into the next room is a little old lady who is crying, shaking, and screaming at a white male who is dancing in the middle of all that broken glass and dishes. He's chanting something religious whatever, the crazy bastard wasn't wearing any shoes or socks and didn't have any shirt on and he's got his blood all over the place, but he just kept dancing and chanting. He didn't even pay any attention to the 4 of us when we entered.

Now he's young, about 6 feet tall and right around 190 pounds. We found out that he was the son of the woman who was crying. As far as a signal 20, like he was, it had been my experience that when you had to fight them, they never directed their anger at any one person in particular and can be equally mad at everyone involved, they fight until subdued. Now violent ODs, overdoses, are different, at least the ones I had encountered, they fight to kill and are immune to pain.

Well I had 3 troops standing on 3 sides of him, and they all had their night sticks in their belt loops. I walked up to him, but out of arms reach, and said to him in a fatherly voice, *"come on son, it's over now, we'll get you some help now."* Well I was kind of edgy to say the least. I figured he'd swing at me and it's off to fight city, but all he did was to step out of all that broken glass, broken dishes and junk and came over to me passively. We put the handcuffs on him, and I told the zone deputy to leave and go to 45th Street with him, that was the Palm Beach County Mental Health Facility, where he would be mentally evaluated.

I used the house phone to call the dispatcher that all was okay and to lift 10-33 traffic, that the zone car was 10-15, had a prisoner, and that he was enroute to 45th Street. I had the south deputy stay at the residence and get the information for the report, also to call 45th Street and advise them that a deputy was enroute with a prisoner.

We all went 10-8, back in service, and nothing else of any great interest happened the rest of the shift.

When I went home that night, I told my wife Claire about

the incident.

****

Several years later the Florida legislature adopted into law, the "BAKER ACT," that's where a deputy or law enforcement officer, having probable cause to believe a person may be a danger to himself or others by acting in an irrational manor, the deputy or officer can take that person into custody can transport him/her to the nearest county mental health faculty for evaluation. They could hold this person for 3 days. But seldom did. Well it had to be 7 or 8 years later my wife brings up the incident out of the clear blue sky, and I was kind of surprised, but said *"yea, I remember it why?"* Well it seems that she had met the boy's mother at one of her religious functions and she had brought the incident up. Claire, my wife, told her that I was the sergeant there that day.

Her boy had straightened out as far as mental problems. The woman told my wife to tell me what happened to him and for God to bless me.

THE DOG - R.B.P.D.

This story's about a dog and his confrontation with the Riviera Beach Police Department, and some never to be forgotten lessons.

It was 1965, and the shift was the day shift. That's 7-3 PM. I was just a gung-ho, that's eager, rookie policeman in the city. Now Riviera, like most big cities, or any city, was divided up into zones. In our city, white officers worked in zones 1 and 2 which were all on the east side of Old Dixie Highway and these zones encompassed US 1, a major highway. These two zones also had a set of railroad tracks belonging to the Florida East Coast Railway, and they also ran from the north of the city to its south boundary. All west of the Old Dixie Highway was considered zones 3 and 4 and all calls to them were worked by black officers. The railroad tracks were part of zones 3 and 4. Now that you have some sort of layout of the city, I'll proceed with the story.

It was early morning, maybe 9 or 10 AM. The dispatcher came on the air with a report of a dog just walking south along the railroad tracks and every once in a while, would just reach out and bite the tracks. Needless to say, its mouth and teeth were all bloody and frothy and you just knew that every time it bit on the tracks that teeth were going to break, as steel is a lot harder than teeth. The call was directed to a black officer since it was in his zone and he had been on routine patrol, he right away acknowledged and he was enroute. Now all police officers and detectives heard the call as we all had radios. Well I happened to be working zone 1 and it bordered on the tracks so I thought I'd back him up should he need it and besides, I was close by. In no time I was in the area of the railroad tracks and there was no one there but me and I see this dog, so I hurriedly checked out as busy at the tracks. I saw him coming closer all the time and I saw him stop and bite the tracks, so I took my night stick with me when I checked out.

Now the call was directed to another officer, but he wasn't there yet and here comes this dog, so I had to act, I just couldn't sit and wait, that's why I took some immediate action. A word about the night stick as it's important. The stick is 20 inches long and maybe 1 1/2 inches in diameter, it was oak and had been used by a New York cop. I don't know how it ended up in Riviera Beach, but it did, and they issued it to me. It had a hole in it and through that was a leather thong so it could be wrapped around your hand for a good firm grip if you had to use it.

The dog is now only 50 feet away from me and getting closer all the time. It was all frothy and bleeding at the mouth and when it saw me, it lay down between the tracks and just took a rest. Much to my relief. Of course, its mouth is still all bloody and frothy, but it never showed any aggressiveness toward me, it just lay there looking at me and let me walk up to it, warily I might add. Naturally the first thing I thought of was rabies. This dog has rabies and I'll have to get shots when all this is over and the dog is secure, and I hear that getting those shots hurt.

By this time I'm really committed to this dog call, so I walked up to him, and he just laid there looking at me. So, I take my night stick, bend over at an awkward angle, and with the thong like a noose. I put it on the dog's head and lower neck like a collar and start twisting it. Well in twisting it tightens up and I anchor the night stick into the rocky area between the railroad ties. So now I'm bent over at this odd angle holding this frothy dog.

At last comes this officer who was assigned the call anyway, but I'm already committed. He sees me bent over holding the dog and I shout to him to bring his night stick. Thankfully the dog is quiet and laying still through all of this. Anyway, the officer brings me his stick and it's also got a leather thong. When he gave it to me, I put the thong end around the back feet and twisted it also until it's tight and then anchor the end between the ties. So there I am, bent over two-night sticks at an odd angle and a rabid dog, kind of like holding a tiger by the tail, what am I supposed to do? am not letting this dog up and now he's antsy and doesn't like being held down, and he's starting to move around.

The officer who was with me went back to his patrol car and had the dispatcher call animal control as they took care of animals and to have them respond. This was a job for them, and we were just assisting another agency, to hell with them.

Well our dispatcher came right back after notifying them that they were on the way as she had explained our situation to them. Now I was involved in holding the dog and I wasn't about to let it go.

After spending 15 or 20 minutes in that position, not daring to let the dog up, who by now was mad at being held, I asked the officer to again have our dispatcher call animal control and see where they were and how soon they would be here? By now my back was plenty sore for being bent over so long and the dam dog was feisty now and I can see I'm lucky it's just a small dog, otherwise I'd be in deep kimchee, cause by now there's no way I'm easing up pressure on the night sticks. There's just no way I'm letting a rabid dog lose so I ask the officer to call our sergeant, Jeff Waites, to see if I could just shoot the dog so at least I could stand up, because it was really hard staying in that bent over position for so long.

The sergeant never did show up as it was just a dog call, rabid or not, and besides there were two patrolmen there anyway. The sergeant just advised the patrolmen to tell me that NO WAY could I shoot the dog and to wait for animal control as they had to put it to sleep and take its head off and send it to a laboratory to see if it did have rabies.

Animal control finally show up after several more minutes and saw my predicament holding down the dog and they just got a long pole with a noose on the end and took the dog and put him into their truck and locked it in. Several weeks later we were advised that the dog we held onto that day had distemper and not rabies.

****

I learned two valuable lessons that day. 1. drive slower on calls of this nature, letting the assigned officer get there first and 2. shoot the animal and then tell the sergeant what I did. Jeff Waites stayed with the Riviera Beach Police Department, retiring years later as an inspector.

THE PAPERBOY SIGNAL 4

This is a story that happened while on the night shift. I had been on the sheriff's department a while as far as seniority, but I still hadn't made sergeant. Now I was a senior man, so I used my ID number, 223, that was issued to me when I joined the department. A 200 number signified that I was a uniform deputy, and it identified me as a uniform deputy to anyone who had a department issued police radio, and it also ID me when I used the radio.

Now on this particular night we had enough troops to cover all 8 zones, so I was a cover car on this night. Now as I remember it was a quiet night as far as any calls to the zones, so the dispatcher did what is known as time checks. This is where the dispatcher would call all the zones in numerical order, and then any cover cars, just get a zone number and a 10-4, okay. That way she knew that all the troops were okay and awake, and she would also call the supervisor(s), the sergeant and Lt. if the shift had one. They would also hear the zone responses and know that all were okay and safe.

When I was a designate cover car and not working a zone, I answered with my ID number. Now three duties of a cover car are just what they imply, you cover or back up zones on their calls that may be violent or have the potential for violence. The nice thing about being a cover car is that you weren't restricted to any one zone as the zone deputies were, you could go anywhere in Palm Beach County and not be questioned or found out of zone as had happened numerous times.

Now on this night all was quiet when the dispatcher came

on with, *"Palm Beach to zones 6, signal 49,"* alarm, and she gave a location on Military Trail that was just north of Lake Worth Road and that the alarm was at a hardware store.

A word about burglar alarms, at this time most businesses had burglar alarms and they were activated once personal left at the end of the workday, and if any window or door was jarred or tampered with, the alarm would set off a noise in the business and also send a signal to the company that installed the alarm and they in turn would call the sheriff's department to respond. A lot of times the alarms were just faulty, but you never knew for sure and so all alarms were responded to and treated as though a crime was committed until proven otherwise.

So when a call went out to zone 6 of a signal 49, I also responded as a cover car and that I was enroute. Now it was very early morning so there was very little traffic on the road. The alarm was on Military Trail, now the Trail, as it was called, ran north and south. It was a 4-lane highway and some of it was divided by a median strip. Where the alarm happened to be the Trail was just a 4-lane.

Now when the signal 49 was dispatched, I happened to be in zone 2 area, so I had a good 2 or 3 miles to go to get there.

Responding to an alarm meant get there in a hurry so I put my blue lights on and put my federal system on so that the siren worked off the horn rim. I started south bound in a hurry. I didn't use the siren as this time of the morning there was no traffic and besides I didn't want to alert anyone. On Southern Blvd. I was doing a good 90 mph, Gun Club Road was passed as I sped south, Forest Hill Blvd. was passed, and I never used the siren as traffic wasn't heavy. All these major roads I had just passed had red lights for traffic control like I said, at this time of the morning. traffic wasn't heavy.

Now just south of Forest Hill Blvd. was another intersection with a traffic signal but this intersection is a Tee, meaning it ended on Military Trail. I was south bound at a very high rate of speed when I see out of the corner of my eye this station wagon east bound and coming up to the intersection, I could see that a young white male was driving.

I found out later that an even younger white male was in the back, asleep, he was the younger brother of the driver and beside his sleeping body were a lot of papers. The two were paperboys on their way to deliver papers on their route.

Well I was running in an emergency mode when I saw the station wagon and it didn't show any signs it was stopping for an emergency vehicle. I hit the horn and the siren went off and I swerved to avoid him, and he still came into the intersection and with me doing 95 to 100 mph. Trying to avoid a collision I served again but still hit him in the left rear and my car veered off to the right.

The collision caused the young boy in the rear to be thrown out the back door of the station wagon, newspapers all over intersection and I thought, *"a hell of a way to wake up!"* My car continued in a south westerly direction. On the southwest corner, the direction I was going, was a closed gas station and I came to rest about 6 inches away from a pump. Needless to say, I didn't make it to the signal 49. I don't know who worked the accident as I went to JFK (John F. Kennedy) hospital. it was ether our department or FHP. (Florida Highway Patrol) My captain was notified that I was involved in an accident while responding to an alarm and he came right over to the ER. One of our troops picked up my wife who was worried, but calm, when she had found out about me being in the hospital. Well anyway, I was treated and released from the ER.

****

I never did find out about whether the alarm was faulty or for real. Years later, and also several wrecked patrol cars later, Captain Sanchez presented me with a certificate. It had an American eagle on it, and it really looked fine, from a distance, but on closer inspection to read it said, *"Sergeant Barton, the second most hated man at the motor pool."*

The driver of the station wagon was cited for failure to yield to an emergency vehicle. Oh yea, I forgot to mention the time of the accident, 2:23 AM. Same as my ID number.

THE REWARD (21A)

This event occurred in Palm Beach Gardens while I was on their police department and just before I had become a member of the Palm Beach County Sheriff's Department.

First a word about Palm beach Gardens it's billed as the, *"Golf Capital of the World,"* as it has several golf courses, which Florida is known to have a few. One of those is PGA sanctioned, (Professional Golfers Association) and it was built with a lot of money from a billionaire named John D. McArthur. Now you may not have heard of John D, but you certainly heard of his sister, Helen Hayes, of some acclaim or James McArthur who played a detective on a series known as Hawaii 5-0.

Well anyway, P.B. Gardens was a middle-class community, it had just a few stores and a few bars or lounges. It even had a hospital built by none other than John D. Of course, it was not in use, but it was still fully equipped and just sat vacant. However, it was always checked by the police department.

Now the police department had a gruff ole police chief named Herb Peck, a retired Pennsylvania State Police Trooper and it also had a sergeant named Hank Nolan.

Sergeant Hank Nolan was the type of guy that could let a speeder, or a reckless driver go by, and he wouldn't bat an eye. But let him see a kid on a bike act a little reckless and ole Hank was on him like stink on shit. and ole Hank was my sergeant.

On the night shift, the police department had only two patrolman and a dispatcher working. The Chief only worked day shift and 3-11 PM for the sergeant, so only grunts worked the night shift. remember RHIP. P.B.G. Police Department was really a retirement community for police officers. Police headquarters was just a modified apartment, and it had no provisions for prisoners etc. In my short tenure on the P.D. I made only one arrest that I remember.

Well back to the story at hand. I was working on the night shift and was on what they call, *"routine patrol"* what else. I worked with another officer named Howard Friess and he had also been a police officer with me on Riviera Beach Police Department. He and another police officer named John Davis had convinced me to leave Riviera P.D. and come to the Gardens.

Anyway, I was enroute to a long since closed club house on what else, PGA Blvd. It was early in the morning, and it was dark. I was just driving slowly toward the clubhouse to check on any possible burglaries or anything suspicious when lo and behold, there laying in the middle of the road was a white male, on stopping I saw that he was all busted up, his clothes torn, and he had bled some. On checking closer I could smell alcohol coming from him. Well the first thing I did was to see if he needed any medical attention because of the blood that I saw. He refused any help, so I ask him for some ID, identification, and of course he had none to show.

Seeing that he was a harmless drunk I called officer Friess to come to my location as the guy was funny since he was sure that his life had been saved and now that he had been found by the police, he would be okay. I put him in my patrol car and told him I'd take him to our station so he could file a report and then I'd get him a ride home. Friess at this time just followed me to the station with his car.

Once at the station and he was cleaned up he praised me and Fries for saving his life and kept insisting that we share in a reward even when we told him that we couldn't accept any reward and that we were just doing our job. Well he kept insisting that we should share in a reward for saving his life but unfortunately, he had no wallet or ID as someone had rolled him, beat him up, as he was drunk, stealing what he had and then dumping him on a dark roadway in Palm Beach Gardens and that's where I found him.

Now to humor him we let him dictate to the dispatcher/typist, his promise to officers Barton and Friess to compensate them for saving his life. What follows are the words, VERBATIM, as were typed on teletype paper.

"I John Delafimont do hereby and herewith decree this to be a legal testament that herewith and herein Barton and Friess having hereby and herewith saved my life are entitled for prolong my life $1000.00 each for apprehending characters who absconded with my wallet and cash on July 17, 1967 at the Red Velvet saloon and dumped me in Timberline Apartments in Palm Beach Gardens, without visible means of propulsion and by the grace of God picked up by officer Barton and officer Friess 3:00 AM and cash will be paid in pictures of Cleveland $1000.00 or ten pictures of Benjamin Franklin."

Well we got John a ride home by taxi and we all had a good laugh.

****

Shortly after this incident I joined the sheriff's department as I was convinced that there was a lot more action for me by none other than soon to be Captain, Lt. Henry Sanchez. Howard Friess also left the department and went into a different line of work rather than be a police officer. John Davis, another Gardens police officer went to the town of Palm Beach as a patrolman. John D. McArthur finally died but his legacy still lives on. If you watch PBS TV (Public Broadcasting Service) on television. He and his wife Katherine have an, *"endowment to the arts"*

Me and Friess never got our promised reward, but we did get a good laugh and I still have the signed promise of a drunk.

THE RUSSIAN

This is about an experience I had while I was a police officer in Riviera Beach. I had just completed my first year as a patrolman and was still a rookie cop, working on the night shift, that's 11-7 AM. They had me working in zone 2, that's to answer all calls in that area when I'm not busy.

Zone 2 runs from the north side of Blue Herron Blvd., to the north end of the city, and there starts the city of Lake Park. The western boundary was the Old Dixie Highway, we also had a zone 1 patrolman who worked from BHB south to the city of West Palm Beach. There were also 2 patrolman, black officers, who work all calls on the west side of the city. In addition to us 4, we had a sergeant overseeing all of us.

Naturally we had headquarters that housed the jail, offices, and our dispatcher. We also had 2 detectives in the city, but they never worked night shift that I know of, and as far as I know they worked their own hours. I used to hear them on the radio on all 3 shifts. So they worked whenever.

Now on the night shift it's the responsibility of the uniform division, which I was part of, when all is quiet and most people are asleep, that doors and windows of businesses in their area are checked to make sure that they are locked, and no damage had been done to them. Every patrolman checks an offense board on his next shift in the lineup room to see if any B&E has occurred in his zone the previous night. If it was a big B&E, he might even get a call at home from a detective.

Well it was the night shift and here I am in zone 2. It's not busy so I'm checking some of the businesses in the commercial area of my zone as I had plenty to check. When doing this I drove real slow with my lights out, always stepping on the emergency brake to stop, that way there was no lights emitted. I had just stopped at a beer distributing business and was up on its loading dock. My patrol car was close by with the door open and I could hear the radio. I guess I was about 4 feet above street level and there was nothing on the dock, just a stack of empty wooden pallets, when all of a sudden, I hear a noise and it sounds like something running toward me. I had no place to go so I got down behind the stack of pallets, it's dark and no lights on and this sound keeps getting closer. Then I see that it's a dog, a BIG dog, it's a Doberman pincer and he's almost ready to start climbing the stairs to the dock to get at me because he sure heard me.

Well I didn't know if he was friendly or what so I picked up a pallet and lifted it over my head figuring I'd give him a big surprise since there was no way I could miss hitting him with something as big as the pallet when he gets close enough. Hell, he had already climbed the stairs and was on the loading dock no more than 20 feet from me. He could dam sure see me and he didn't act to friendly and I could then see his teeth and knew he wanted a piece of me.

I was just ready to throw the pallet at him when I heard this deep voice and all it said was STOP, and the dog stopped right in front of me. Well with that I lowered the pallet down but only in front of me, I still wanted something between me and the dog. The dog just paces around and here comes this guy. Now this guy comes into sight, and he looks like he'd be a handful if you had to arrest him, the dog stopped and ran over to him.

I started talking with him wondering what he's doing out at this late time. He had to be 5' 5" or so and well over 225 pounds. He gave me his name and address which was close by and explained that he was just out walking his dog in the cool morning air, when the dog must have heard me on the dock and started running in my   direction. He said goodnight and continued to walk his dog and I finished my checks in that area, still leery of my encounter with the dog. I then got in my car and left the area.

When I was in my car, I ask the dispatcher for a 10-55, meeting with the sergeant at his convenience. The sergeant was the shift commander for the entire city, so I didn't know if he was busy or what. He must have been on what we call ROUTINE PATROL cause he agreed to meet me. When I saw him, I told about the guy and the dog on the loading dock. The sergeant listened to me and when I was all done said he knew the guy and said, *"Oh I see you met the Russian".*

The sergeant said he had met him some time ago but under different circumstances. He went on to say that they had been trying to arrest him and when they finally got the cuffs on him, he just roared and snapped the handcuffs.

****

Got to tell you, I'm glad I just met the Russian and his dog and I didn't have to arrest him. The almost run in with his dog was enough for me on that dark morning.

SKUNK APE

The final story in my book is about the Skunk-ape. Worldwide it is known as the Yeti, the Abominable Snowman, in the northwestern states it called Sasquatch. And since time immoral man has tried to catch it and explain it and even wrote stories about the elusive snow man or whatever you call it in your neck of the woods. It has seen described as up to 8 feet tall, all covered with hair, and walks like a man and could weigh 5 or 6 hundred pounds. In Florida it was called a Skunk-ape.

Now the sheriff's department had two deputies that followed, and kept track of, all calls involving the Sasquatch and it was a standing order that the complaint desk would notify these two regardless whether they were on or off duty. As for myself, I never thought about it or even cared, ...until one night on the 4 to 12 PM shift and I was the sergeant, so far, no calls of any serious consequences and all the calls so far were minor in nature. I had just turned west on Lake Worth Road when the dispatcher came on the air with a minor disturbance call for zone 6, that it involved several pigs. Now Lake Worth Road is in zone 6's area since it was a minor call and I was close, so I came right back to the dispatcher and told her to 10-22, disregard, zone 6 and assign that call to me. That meant a case number, a complainant address and time I was dispatched. The call was only 2 miles away and it involved a couple of pigs, so how involved could it be. Hell, I'd be done in no time. Well I went 10-97, arrived, in 2 or 3 minutes from the time of dispatch. The complainant lived on the north side of Lake Worth Road west of the Florida turnpike. This area was quiet, rural, and mostly woods. I was met by a female who was all mad and nervous and as I parked, she said, *"Something just killed my pigs and it stinks, I never saw what it was I just heard the pigs squealing, and when I went outside to check on them, they were dead and whatever killed them was gone."* I told the female complainant to go back into her house and I would check it out.

The time was early night and there was no moon out, so it was dark, and being rural there were no houses in the immediate area, and what there were, were off in a distance. Since it was dark, and I was away from civilization, I went and got my K-Lite flashlight and my 12-gauge shotgun out of the car.

Now I didn't know how much land or property the complainant had but I guessed it to be several acres, so as I walked away from her house it got darker and more woodsy and quiet as I looked for her pigs, both dead from what she had told me, when I ran across what looked to be a pen and when I looked inside, holy shit, I see two pigs that looked to be about 125 to 150 pounds each and both are dead.

The whole place smells and it's real quiet, and there's blood and guts all over the pen. It looked like each pig had been picked up, pulled apart, and then thrown back down, and the whole place stunk like a skunk had done its business. But it had to be something much bigger and stronger than a skunk to lift a pig, pull it apart and throw it back down, and besides it wasn't a skunk smell.

Now up to this time I carried my k-lite in my left hand and my shotgun in my right, but after seeing this mess I jacked a round into the chamber and put the flashlight right under the barrel holding it there with my left hand so that anywhere the light goes, so would a 12-gauge buck go if it had to. I really felt eerie going around the property checking for whatever might be out of the ordinary but as luck would have it I didn't find anything other than it smelled all over the property.

I know there were two dead pigs because I saw them, and they were dead. How do you explain that, and besides it stunk? Well I checked what I could and walked around the property right up to the trees that started the woods. All this time I felt spooky and eerie. Well after checking all around and not finding anything, I was glad, I finally secured. The dispatcher gave me my times and I was 10-8, back in service. The rest of the shift was uneventful, so I went to road patrol as it was almost shift end. I told the oncoming shift, night shift, and their sergeant about my pig call. It was at that time that I found out Florida had what was called a Skunk-ape and that it was elusive and the reason they called it a Skunk-ape was because it stunk. Well I told them that I never saw anything, but I did smell something, and I did see two dead pigs that were just tore apart.

Now I don't believe or disbelieve in the Skunk-ape as I never saw one or even heard about one, but I'll leave that judgment to someone else. It's easy to relate this story when you're in a well-lit crowded place with people around, but it's an entirely different story to be out in a dark, rural place with two dead pigs that you saw were pulled apart and the whole place stinks.

****

At the beginning of this story I told about two members of the sheriff's department who were seekers of the Skunk-ape who instructed the complaint desk to call them whether on or off duty. Their names are Marvin Lewis and Ernie Milner. I don't know if they ever followed up on my pig call.

THE WARRANT HENRY FRYESON

This story is about a warrant, sometimes called Capias.

Naturally it's a court order to arrest someone and put him/her in jail for whatever reason. This one is for a black male whose name is Henry Fryeson, and the capias is from the court of domestic relations for nonpayment of child support.

I'm the road sergeant, it's the 4-12 PM shift and I happened to be in the Delray substation so I'm in the south end of the county. I was speaking with the substation commander and a detective named Gil Brenner when Gi says, *"Henry is a big guy and he won't be muscled, just talk nice to him and he won't be any trouble."* Gil must have known Henry from past experience.

Now warrants/capias have a work sheet and on it, it tells you the subjects to be arrested name, home address, where he/she might work, and maybe a vehicle description and tag number, if it's available.

Gil tells me he's known Henry for the past several years and that he works at FPL, (Florida Power & Light) and they have a storage yard in Delray Beach. The yard is where crews work out of and they also store electrical equipment, their trucks, transformers etc. there, and this is probably where we would find Henry.

Well with that information I gave the capias to a deputy named Derrick who was working in the south end at the time. Now with all that information I told Derrick to go an arrest that guy. I told him to be sure and talk nice to this guy as he's pretty big and could get mean.

Deputy Derrick is a normal size guy, around 5' 9" or so

and about 180 lbs. I had him and his auxiliary man, an auxiliary deputy is a man who has a civilian job and puts in time as an extra deputy and rides with a regular deputy sheriff a number of hours per month, go 10-8, in service. They were to go to FPL yard and arrest this Henry Fryeson and since his radio is a portable one, and on, I would hear it. Well I stayed at the substation and continued talking with the commander and Brenner about cases being worked in south county.

The radio was on, and I heard Derrick go 10-6 10-49, out executing a warrant, at the FPL yard. With his radio on I could hear any unusual events or if he had any trouble. Well time passed and still no word from zone 8, Derrick and so after he's been out maybe 15-20 minutes, I started to get concerned so I tell Howe, the CO, and Brenner that I have to go and check up on the troops at FPL.

I did a hurried 10-8 and it didn't take me 5 minutes to get to the FPL yard and check out. What I see is Derick and his A-man standing outside of the yard talking to this big black guy and he's looking down at both deputies. He had to be 6'8" and looked close to 300 pounds. I saw all this as I parked my car across the street from where they were. I figured no way am I letting this guy get his hands on me or the two deputies.

I parked the car and got out, slammed the door, and started towards the three standing there when this black guy hearing the door slam turned sees me and hollers, *"Bob, how you doing?"* I have to tell you, my heart sank, he knew me. I got closer and saw that I knew him also. Henry had been a police officer with me when I still had been with Riviera Beach so many years ago. I didn't get to know him well as he was black, and black police officers worked on the west side of town, so I only knew him from lineups. I had never done any casework with him. I know from past experience he was a hell of a backup though. Because I could hear everything going on the radio.

Well since I knew Henry, I told Derrick to go 10-8 and give me the capias, I would take care of it. I told Henry that I had a capias/warrant for him and that he had to go to jail. He knew about the problem and ask me to tell his boss in FPL, the foreman, that he was going to jail and that he wouldn't be into work for several days.

I went to FPL yard, found the foreman, and told him about Henry and in talking with him, he tells me that he seen Henry pick up a Chevy Biscayne, mid-sized car by the front end, THAT'S THE MOTOR END. So you know that his 300 pounds wasn't just fat, he also had a chance to try out for the Miami Dolphins. I went back outside and told Henry to get into my car as he was going to jail. Now he asks me if he could ride in the front seat, and I said, *"sure"*.

Anyone knows that any prisoner rides in a back seat of a patrol car where he can or she can be secured, and not cause any harm.

I started for the substation with Henry as a prisoner in the front seat as my passenger. Anyone seeing my patrol car would just think I had a passenger and not a prisoner. On the way ole Henry says to me, *"you know I wouldn't go to jail if I didn't want to,"* And I said, *"yea,"* grateful we didn't have to fight him as I could just imagine the 3 of us trying to arrest him.

At the Delray substation I turn Henry over to a vice agent named Edwin Golvin, who also happened to be black. Vice had their office up north in West Palm Beach and Golvin happened to be going to the office and the jail was there also.

****

Several years later I saw Henry Fryeson at a Lil-general 7-11 store on Boca Raton Road. He had several surgeries on his stomach and was just a shell of the man he used to be. Detective Gil Brenner died in an automobile accident. Vice agent Golvin finally made sergeant and returned to the uniform division. Me, I was always grateful that Henry was pro law enforcement and didn't cause any trouble with the warrant.

TOM BRODIE MIAMI

This is about a police academy. The year was 1968 and to date no police academies existed in Palm Beach County for anyone aspiring to be a police officer. Myself, I had been in law enforcement for almost 5 years. Two years in Riviera Beach, one year in Palm Beach Gardens and now I was in my second year on the sheriff's department.

Up to this time all law enforcement related courses, such as laws, criminal as well as civil, rules of evidence, court procedures etc. had to be learned on the job since there was no police academy, at least not in Palm Beach County. Present police officers were required to take all the above-mentioned courses and they were able to take them at their leisure when available, just as long as they were completed.

The recipients of these classes were awarded a certificate that stated that the course was successfully completed. These certificates could be for any number of hours and at the time no police certification existed, at least in Palm Beach County. Up to this point, a police officer could have any number of hours of law enforcement experience to his credit, and it was assumed that his schooling or training in that field would continue through entire career.

For myself I was advised that I WOULD ATTEND these courses as given. The state of Florida issued certificates to those people qualified to teach law enforcement related courses, and only after taking state approved tests in that field.

Myself, I attended these courses when I could, and it just so happened that the teachers happened to be police officers in the city of West Palm Beach.

Now POLICE STANDARDS nationally went into effect in 1967, meaning that anyone who was a police officer at the time of its enactment received a certificate from the police standards council at that time, automatically grandfathered in, meaning they received a certificate that they were certified police officers. On the bottom of that certificate was a gold-colored seal, all others after that year received the same certificate but the seal was blue in color. These basically said that the recipient had successfully completed the required hours. Each year the number of hours needed to complete the course and be eligible progressively increased.

In 1968 I was told that myself and 3 others from our department, Dick Webb, Steve Quackenbush and Ralph Wiles would attend a police academy in Miami Florida. It was called PSD, (Dade Public Safety Department). We were the first of our department to attend a certified police academy.

At this time, I won't go into details about the police academy as that's another story.

The academy had various instructors, the Public Safety Department, FBI and practicing lawyers from the state of Florida. Naturally all had experience in the field that they taught, and they were more than qualified to teach by the police standards council as well as the state of Florida.

One such instructor, Tom Brodie, who was a member of PSD at the time, stuck in my mind and really impressed me, taught about bombs, explosives etc.

The Sheriff at this time was an E. Wilson Purdy, and Tom Brodie was a captain on Dade's Sheriff's Department. Captain Tom spoke to us about explosives and also showed us various bomb scenarios and explained the various ways to handle such calls and just how far we, as novice police officers, should go when we, as police officers, got a call of a potential bomb, and just who we should notify and call in. He even showed us a video of Mickey Rooney as a mad bomber.

Captain Brodie was an acknowledged expert in the field of bombs and explosive devices and the handling of such. He had written several books on the subject and was in demand worldwide, traveling to Japan to teach their department, he also traveled to New York to teach the NYPD.

I'm sure he must have started his career in the military who called it, EOD, (Explosive Ordinance Disposal). After we had attended several classes with Captain Brodie, he announced that we were going into the field for a live firsthand exercise.

PSD has a bomb truck that they used to transport bombs, explosives etc. This truck was a converted deuce and a half military truck, it had ten wheels. What they had done was to remove the back end and put in a heavy layer of sand as its base. Mounted on this sand was a very heavy, maybe 1" thick circular vat open at the top so that any explosive would release its energy harmlessly out the open top, just going up.

Now you've got to understand that it was just too dangerous to move certain objects or bombs, so they were blown up in the place they were found. The majority of these devises were placed in the bomb truck and taken away and exploded so that no one was harmed and nothing damaged.

Now Brodie said we all had to go to a large vacant lot, and he would demonstrate the truck to us as it might be used. Now by all, I mean the entire class of police officers in attendance. The class number was #45. It contained officers from all over south Florida.

Well we had all gone out to this lot in Miami and when we

got there, there stood Captain Tom Brodie behind the big bomb truck. First, looking at Brodie, it looked like he had a bunch of flares in his hands, but a closer inspection showed it to be 7 sticks of dynamite that were taped together in a bundle and a fuse sticking out of it. I don't know much about dynamite, but I do know that it comes in different strengths and that any strength is dangerous. He showed the bundle to all the class and then had all move away to a safe distance, or what he said was a safe distance. He told us then that he would light the fuse and threw it into the back of the truck in the steel container to show us that the truck was able to withstand the blast.

I figured that he would light the fuse, throw the dynamite into the vat and run as he was no more than 6 or 7 feet from the vat, but what he did was light the fuse, throw the dynamite into the vat and just stood there with the dynamite ready to go off. He never made any attempt to move to safety when, WHOM, the dynamite went off and Brodie just a few feet away. I don't think he even batted an eye because I was watching him. Now out of this vat on the bomb truck comes this God-awful scream and up rises this smoke ring, it's got to be 4 feet in diameter and thick, it went up about 200 feet into the air, screaming all the way and finally dissipated.

I've got to tell you I was really in awe; I had never seen anything like that.

****

Tom Brodie finally retired from PSD after a few more years, I think as a Major. The four of us from Palm Beach County graduated from the academy. Palm Beach County finally got its own police academy at Palm Beach Junior College, as far as I now no other deputies attended PSD or any academy other than our own.

THE TRAINING OFFICER

The Training Officer. The name itself conjures up reverence and respect. Well at least from the new troops in the division who read every written word, attend every seminar, ESPECIALLY SINCE ITS MANDATORY, just like it was decreed from the bible. His knowledge is vast, supposedly, in matters of criminal law and most would think he was just a credit away from passing the bar exam, and also that his experience in the field would be vast, well at least to the new troops. However, on the other end of the spectrum was the detective bureau. Most thought he was a regular pain in the ass, what you sit on and that all he does is hand out material to justify his existence. Besides they don't want to read it and most probably won't anyway, and that's all he is, is a sergeant or a Lt. who couldn't make it as a road supervisor, or even as a supervisor of detectives. Now top management in all their vast wisdom, had to find a slot for him so he would not be an embarrassment to the department, nor would he be in the position as a road supervisor where a faulty decision by him could subject a deputy or himself to harm.

Alas and behold! our department was fortunate enough, or unfortunate enough, to be endowed with a training officer of the caliber of *"Sgt. R. Lopez"*.

Now in all fairness to all those training officers on practically every law enforcement, a word about the true function of a training officer. His is truly a demanding responsibility as it is his duty to correlate the decisions of the US Supreme Court along with the decisions of the Florida Supreme court and in turn get an interpretation from the states attorney's office on the effect and application that the department was to take. Once this information was gathered, it was the job of the training officer to have it printed up and have it disseminated to the entire department and it was known as, *"The Training Bulletin"* and it was also numbered. A few brief examples are the MIRANDA decision, stop and frisk, searches etc., and a continuous stream of decisions that affect law enforcement agencies, they all require his being cognizant or on top of all things pertaining to law enforcement Now these are in addition to countless in service training courses that he must set up for the department personal as well as lectures, movies pertaining to the laws of Florida such a man was Richard Lopez, a sergeant no less, and a transplant from Florida Highway Patrol. Who, after being a traffic cop for roughly 6 years affectionally known as a yo-yo cop, an assignment on the Florida turnpike, that's 20 miles north and 20 miles south, looking for traffic violations? This being his only exposure to crime and corruption, this enhanced his criminal expertise greatly. The result being the sheriff's department gladly hired him, but not as a lowly deputy sheriff to be thrown into a zone to answer calls, but he went directly to the detective bureau as a detective sergeant, thank heaven for political affiliations. Of course we on the road didn't know that at the time, this move alone by the administration greatly enhanced the already faltering morale that all departments suffer at some time. The grunts on the road knew that with this move, they would be grunts all the longer and just be slick sleeves.

But wait! Did someone goof? A certain Richard wrote a pretty good almanac, but this Richard was a piss poor detective. Well not to admit defeat and to show his versatility he suddenly appeared at road

patrol as a uniform sergeant in charge of a shift and having approximate 7 to 10 troops under his direct supervision, assisting them with on-the-spot decisions in various calls. This is required by road sergeants on a routine basis. But alas wait! Something was not right, Palm Beach sheriff's office's little leprechaun in a green uniform with 3 gold stripes on his arm was doing such a good job as a road sergeant that the staff must of thought he would an even gooder in a position more of a researcher for the department into legal aspects. One with less exposure and thus, our *"Training Officer"* came into being. Now Sergeant Lopez had already received his associate degree and was at present going to Florida Atlantic University in Boca Raton, Florida. Also, in Palm Beach County. And he was working towards his bachelor's degree. His new position was most welcome I'm sure, so now it's school in the evening, no evening or night shifts for him, and golf with the sheriff, chief deputy and several of the captains on the weekends. Well life as a cop was tough and brutal but Sergeant Lopez could handle it. At this time, I had been a road sergeant for about 2 years and having spent most of my time on the 4 to 12 shift, which was the busiest shift, but I liked it as my days were free to go diving or even if it was bad, I'd go and beach comb. I was glad to see Sergeant Lopez off the road as were most all his troops, especially his shift in his new position as training officer so he wouldn't make any more awkward decisions as he frequently did on the day shift, and myself and my troops had to straighten things out. Well anyway he was gone from the road, and we all breathed a little easier. The training bulletins he passed out were a small price to pay just to be rid of him and in all truth, the bulletin information was good information until are you ready for this. Apparently, Amy Vanderbilt had gotten word that members of the sheriff's department were more than able to handle law and order within the county but alas! They were sadly lacking in the manly art of table etiquette. This apparently led to interdepartmental *"contempt and gossip"* and some individuals even suffered a loss of prestige. But wait, our training officer would never let us stumble blindly through life, never knowing the fork from the spoon etc. For myself as well as my troops and even most of the department it was a welcome relief to know that Sergeant Lopez was busy risking life and limb, cutting short his golf game, working unceasingly to come up with the ultimate training bulletin. It had to rank with *Gone with the Wind*, Call of the Wild, and some would say, a sequel to *the 10 Commandments*, probably because of the numbered directives. Finally a day never to be forgotten, August 10,1971, now not to be shared only the members of the department, for it had progressed in greatness far beyond the department alone, so why not tell the world, well at least the gold coast of Florida. So, with the able assistance of our paper, the Palm Beach Post Times on that day printed the training bulletin. Not in its entirety but close to it, the immortal words of Sergeant Lopez our training officer.

The following is the article that was printed by the, *Palm Beach Post Times*, newspaper on August 10,1971. Unfortunately, my talents lay in being a road sergeant and all I can do is copy the words:

Palm Beach County sheriff's deputies who don't know how to hold a knife or a fork will be able to breathe a little easier now, the technique is spelled out in *"The Training Bulletin"* issued by sheriff, William Heidtman, it was specifically designed to avoid interdepartmental, contempt and gossip, and loss of individual, prestige. The bulletin covers a multitude of business and social faux pas which could reflect on the integrity of the sheriff's department. Among them are:

How to act when a woman enters the room, how to, break bread, with your hands, how to hold a spoon, like a fork, how to respect rank, salute. How to tell your wife about your work.

The following is the printed words of the newspaper.
SUBJECT: *Sheriff's Office Customs*

There are several customs and rules of conduct which should guide members of the Palm Beach Sheriff's Office.

1. While the sheriff's office is not a military organization, it does in a great many ways closely relate to one and the officer/deputy sheriff relationship of its members. It should be based on the military saying that "familiarity breeds contempt," excessive social association between officers and deputies may lead to the following,

   - Contempt of the deputy sheriff by fellow deputies.
   - A loss of prestige by the officer.
   - Gossip about the members involved.

2. A commissioned officer at the Palm Beach County sheriff's office is to be respected for his position. All officers of the rank of lieutenant and above are entitled to a salute, for routine purposes a salute is customary on the first meeting in the morning, no more is necessary during the day while working in close proximity. All visiting officers are entitled to a salute.

3. Deputy sheriff's should recognize that rank has its privileges as a byproduct of past accomplishments and position. Along with the privileges attained with the rank there are additional responsibilities of administration and command. When a man is made an officer of the Palm Beach County Sheriff's Office, he is no longer responsible for himself but may bear the responsibility of a group of men. Respect of channels is important to efficient administration and to the morale, regardless of

who he is, every man wants to feel useful, respected, and important. when members start going over their heads and not respecting channels, morale and efficiency suffer. Supervisors will gladly submit suggestions and requests to the upper echelons.

4. Temper and Profanity; Neither temper nor profanity have a place in the Palm Beach County Sheriff's Office. Profanity denotes the lack of expression, vocabulary, and good breeding. Temper denotes a lack of self-control.

5. Members should avoid any conversation which could be considered gossip.

6. Personal indebtedness is a thing to be avoided if possible.

7. At times, members of the Palm Beach Sheriff's Office and their families should develop close relationships, as deputy sheriff's wives invariably wind up getting together. It must be remembered that gossip travels through these channels.

8. The way members act in public has a direct relation to the way the public will feel about the Palm Beach County Sheriff's Office. Loud laughter and joking are good morale builders, but such conduct in public is out of place.

9. The PBSO prohibits the use of intoxicants while on duty, unless on specific assignment. Even more, members must be careful while drinking while *"off duty"*. Every man is a member of the PBSO 24 hours a day.

10. Every man has his own morals or code of ethics. Some are loose and some are more rigid in their convictions. A man who is loose morally is usually careless with truth.

His morals also control his honesty. Commandments in the bible should serve as a guide for the rules of conduct for members.

SUBJECT: Etiquette - Table Manners

Members are expected to display table manners and eating habits of officers and gentleman at all times.

Manners at the table consist not only of doing the right thing at the right time but doing it with poise and without awkwardness. Some of the items that will distinguish members as officers and gentleman of PBSO are as follows,

1. When any member of PBSO enters a restaurant or eating establishment try to be seated facing the entrance or cash register. Never have your face to the wall or your back to the entrance.

2. When there is a group of six or more, it is better to call a restaurant or eating establishment and let them know in advance that the group is coming, this will make for better seating arrangements and for better service. In most places a check is presented to be paid when leaving the establishment. It is much more convenient and has a much better appearance if the check is paid for by one individual. Each man should make a mental note of the cost of his meal and reimburse the paying deputy sheriff after he is outside the establishment.

3. It goes without saying that all ladies in the party are to be seated before any of the men sit down. It might also be pointed out here that the gentleman will rise at any time a lady or commissioned officer stops at the table.

4. Loud talking and laughter are out of place while the meal is in progress.

5. On being seated the first thing to do is spread the napkin in your lap without tucking it under your belt, it should be unfolded. Watch the host or hostess.

6. Use the right implement for each course. Salad forks are not furnished in most cases except on formal occasions However, implements for all courses may sometimes be laid on the table when the meal is served. A mistake is of no great consequence. Your best bet is to do one of two things, work from the outside in.

- THE KNIFE
  - Use it only when needed. Do not use it on bread except for spreading butter. Do not use it on vegetables.
    Hold it in the palm of the right hand with the index finger along the back of the knife.
  - Cut only one bite at a time lay the knife handle to the right with the cutting edge toward you on the top edge and across your plate. If you are left-handed, place the knife on the left side of the plate with the cutting edge toward you.

- THE FORK
  - It is used as an aid in cutting meat. Hold in the left hand with the handle in the palm, the tines turned downward, and the forefinger extended along the back.
  - When you eat with it, Hold it like a pencil.
  - When you have finished using it, place it's tines upward near the center of the plate.

- THE SPOON
  - Used for soups, desserts, coffee, and tea only.
  - For soup, (hold spoon same as fork) always dip away

from you and hold the spoon sideways to your mouth, tipping it so that the liquid flows into it, no noise.
- For desserts, hold the spoon as you do a fork.
- When using a spoon to stir coffee or tea, don't stir any more than necessary and avoid noise.

There are other items to keep in mind.
- Don't be a course straggler. The table is not a conversation place.
- If you finish a course first, wait until the others are ready to start the next one.
- Break bread with your hands, then butter a piece at a time, bread should never be cut.
- Don't get up from the table until everyone is finished.
- When you tip, 15% is a fair figure.

If you have any questions concerning this bulletin, please contact Sgt. RICHARD LOMAN, training officer or captain HENRY J. Sanchez, the director of personal and training, PBSO.

Well needless to say life somehow for the training officer took a dramatic decline in his popularity ratings even with the new troops who at first had been so faithful at the start, now all personnel where subject to public ridicule and smirks every time they went 10-40, or out for a meal, and as a result of all the widespread publicity were practically always approached by some citizen who good naturally would comment to the deputy, *"Oh! I see you are using the salad fork on your salad, Gee, you sure learn fast."* Comments like this, and more, made for many a deputy almost getting into a fight himself, writer can vouch for that, especially when he has had a bad day with maybe a couple of domestics and maybe a fight or two or even a robbery or whatever. He still has to do all the paperwork, reports, and all he's trying to do is rest and get a quick meal and some peace and quiet, so it was quite evident that the deputy's thoughts fondly return to the training officer. At the end of his masterpiece, if any questions about the bulletin still cloud the minds of any member of PBSO that he should contact him or captain Henry J. Sanchez, the director of personal and training.

Now captain Sanchez could immediately if not sooner dispelled any doubts or questions a deputy might have on proper etiquette. He is an ex-combat marine veteran from WW II, he was also retired from West Palm Beach police department and now had been on the sheriff's department about 7 years and was next in command, Captain Yule was the commander. He had just been reassigned to the training and personal department., to which he was really choked up to be in, I'm sure. He had a voice that was about 4 or 5 octaves below middle C. so no wonder his nick name was hollering Hank, of course no one said it to his face. Well to this day I never did find out how the training bulletin got past him and a word to the wise, *"don't ask"*. Well anyway to us on the road it seemed just a short time when LO and BEHOLD, our training officer had a replace- met and Sergeant Lopez left the department to take the position of Director of Public Safety, they put him in a position of county government and in a supervisory capacity over various county programs. The most notable one being the head of animal control. A position of great responsibility and one in which he continued educating his dog catchers in proper etiquette. It Was later found out that the material for the training bulletin, had been plagiarized from the Florida Highway Patrol and was in their training manual.

****

Several days after the bulletin appeared in the Post Times, they wrote a short commentary as follows:

When using the spoon should sheriff's deputies laugh or cry over the ridiculous training bulletin that is so chock full of little admonitions and homilies? The deputy might want to cry over that bulletin issued by sheriff Willard Hestor because it treats them like pre-kindergartners.

Then again, the bulletin which makes such regulations as a *"temper denotes a lack of self-control, the knife is an aid to cutting meat"* is a real laugh. Its *"do's and don'ts"* must make a deputy wonder whether they are reading Emily Post's etiquette Book or a PBSO training manual.

The bulletin contains such items as, *"a man who is foot loose morally, is usually careless with the truth,"* or when *"using a spoon to stir coffee or tea, don't stir any more than necessary and avoid noise, personal indebtedness is a to be avoided, when possible,"* and on and on it goes.

In conclusion, the name of the training officers, Lopez & Sanchez are listed in case there are any questions. Come to think of it, I do have a couple. *"Is this bulletin really necessary? Isn't it a bit insulting to men who aspire to have a law enforcement career?"*

Sounds like a forerunner of a Hollywood flick, don't it?

TREVINOS DANCES

The sheriff's department used to, and still does I believe, get extra duty details that call for off duty deputies to pick up some extra cash working security jobs such as construction sites and dances around the county. This of course on their days off. Now these jobs are all in the unincorporated area of the county.

Wellman's Dance Hall on Lake Worth Road and the Florida Turnpike was frequented by Mexicans and Puerto Ricans. Trevino's on Delray Road was another dance hall frequented by the above, and all the attendees were either Mexicans or Puerto Rican and all were migrant laborers. Now the dances are always a big event with live bands and crowds of 2 to 3 hundred is the usual, so security details called for 3 or 4 deputies to work a dance. Sometimes they had a really big band and it even called for more deputies to work and keep order. It just wasn't feasible to have a zone car standing by for the duration of the dance as he had calls to answer and other duties to do. So a roster, list, was put up and those wishing extra duty signed up for a date to work. Now like most cops, I was never financially solvent, so I signed up to work Trevino's dance on a Friday and Saturday night while I was off or working the 7 to 3 PM shift or the 11 to 7 AM shift getting someone to cover for me for an hour or so. The dances usually were over at 12:00 midnight. I was always in the south end zones, that's where all the labor camps were anyway and besides, I enjoyed working the dances. Now when I worked at Trevino's it was usually Lt. Bendick, me and Dave Smith, a slick sleeve like me.

When these details first started, we didn't have the use of a patrol car so we would meet at road patrol in West Palm Beach airport and drive the 18 or 20 miles to Delray Road in one of our cars. We would switch driving from week to week. We would advise the dispatcher by land line, regular telephone, that we were on a dance detail at Trevino's and just to have the zone car check on us from time to time as he could. Now since Bendick was an officer he got to take a walkie-talkie along. Me and Smith had K-Lite flashlights plus our side arms. As we were in uniform, I also carried an iron claw, a single hand cuff, that worked like a ratchet would, and I also took my model 97 Winchester shotgun but put it in the trunk of the car since the migrants had a tendency to get rowdy at times.

Well this time down was my turn to drive, and we put all the gear we were taking into the trunk of my Ford. Well it was a Saturday night dance and we got there around 8:00 PM and it was just starting to pick up, Trevino's is a large 2 story building. The first floor has a large bar on one side and a Mexican restaurant on the other. The entire second floor is one big dance hall. Now it sits on the north side of Delray Road and has a large parking area in front of the building that also extends to the east side. Now just east of all this Trevino has a small store. Well, we park right in front of the building entrance so we could keep an eye on our personal cars because they did have a tendency to get vandalized.

We checked in with Oscar Trevino, the owner and operator of all, and the way we worked the detail was to have one deputy on the dance floor, there usually wasn't any trouble on the floor anyway, it was always the bar or parking lot. The other 2 deputies worked the parking lot and sometimes the bar, mostly the parking lot were all the fighting, cutting, or shooting took place. We would rotate around the 3 positions every hour or so, so that everyone worked the dance etc. Zone 8 would stop by when he wasn't busy, check on us, or just to shoot the breeze. If we had to make an arrest for CCW (Carrying Concealed Weapon) or DC (Disorderly Conduct) he would transport the prisoner to the county jail we would draw a case number, do a report, and file the case with the county solicitor's office.

Well this night had its usual fights and drunks. What we usually did with them is to put them in their cars and hide their keys or else let a friend take them to whatever labor camp they were from. Now remember Trevino's is way out in rural Palm Beach County. We did have to arrest those that didn't have anyone to take them home/camp. Now this particular night wasn't too bad as we didn't have to arrest anyone, nor did we have any serious trouble. So it's right at 12:00 midnight, the dance is over, and everyone is emptying out of the building, that's the bar, restaurant, and dance hall into the parking lot.

Now there's more in the parking lot who are drunk or closed to it and feeling no pain as they get into cars. By now all 3 deputies are in the lot area with our flashlights trying to keep some sort of order and now all cars are starting to move. Some like to gun their engines and peal out. Usually if a deputy hollered out some nice words they would slow down and drive normal, until out of sight.

Well, a white Mustang with 5 or 6 Puerto Rican males was speeding west from the east end of the parking lot. Dave Smith was up by the bar/restaurant area, and I was at the main entrance and close to my car. Bendick was near the speeding Mustang, and I saw them swerve and try to hit him, Bendick, but he was able to jump out of the way as it flew by, and I saw him take his service revolver out. Now the driver was in front of me, and he had to turn east on Delray Road or go west, same road, well he did a U-turn and went east on Delray Road. Seeing all this I ran to my personal car, opened the trunk, and grabbed my shotgun and jacked a round into the chamber as I was running out into the roadway. The Mustang by now was east bound on Delray Road and was maybe 2 or 3 hundred feet away from me when I pulled the trigger. The muzzle, or business end, was pointed down toward the roadway so that the round would bounce of it before it hit the car. Well everyone in that lot had to hear some or all those pellets hit the back end of the Mustang, but it never stopped, in fact it seemed to speed up. I ran back to check on Bendick, and he was okay, just mad as hell. We advised all south end units, uniform, and detectives, at the Delray substation of the incident. For all that, we didn't hear any more from, or about, the Mustang. We also checked at all the hospitals for any bullet type wounds especially Mexicans or Puerto Ricans involved, all reports were negative.

****

In the following days as I worked in the south end of the county, I checked all the labor camps and packing houses for a white Mustang with bullet holes in the trunk area but never found one We had also put out a BOLO, (Be on the Lookout) We never got any response. The driver would have been charged with aggravated assault plus any of the others through NCIC or FDIC or Palms. All are computer checks on individuals. On future details at Trevino's dances no white Mustang ever showed up and I got to admit that the traffic at the dances was a lot more orderly.

WELLMAN'S SERGEANT MILES

This is a story about a dance hall, Wellman's dance hall to be exact. Now this dance hall is located on Lake Worth road just west of the Florida Sunshine parkway or the turnpike. Now as a dance hall, Wellman's catered only to migrant labors and so that meant Puerto Ricans and Mexicans. One thing they had in common was they liked loud music, and another was they didn't particularly like each other, and they were all migrant labors. So on any weekend when the dances were held you could hear loud music as it was live and the migrants were off work, just got paid, and wanted to get liquored up and drink and let off some steam and Wellman's was the place to do it. Being that both Puerto Ricans and Mexicans liked each other so much there were always fights and cuttings and an occasional shooting. So the sponsors ask the sheriff's department to assist them in maintaining some sort of order and if needed to make an arrest as Wellman's was in the county area and any deputy could make an arrest if he had to.

Now this particular night, a 3-11 PM shift, a dance was held, and it was no different from any other night. They had asked for 3 deputies to work the dance, also a sergeant to oversee all. So that meant a total of 4 troops. This also meant that the dance detail had the benefit of all the sheriff's department should they need it and so they were also supplied with a patrol car, green & white, and it was at their disposal. The troops working the detail were also off duty, some worked on the day shift, some on the night shift, and all worked to make extra money as at the time the sheriff's department didn't pay so well and sometimes it was hard to pay attention. All deputies and some detectives worked details when they could.

Now the sergeant on this detail was a Robert Miles, he was also retired out of the Marine Corps, so he was pretty squared away, meaning he was pretty sharp.

Myself and the shift was working in zone 6 being that Wellman's was in my zone. I was supposed to stop by and check on the detail and just shoot the breeze when I wasn't busy. Well I stopped by this particular evening, and you could hear the loud music long before you actually got there, and when I got there, I saw a Puerto Rican male in the back seat of the dance details patrol car. He was in the cage on the back seat, he wasn't cuffed and was kicking at the window that looked like it was going to break if something wasn't done to stop him.

The dance detail had apparently arrested the male and put him in the back seat. I had just pulled up to check on the detail when I saw the PR/M kicking violently at the window. I ask Sergeant Miles what he was going to do about it to stop it and he said he wasn't going to do anything.

Well when I heard that I took my gas billie, now back then all on duty deputies were issued gas billies and we were taught if you have to shoot someone, to aim it at the chest as in addition to being tear gassed, the wadding also came out and it would hit whoever you gassed, and it burned them, needless to say, I don't ever remember gassing someone and just aiming at the chest.

Well the PR/M was kicking violently at the right rear window, so all his attention was centered on it. So, I opened the left rear door and when he heard it open, he turned and looked at me and I shot him with the tear gas. Well that immediately took his mind off kicking anything else, I slammed the door shut and told Sergeant Miles that I didn't think that his prisoner would kick anything else, and that I had to leave.

213

****

Now I never did hear any more about their prisoner and I didn't even have to do any paperwork.

Later I made sergeant. At one of Sheriff Heidtman's *"annual surprises,"* his birthday party, I got into a confrontation, fight, after indulging in some suds and spirits about Sergeant Miles when someone called him a chicken, and I got into this fight with a big, retired cop from New York City named Richard Rhome who had had trouble with Miles. The sheriff wasn't very happy with this going on at his *"annual surprise"* and we both got sent home.

www.ingramcontent.com/pod-product-compliance
Lightning Source LLC
Chambersburg PA
CBHW070501160726

48003CB00004B/1365